A THEOLOGY OF THE CROSS

OVERTURES TO BIBLICAL THEOLOGY

The Land
by Walter Brueggemann

God and the Rhetoric of Sexuality
by Phyllis Trible

Israel in Exile
by Ralph W. Klein

The Ten Commandments and Human Rights
by Walter Harrelson

A Whirlpool of Torment
by James A. Crenshaw

Texts of Terror
by Phyllis Trible

The Suffering of God
by Terence E. Fretheim

Faithfulness in Action
by Katharine Doob Sakenfeld

New Testament Hospitality
by John Koenig

The Tragic Vision and the Hebrew Tradition
by W. Lee Humphreys

Jesus, Liberation, and the Biblical Jubilee
by Sharon H. Ringe

From Darkness to Light
by Beverly Roberts Gaventa

The Mighty from Their Thrones
by J. P. M. Walsh, S.J.

Biblical Perspectives on Aging
by J. Gordon Harris

The Economy of the Kingdom
by Halvor Moxnes

Holiness in Israel
by John G. Gammie

The Feminine Unconventional
by André LaCocque

Theology of the Cross
by Charles B. Cousar

Editors

WALTER BRUEGGEMANN, Professor of Old Testament at Columbia Theological Seminary, Decatur, Georgia

JOHN R. DONAHUE, S.J., Professor of New Testament at the Jesuit School of Theology, Berkeley, California

ELIZABETH STRUTHERS MALBON, Associate Professor of Religion, Virginia Polytechnic Institute and State University, Blacksburg, Virginia

CHRISTOPHER R. SEITZ, Associate Professor of Old Testament, Yale Divinity School, New Haven, Connecticut

The Death of Jesus in the Pauline Letters

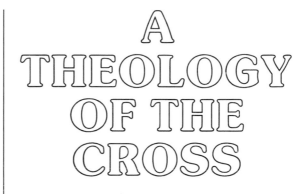

A THEOLOGY OF THE CROSS

CHARLES B. COUSAR

FORTRESS PRESS   Minneapolis

For
Irving Blanton Cousar
and
Robert Wilbur Cousar

A THEOLOGY OF THE CROSS:
The Death of Jesus in the Pauline Letters

Copyright © 1990 Augsburg Fortress. All rights reserved. Except for brief quotations in critical articles or reviews, no part of this book may be reproduced in any manner without prior written permission from the publisher. Write to: Permissions, Augsburg Fortress, 426 S. Fifth St., Box 1209, Minneapolis, MN 55440.

Scripture quotations, unless otherwise indicated or translated by the author, are from the Revised Standard Version of the Bible, copyright © 1946, 1952, and 1971 by the Division of Christian Education of the National Council of Churches.

Library of Congress Cataloging-in-Publication Data

Cousar, Charles B.
    A theology of the cross : the death of Jesus in the Pauline
letters / Charles B. Cousar.
        p.   cm.—(Overtures to biblical theology : [24])
    Includes bibliographical references.
    ISBN 0-8006-1558-1 (alk. paper)
    1. Bible. N.T. Epistles of Paul—Criticism, interpretation, etc.
2. Jesus Christ—Crucifixion.   3. Paul, the Apostle, Saint—
Contributions in theology of the cross.   I. Title.   II. Series.
BT453.C68   1990
232.96′3′09015—dc20   90-31424
                                                                                            CIP

The paper used in this publication meets the minimum requirements of American National Standard for Information Sciences—Permanence of Paper for Printed Library Materials, ANSI Z329.48-1984. ♾™

Manufactured in the U.S.A.   AF 1-1558

94   93   92   91   90   1   2   3   4   5   6   7   8   9   10

Contents

Editor's Foreword

The cross is relentlessly a scandal for Christian faith. Because the event of the cross is a dynamic phenomenon in the memory, narrative, and life of the church, the exact "bite" of the cross for faith is not static or stable. It is a memory that insists on beginning present reality; it is a concrete event that restlessly becomes paradigmatic in various contexts and circumstances of the life of the church. For that reason, its claim, power, and threat must repeatedly be reasserted and rearticulated.

For all modern theology, Martin Luther looms large and dominating for all subsequent reflection on the cross. Luther's remarkable sensitivity and daring affirmation have been generative of enormous critical insight, mostly Lutheran and German. That risk and pivotal discussion have come to contemporary culmination in the work of Ernst Käsemann, who has written on the theme most poignantly and penetratingly. Because the cross is endlessly relentless in its claim and restless in its critical voice, however, even Käsemann's rendering is not final.

Cousar's book demonstrates that we can and must move beyond even Käsemann in our own obedient act of understanding and response to the cross. It is clear that much of the German discussion discerned the cross in the crucial but narrow categories of "justification." Cousar's careful and acute exposition shows effectively that the cross cannot be contained in such a single category, but functions as a norm and singular definitional voice on a broad range of theological, interpretive, and ethical issues.

Cousar's bold rereading of Paul carries our understanding of the cross in two remarkable and telling directions. On the one hand, Cousar is concerned to transpose the interpretive conversation from a German context to a North American matrix. While the courage of Barmen will no doubt continue to ring in our ears, Cousar proceeds from the awareness that our North American dominant cultural values are massively resistant to a theology of the cross, precisely because the cross places suffering at the heart of God's character and at the heart of meaningful, faithful human life. Cultural resistance to meaningful suffering has as its counterpart theological resistance to the cross that issues either in resistant disregard or in resistant distortion and trivialization. Thus attention to the cross requires, in our self-indulgent context, a very different set of categories for life and understanding. The shift of categories surely touches every aspect of life, socio-economic and epistemological, as well as ethical.

On the other hand, Cousar is at his most imaginative and suggestive when he brings the norming power of the cross to bear upon our conventional categories of systematic theology. In chapter 1 he offers a remarkable critique of the "classic attributes" of God—power, righteousness, wisdom, faithfulness, freedom, and love. His argument permits the conclusion that our common uses of such "attributes" "merely mask the desire for control, for moral superiority, and for maintenance of the status quo." The cross thus requires "an entirely different way of thinking about God." In chapter 2 he considers the salvific meaning of Jesus' death and the rich range of language used by Paul to witness to that meaning. Cousar takes up this language for a critical review of the "historical" views of the atonement—the subjective, the objective, and the "classic" views. It is evident that the rich use of metaphor and symbol that Paul found indispensable has been lamentably reduced and flattened in order to arrive at historical "theories." Careful textual study requires us to return behind these "views" if we are to engage the witness of the text seriously. In chapter 4 Cousar takes up two of the classic "marks of the church"—unity and holiness—and shows in yet a third dimension how the cross critiques our usual ways of characterizing the church, for seen under the scandal of the cross the characterization of the church is much more an endless process of reform and redefinition that is never settled. On these fronts of doctrine of God, doctrine of salvation, doctrine of church, this book requires us to engage in radical rethinking that cuts underneath our common conclusions and our conventional quarrels.

Cousar is subtle, almost sneaky, in the way he shows Paul's theology of the cross to be more radical, more dangerous, and more pertinent than we have been wont to think. In my judgment, his approach to biblical theology does three things that make this not only an important but a compelling and attractive book. First, he is in touch with the issues of the day, ethical and intellectual, and understands the profound crisis now facing the North American church. Second, he writes with clarity and simplicity so that the argument is available and not to be avoided. Third, and most important, he builds the case text by text, for he understands that biblical theology is inescapably exegetical. Cousar's book, as much as any I know, will permit the dangerous discussion of the cross to be a genuinely North American discussion. We need not be imitators of the Germans, splendid as that is, but perhaps can be more fully imitators of Paul.

It is a delight to welcome my colleague, Charles B. Cousar, as a contributor to the Overtures series. His book has a chance to make a difference, even in the church as it thinks "through the cross" and not past it.

Walter Brueggemann

Preface

This book has been in the incubating stages a long time. I first became interested in the topic during a sabbatical year spent in Tübingen when I listened to Ernst Käsemann lecture on 1 Corinthians. The year was 1968–69, when a great deal was happening in Germany—student protests, sharp debate in the church, an agonizing watching of traumas taking place in eastern Europe. Käsemann's passionate affirmation of Paul's theology of the cross was timely for the circumstances of that year. It challenged students to consider what they were about and what they wanted in their demand for reform; it confronted the church's quest for religious security and questioned the search for a safe haven of redemption without the risks and ambiguities of faith; it provided a context for discussing the painful struggles for freedom in Czechoslovakia.

In the ensuing decades, many lectures, several articles, and a commentary on Galatians have sharpened my interest in Paul's theology of the cross and the conviction that the texts in his letters that speak so powerfully of the crucified Christ still have a cutting edge and, if anything, an even sharper edge than twenty years ago.

The last portion of the twentieth century in North America in many ways presents a different scene from Germany of the late 1960s. The economic and political landscape is not the same. The church here faces a peculiar set of problems, as it seeks to define itself in a world where the rich are getting much richer and the poor much poorer. Moreover, the frantic pursuit of success and self-indulgent consumerism are not simply "out there" in the society distinct from the church, but are "right here" in the homes and the garages of those of us who are church members. In such a context Paul's interpretation of Jesus' death and its impact on the Christian life may be terribly difficult to hear. His dominant themes sound alien and jarring, but for just that reason it is all the more urgent that we listen to Paul.

I am indebted to several institutions and a number of people who have in varying ways contributed to this enterprise. I am grateful to the Association of Theological Schools in the United States and Canada for a faculty research grant and to the Board of Directors of Columbia Theological Seminary for a sabbatical leave, spent in Cambridge, England and Berkeley, California. Beverly R. Gaventa, S. C. Guthrie, Jr., and Richard B. Hays were gracious enough to read the manuscript and to make insightful suggestions for its improvement. Christine Wenderoth, the associate librarian at Columbia, tracked down a number of difficult references for me. Walter Brueggemann and the late John A. Hollar were supportive editors, hearing me out on requests and gently guiding me toward deadlines. More than anyone else, Betty, my wife, has been my constant companion through the entire project. She has patiently listened while I "talked through" the arguments of various chapters, has given me the freedom to work, and has never lost faith. The book is dedicated to my parents, whose unwavering commitment to the crucified Christ, in both good times and bad, has profoundly shaped my own life as well as the lives of others.

Charles B. Cousar

Abbreviations

AB	Anchor Bible
BDF	F. Blass, A. Debrunner, and R. W. Funk, *A Greek Grammar of the New Testament* (Chicago: University of Chicago Press, 1961)
BiblZeit	*Biblische Zeitschrift*
BJRL	*Bulletin of the John Rylands Library*
BTS	Biblisch-theologische Studien
BZNW	Beiheft, *Zeitschrift für die neutestamentliche Wissenschaft und die Kunde der älteren Kirche*
CBQ	*Catholic Biblical Quarterly*
EvTh	*Evangelische Theologie*
ExT	*Expository Times*
HDR	Harvard Dissertations in Religion
HeyJ	*Heythrop Journal*
HNTC	Harper's New Testament Commentary
HR	*History of Religions*
HTK	Herders theologischer Kommentar zur Neuen Testament
HTR	*Harvard Theological Review*
ICC	International Critical Commentary
IDB	*Interpreter's Dictionary of the Bible,* ed. George A. Buttrick (New York: Abingdon Press, 1972, 1976), 4 vols., supplementary volume
Interp	*Interpretation*
JBL	*Journal of Biblical Literature*
JourRel	*Journal of Religion*

JSNT	*Journal for the Study of the New Testament*
JSNTSS	*Journal for the Study of the New Testament* Supplementary Series
JSOT	*Journal for the Study of the Old Testament*
JThC	*Journal for Theology and Church*
JTS	*Journal of Theological Studies*
KEK	Kritisch-exegetischer Kommentar über das Neue Testament
NCB	New Century Bible
NovTest	*Novum Testamentum*
NTS	*New Testament Studies*
PC	Proclamation Commentary
PerspRelStud	*Perspectives in Religious Studies*
RevExp	*Review and Expositor*
RSV	Revised Standard Version
SB	Stuttgarter Bibelstudien
SBLDS	Society of Biblical Literature Dissertation Series
SBT	Studies in Biblical Theology
SNTSMS	Society for New Testament Studies Monograph Series
TDNT	*Theological Dictionary of the New Testament,* ed. Gerhard Kittel and Gerhard Friedrich, trans. Geoffrey W. Bromiley (Grand Rapids: Wm. B. Eerdmans, 1964–1976)
WBC	Word Biblical Commentary
WF	Wege der Forschung
ZNW	*Zeitschrift für die neutestamentliche Wissenschaft und die Kunde der älteren Kirche*
ZThK	*Zeitschrift für Theologie und Kirche*

Introduction

"He was crucified in weakness" is a shocking way to put it (2 Cor. 13:4). The verse might even be translated, "he was crucified as a weakling."[1] Standing where Paul stood, beyond Easter, one might have anticipated in the recounting of Jesus' death a sublime halo or a hero's mantle or some word of support to ease the sense of Jesus' helplessness. Instead the apostle offers only a stark statement of a shameful and abject incident. Furthermore, such unadorned assertions are characteristic of Paul. His letters are punctuated with reminders of the manner and meaning of Jesus' death. He writes of course not as a historian describing the details of how, where, when, and by whom Jesus was killed, but as a pastoral theologian interpreting the import of Jesus' death both for the congregations under his care and for himself. The blunt language assumes a theological function in addressing communities struggling with their own identities and with the complications of being Christian in a sometimes hostile, sometimes indifferent, world.

This book investigates the importance and role of the death of

---

1. The phrase translated in the RSV "in weakness" (ἐξ ἀσθενείας) is difficult to interpret. The prepositional phrase is probably to be taken as a rhetorical parallel to the corresponding phrase "by the power of God" (ἐκ δυνάμεως θεοῦ) and to be rendered "he was crucified as a result of his weakness" or "he was crucified as a weakling." See Rudolf Bultmann, *The Second Letter to the Corinthians,* trans. Roy A. Harrisville (Minneapolis: Augsburg, 1985), 243; and Victor Paul Furnish, *II Corinthians,* AB (Garden City, N.Y.: Doubleday, 1984), 571.

1

Jesus[2] in the letters of the apostle Paul.[3] The task is fraught with complexities because there is no univocal role assigned to Jesus' death in the letters nor is there one fixed language employed in its depiction. Sometimes the death is spoken of as a self-giving on Jesus' part (Gal. 2:20), at other times as a giving on God's part (Rom. 8:32); sometimes the language of crucifixion is used (1 Cor. 1:23), at other times not (2 Cor. 5:14); sometimes believers as a community are made participants in Jesus' death (Rom. 6:1-11), at other times the death imparts significance to the individual (1 Cor. 8:11); sometimes the death is asserted exclusively (1 Cor. 2:2), at other times it is linked to the resurrection (Rom. 4:25); sometimes it is affirmed as the event by which God effects atonement for human sinfulness (Rom. 3:24-26), at other times it is identified as the cause for persecution (Gal. 5:11). Without blurring the ambiguities and without trying to push Paul into the role of the dogmatic theologian, we shall seek to make sense out of the variety and complexity of what he states about Jesus' death. This will entail an exegetical consideration of a selection of those passages that specifically treat or in some fashion allude to his death, with a particular eye to how the passages function in the arguments of the particular letters.

This study is undertaken in the awareness that the Christian community of the west (of which the author is a part) finds Paul's gospel hard to hear. It is not merely the remoteness of the contextual issues, like circumcision and wearing veils, that we find difficult to translate; it is the problematic at the very heart of Paul's message. The optimism, which has been the vision of society in North America, has had its heyday and, though in many quarters the illusion lives on, cracks are clearly visible in the wall. Outbreaks of terrorism, the vagaries of our economic

2. I am using "Jesus," "Christ," and "Jesus Christ" as interchangeable terms, following the conclusion of Kramer that in the Pauline corpus the three increasingly become names, except where the context indicates differently. See Werner Kramer, *Christ, Lord, Son of God,* trans. Brian Hardy, SBT 50 (Naperville, Ill: Alex R. Allenson, 1966), 201–2.

3. The customary seven letters are taken here as authentically Pauline—Romans, 1 and 2 Corinthians, Galatians, Philippians, 1 Thessalonians, and Philemon—though it is acknowledged that a case can be made for the Pauline authorship of at least three others (Ephesians, Colossians, and 2 Thessalonians).

life, the failure of science immediately to eradicate AIDS, our inability to distribute food to a starving world, and the constant threat of nuclear "accidents" have undermined a placid security. Technology, while solving many problems, has created a host of others, not to mention more sophisticated weapons with which to wage our wars. What inevitably ensues, then, is that hopes for the world, perhaps expressed in idealistic terms, yield to an almost desperate individualism. The dreams for the larger community are reduced to dreams for "me." The contemplation of the massive problems facing humanity as a whole leaves one only with nightmares, thereby insuring a retreat into the self.[4]

A single vignette will suffice. In 1939 Budd Schulberg, a young Hollywood author, wrote a book, *What Makes Sammy Run?* The main character, Sammy Glick, a selfish, cruel climber, moving from copyboy to Hollywood producer, became something of a symbol for the back-stabbing hustlers who clawed their way to the top. In 1987, nearly fifty years later, Schulberg reflected on what happened to Sammy. "The book I wrote as an attack on anti-social behavior has become a how-to book on looking out for No. 1." Schulberg got his first clue when he spoke to a college gathering, and a student later told him, "I love him. I felt nervous about going into the world and making it. But reading 'Sammy' gives me confidence. It's my bible." Schulberg reflected on the incident, "I asked myself, 'What have I done?' From the anti-hero of the '40s to the role model hero for the yuppies of the '80s."[5]

In the face of this national transformation of mood, Christianity, for the most part, has continued as "the official religion of the officially optimistic society."[6] No doubt shaped in part by the wishful thinking of the prevailing culture and in part drawing on certain dimensions of its tradition, the church has found it difficult to confront its own triumphalism, much less the residual

4. For ample documentation of this, see Robert N. Bellah et al., *Habits of the Heart: Individualism and Commitment in American Life* (Berkeley: University of California Press, 1985).

5. From *Newsday*, reported by Richard Reeves, "Whatever It Is, It Still Makes Sammy Run," *International Herald Tribune,* August 19, 1987.

6. Douglas John Hall, *Lighten Our Darkness: Toward an Indigenous Theology of the Cross* (Philadelphia: Westminster Press, 1976), 73–106.

triumphalism of society. Clinging to a dated dream of the past is much easier than the birth pangs of a new vision! In many quarters employing the language of the nineteenth century, the church still speaks in expansionistic terms, of positive thinking, of restoring prayer to the public schools, of making North America again the promised land. To put it in the categories of theology, the church has tended to follow a militant, exalted Christ. Such a Christology is more easily accommodated to the pressures in which we live and certainly makes the church more attractive to a larger proportion of an upwardly mobile population. Paul, too, writes of "the Lord Jesus Christ," risen from the dead by God's power, exalted to the place of authority and rule, from whose love we can never be separated. And yet such texts appear as a piece of the message called in one of his letters "the word of the cross" (1 Cor. 1:18). Paul constantly reminds his readers that the risen Christ is none other than the crucified one, whose wounds cannot be removed by exegetical surgery. The crucifixion of Jesus is not only a past, datable, verifiable fact in the church's memory, but also an ever-present reality to guide and determine the church's life. It is precisely this dimension in Paul's letters that makes them hard to read and accept.

We do well, then, to acknowledge at the outset that an understanding of Jesus' death transcends merely an academic exercise. When the church opens its sacred book and encounters again those passages announcing a crucified Christ, it discovers "the strange new world" of which Karl Barth spoke in 1916. The strangeness, however, is not that we expect to find there *only* history or morality or religion—like the liberals whom Barth was addressing. We are the generation that has debated endlessly the nature of biblical authority and inspiration. In various parts of North America congregations and denominations have vigorously fought and divided over the extent to which the Bible can be identified with the Word of God. But our debates have not lessened the distance between the world of the text and the world in which we earn our living, educate our children, care for aging parents, and seek to function as responsible citizens. Being a postliberal, a liberal, an evangelical, or even a fundamentalist with regard to biblical authority provides no magical power to reduce the oddness of these Pauline texts, to make "the strange, new world" more familiar or comfortable.

Pastors who face their congregations Sunday after Sunday know about the strangeness when they seek to preach from Paul's letters. How are they to interpret "I will all the more gladly boast of my weaknesses, that the power of Christ may rest upon me" (2 Cor.12:9) to the middle-management executive who faces a loss of job if his or her company is bought out? What will the college professor make of a God who declares "I will destroy the wisdom of the wise, and the cleverness of the clever I will thwart" (1 Cor. 1:19)? How can a generation fed on a diet of positive thinking, of self-assertion, of rampant consumerism contemplate even for a moment Paul's vow, "God forbid that I should boast of anything but the cross of our Lord Jesus Christ, through which the world is crucified to me and I to the world" (Gal. 6:14)? The pastor reminds us that when the Pauline texts are clarified, when the academic problems have been finally resolved, the strangeness remains.

Though not always evident on every page, my primary conversation partners for this study of the death of Christ in Paul are the German New Testament scholars of the 1960s and 70s who produced such a rich corpus of literature on the "theology of the cross." In part their contributions were evoked by the needs of the church, and by pastors and church members who sensed a confusion over the heart of the faith—namely, the death and resurrection of Jesus Christ. How crucial is Jesus' death? Is it a unique event in which the crucified Jesus vicariously bore the divine judgment against human sin? Are the categories by which the death is depicted in the New Testament disposable categories of a past age, which now must be replaced? Is Jesus the object of faith or merely the example of how to remain faithful throughout life? A movement under the slogan "No Other Gospel" arose in the middle 1960s, challenging the seemingly radical approaches of many professors in the theological faculties of the universities, and insisting on the historicity and objectivity of the death and resurrection of Jesus as a basis for salvation. In response, the council of the *Evangelische Kirche der Union* in 1964, through its theological committee, initiated three studies to address the issues, one dealing with the resurrection[7] and two concerned with the more pressing issue, the meaning of the death of Jesus. In the latter two studies, contributors to various aspects of the topic from a New Testament perspective were Ernst Käsemann, Hans Conzelmann, Ernst Haenchen, E. Flessemen-van Leer, Eduard Lohse, and Wolfgang Schrage. One of the studies contained an official report of the theological committee, which was then approved by the church's governing synod in 1968.[8]

Simultaneous to and in the aftermath of these discussions, a number of articles and monographs appeared addressing the death of Jesus. In addition to the essays officially prepared for the study by Käsemann and Schrage, those most significant for the investigation of Paul have come from Gerhard Delling,[9] Ulrich Luz,[10] Wolfgang Schrage,[11] Peter Stuhlmacher,[12] and H. W. Kuhn.[13] Two Roman Catholic scholars, Franz-Josef Ortkemper[14]

---

7. The English edition is *The Significance of the Message of the Resurrection for Faith in Jesus Christ,* ed. C. F. D. Moule, trans. D. M. Barton and R. A. Wilson, SBT 8 (London: SCM Press, 1968).

8. The published studies on the death of Jesus are Fritz Viering, ed., *Zur Bedeutung des Todes Jesu* (Gütersloh: Gerd Mohn, 1967); and idem, *Das Kreuz Jesu Christi als Grund des Heils* (Gütersloh: Gerd Mohn, 1967). The editors of *Interpretation* (24 [1970]: 131–242) made available to English readers translations of three of the articles from the first study (those by Käsemann, Conzelmann, and Haenchen) plus an article from the second by Walter Kreck and the final report of the theological committee. The account of the discussion in the German church can be found in Fritz Viering, *Das Kreuzestod Jesu: Interpretation eines theologischen Gutachtens* (Gütersloh: Gerd Mohn, 1969).

9. Gerhard Delling, *Der Kreuzestod Jesu in der urchristlichen Verkündigung* (Göttingen: Vandenhoeck & Ruprecht, 1972).

10. Ulrich Luz, "*Theologia crucis* als Mitte der Theologie im Neuen Testament," *EvTh* 34 (1974): 116–41.

11. Wolfgang Schrage, "Leid, Kreuz und Eschaton: Die Peristasen-Katalog als Merkmale paulinische *Theologia crucis* und Eschatologie," *EvTh* 34 (1974): 141–75.

12. Peter Stuhlmacher, "Eighteen Theses on Paul's Theology of the Cross," in *Reconciliation, Law, and Righteousness,* trans. E. R. Kalin (Philadelphia: Fortress Press, 1986). Stuhlmacher's theses were first developed in a seminar in 1975 and published in German in 1981.

13. H. W. Kuhn, "Jesus als Gekreuzigter in der frühchristlichen Verkündigung bis zur Mitte des 2. Jahrhunderts," *ZThK* 72 (1975): 1–46.

14. Franz-Josef Ortkemper, *Das Kreuz in der Verkündigung des Apostels Paulus: Dargestellt an den Texten der paulischen Hauptbriefe,* SB 24 (Stuttgart: Verlag Katholisches Bibelwerk, 1967).

and Karl Kertelge,[15] also made substantial contributions to the dialogue.

I use the phrase "conversation partners" advisedly. There is no effort here to survey in detail or critique what emerged from these studies during this particular decade or so. Perhaps such is the task for a later historian. Those mentioned above do not by any means agree among themselves on all the important aspects of the theme nor can they be classed as a "school." They may in fact be surprised to find themselves grouped together. But during a particular period and in a common setting they have addressed the same topic. The Lutheran tradition, which undergirds most of the studies, and the German context from which they emerged are unique and are certainly different from my own tradition and context. One cannot help thinking, however, that the texts in Paul that occupied much of the energy of these "conversation partners" are texts that demand careful reflection by the church of North America today, as it struggles for a new self-understanding amid a society in many ways turned in on itself. It is the texts and not the "conversation partners" on which I wish to focus in this study.

"THEOLOGY OF THE CROSS"

In this introduction one issue of crucial significance warrants clarification before we begin to examine the texts themselves. The phrase "theology of the cross" has carried special meaning in the discussions about the death of Jesus because, with greater or lesser precision, it has been employed as a slogan for a particular stance within the history of interpretation. Historically its use actually embraces a theological concern much broader than merely the Pauline letters. The term was first used in 1518 by Martin Luther in the series of statements prepared for the Heidelberg disputation.[16] He strongly objected to the scholastic theo-

15. Karl Kertelge, "Das Verständnis des Todes Jesu bei Paulus," in *Der Tod Jesu: Deutungen im Neuen Testament,* ed. Karl Kertelge (Freiburg: Herder, 1976), 114–36.
16. See especially Theses 19, 20, and 21. *Luther's Works,* ed. Jaroslav Pelikan and Helmut T. Lehmann (Philadelphia: Fortress Press, 1957), 31:52–53.

logians of the day who attempted by rational process to discern the invisible nature of God from the obvious works of creation. In line with Rom. 1:18-25, Luther argued that the knowledge of God does not derive from speculation about the works of creation. The theologian who assumes that the invisible things of God can be perceived from the visible does not deserve to be called a theologian at all. The effort to do so is pretentious and deceiving. It can lead only to calling the good bad and the bad good. Instead, Luther maintained that it is only "through suffering and the cross" that God can be known at all, and then, as with Moses (Exod. 33:23), it is only the backside of God, God hidden in the revelation, that is finally known. The "theology of the cross," then, designates a theology of revelation and not a specific view of the atonement.[17] It is not to be thought of as one doctrine set alongside other doctrines, but as a theological method, a way of doing all theology.[18]

Luther is followed by "exemplars of a thin tradition"[19]—Søren Kierkegaard, Martin Kähler, Adolf Schlatter, Dietrich Bonhoeffer, and to some extent the young Karl Barth, Paul Tillich, and Reinhold Niebuhr. In more recent days, however, the tradition has been reclaimed by two prominent voices in Germany, Jürgen

17. Luz warns that almost every theology mentions the crucifixion and wants to claim for itself the right to be a "theology of the cross"—even the theology at Corinth opposed by Paul and the scholastic theology attacked by Luther. In line with Luther, Luz proposes three marks of a true "theology of the cross." (1) It understands the cross as the exclusive ground of salvation, with the result that all other saving events (such as the resurrection and the parousia) are considered in relation to it and all current understandings are critiqued by it. (2) It understands the cross as the starting point of theology, in the sense that it is not merely an isolated component of theology, but theology itself pure and simple, in the light of which all issues are at stake. (3) It understands the cross as the hub of theology, in the sense that from it statements of anthropology, views of history, ecclesiology, ethics, etc., radiate. Luz lists only Paul and Mark among New Testament witnesses as theologians of the cross in this exclusive sense (*"Theologia crucis,"* 116).
18. See the classic statement written originally in 1929 by Walther von Loewenich, *Luther's Theology of the Cross,* trans. H. J. A. Bouman, 5th ed. (Minneapolis: Augsburg, 1976); Alistair E. McGrath, *Luther's Theology of the Cross: Martin Luther's Theological Breakthrough* (Oxford: Basil Blackwell, 1985).
19. Hall, *Lighten Our Darkness,* 115–37.

Moltmann[20] and Eberhard Jüngel,[21] and one in North America, Douglas John Hall.[22]

ERNST KÄSEMANN ON THE DEATH OF JESUS

Our concern, however, is not with the broader theological tradition, nor even with the "theology of the cross" as the proposed center of the New Testament, but with the letters of Paul. Unquestionably the most vigorous and articulate advocate of understanding Pauline thought as a "theology of the cross" is Ernst Käsemann. In the post-Bultmannian era his influence has certainly been the most dominant in shaping the discussion in Germany, and accessibility of his works in other languages has made his voice resound in academic circles throughout the world. While nearly all his writings dealing with the apostle argue for the cross as the canon of Pauline interpretation, it is his essay prepared as a part of the study sponsored by the *Evangelische Kirche der Union* that has become a landmark in modern interpretation.[23] The essay is not a detailed, exegetical piece, surveying all the relevant passages, but a passionate affirmation of the "theology of the cross" and a challenge to theologians and church officials to follow Paul's lead. It is significant that the title in German (no doubt reflecting the original assignment made by the theological committee) is not "The Pauline Theology of the Cross" but "The Saving Significance of the Death of Jesus in

20. Jürgen Moltmann, *The Crucified God: The Cross of Christ as the Foundation and Criticism of Christian Theology,* trans R. A. Wilson and John Bowden (New York: Harper & Row, 1974).

21. Eberhard Jüngel, *God as the Mystery of the World: On the Foundation of the Theology of the Crucified One in the Dispute between Theism and Atheism,* trans. D. L. Guder (Grand Rapids, Mich.: Wm. B. Eerdmans, 1983).

22. Douglas John Hall, *Lighten Our Darkness;* idem, *God and Human Suffering: An Exercise in the Theology of the Cross* (Minneapolis: Augsburg, 1986); idem, *Thinking the Faith: Christian Theology in a North American Context* (Minneapolis: Augsburg, 1989).

23. Ernst Käsemann, "Die Heilsbedeutung des Todes Jesu nach Paulus," *Zum Bedeutung des Todes Jesu,* 13–34. Two translations of this have appeared in English: "The Pauline Theology of the Cross," *Interp* 24 (1970): 151–77; and "The Saving Significance of the Death of Jesus in Paul," in *Perspectives on Paul,* trans. Margaret Kohl (Philadelphia: Fortress Press, 1971), 32–59. The citations here come from *Perspectives on Paul.*

Paul" (*Die Heilsbedeutung des Todes Jesu nach Paulus*), though, as we shall see, the latter is clearly interpreted in light of the former. Because of the powerful influence of Käsemann and in order to define more precisely the issues surrounding a consideration of Jesus' death, we shall examine in detail his monumental essay and then raise a methodological issue that will give a slightly different cast to our own study.[24]

Käsemann begins his essay with an unabashed confession. "It must be asserted with the greatest possible emphasis that both historically and theologically Paul has to be understood in the light of the Reformation's insight. Any other perspective at most covers part of his thinking; it does not grasp the heart of it" (32). By "the Reformation's insight" Käsemann means primarily Luther's perception that all theology must be seen as a "theology of the cross." On the surface such an emphasis on the Reformation might suggest a return to an era when ecclesiastical dogma dictated the results of the exegetical process. As a matter of fact, ecclesiastical control (or perhaps better, ecclesiastical domestication) is exactly what Käsemann is opposing. There has been in his perception no unbroken confessional tradition continuing the insights of the Reformation; instead, the church's theology as well as the discipline of exegesis (excepting those "exemplars of a thin tradition") has consistently blunted the sharpness of what the reformers argued, usually in the interest of a less onesided and a more ecumenical approach.

When Käsemann turns to Paul, he consistently draws a distinction between the texts that Paul inherits from the liturgical tradition of the early church and those that emanate from Paul himself. The latter are more characteristically Pauline and for Käsemann carry more weight. In line with this, he begins with the passages emphasizing "the scandal of the cross," because crucifixion language (not appearing in the texts from the received tradition) represents a distinctively Pauline contribution. This becomes Paul's way of underscoring not only the fact that Jesus

---

24. See the thorough treatment of Käsemann's "theology of the cross" in connection with the NT canon in Bernhard Ehler, *Die Herrschaft des Gekreuzigten: Ernst Käsemanns Frage nach der Mitte der Schrift*, BZNW 46 (Berlin: Walter de Gruyter, 1986), esp. 300–13.

died by a means of a punishment reserved exclusively for criminals, but also that he died as one cursed and forsaken by God (Gal. 3:13; cf. Heb. 13:12-13). The message of a crucified Messiah was so radical that it became for Jews a stumbling block and for Greeks folly (1 Cor. 1:23).

Käsemann makes two indispensable observations about Paul's use of crucifixion language as opposed to other terms for Jesus' death. First, the "theology of the cross" is from beginning to end a polemical theology. In fact, it loses its force and vitality when employed in nonpolemical contexts. "It was always a critical attack on the dominating traditional interpretation of the Christian message, and it is not by chance that it characterized Protestant beginnings" (35). By "polemical" Käsemann does not mean an argument used in a conflict situation between Christians and non-Christians, but an argument used in an intramural challenge. It was the legalistic piety of Jewish Christian circles and the enthusiasm of Hellenistic Christianity that became the object of Paul's attack. To put it another way, Paul is aware that the world has so infiltrated the church that within the Christian communities can be found those who are "enemies of the cross" (Phil. 3:18; Gal. 6:12). The question with such groups is not whether they remain suitably religious, but whether they find their foundation and criterion in the cross even in their everyday life.

Käsemann's second observation follows from the first. "Hostility to the cross is the leading characteristic of the world" (37). Paul's ministry is an example of what living under the shadow of the cross entails. He mentions afflictions, perplexities, persecutions, and the like not as a special badge he wears as an apostle, but as evidence of what the church continually discovers when taking seriously the crucified Jesus. Religion in general may be tolerated or even revered by a surrounding society, but the cross will evoke rejection.

But what of those passages in Paul where Jesus' death is referred to as having atoning significance? Käsemann feels that most of these references are a part of the tradition Paul has inherited from the church before him and that, when they appear in his letters, they are revamped and given a new depth and often a different direction. The traditions that speak of Christ's death as a sacrifice for sins or as a vicarious or representative act for sinners or as a redemption for enslaved people are employed to express the benefits of grace for the human community. Paul is more interested in the anthropological thrust of Jesus' death than in what it may have meant for God. About the language of sacrifice, Käsemann writes, "The cross's consequences for men [and women] dominate all Paul's statements to such an extent that the consequences for God simply do not enter his field of vision, and other concepts occupy the foreground so exclusively that for this reason alone no essential significance can be attributed to the theme of sacrifice" (43).

Paul, according to Käsemann, is engaged here in two radical moves in his treatment of the received tradition. On the one hand, he is interpreting the traditional texts existentially. What had been adapted to liturgical forms and uses in the pre-Pauline church needed to be brought back to earthly realities, to the lives of those for whom the death occurred. This Paul does by consistently putting the traditional language to an anthropological use. On the other hand, Paul radicalizes the tradition by stressing Jesus' death for the ungodly. For him the liturgical forms simply did not convey with sufficient sharpness the shocking and paradoxical meaning of the death for rebellious humanity. The cross is not a nicety. It exposes humans as always the sinners, unable alone to achieve salvation; it crushes the illusions of transcendence and self-righteousness.

Two texts in Romans, neither from the received tradition, become decisive in Käsemann's understanding of Paul. They speak of God "who justifies the ungodly" (4:5) and Christ who "died for the ungodly" (5:6). These texts provide the crucial link between the death of Jesus and what for Käsemann gives the death its true interpretation—justification by faith. He comments:

> Despair ends on the cross of Jesus because pride ends there as well; the rebel's presumption as well as the arrogance of the devout, alienation from God together with holy places, foolishness at the same time as the illusions of those who think themselves wise. Before God who humbles himself, self-transcending man comes to an end; even the mask of Christianity cannot save him. The dying

Son of God does not give life without killing; he pardons but as judge; he glorifies us by humbling us to the deepest degree; he illuminates by confronting us inexorably with the truth about ourselves; he heals by placing us among the poor in spirit. . . . All this can be brought down to a common denominator: the justification of the ungodly is for Paul the fruit of Jesus' death, and nothing else. And this means *regnum dei* on earth [45-46].

Any treatment of the "theology of the cross" in Paul must face the question of how the resurrection of Jesus relates to his death. Käsemann is highly critical of those who in answering the question have set the cross and resurrection in a coordinating or dialectical relationship or have treated the two as "only links in a chain" (47), together with Christ's preexistence, incarnation, exaltation, and return.[25] The problem with such answers is that they blunt the insight of Luther and end up as attacks on the Reformation basis of Protestantism. Käsemann singles out the 1933 study of Walter Künneth, which stresses the resurrection as "the key-signature" to statements about the cross and poses the connection between the two in this way: "Cross and resurrection stand in the relation of riddle and interpretation. . . . The cross is, to be sure, the presupposition for the resurrection of Jesus, but it is the latter that gives the former its meaning."[26]

In response, Käsemann notes that for Paul Jesus' resurrection is not understood as the revivification of a dead person, but as the inauguration of the general resurrection of the dead. It is the beginning of the rule of Christ as the Lord of the church, the *destined* Cosmocrator. To be sure, other Christologies in the New Testament affirm the heavenly exaltation of Jesus immediately following his death. But the pitfall of these Christologies is that the cross can then easily become merely a way station on the journey to the exaltation and an incident that retains for the church only historical relevance. The enthusiasm of the Corinthian congregation resulted from just such an inadequate Chris-

---

25. See Käsemann's critique of *Heilsgeschichte* in "Justification and Salvation History in the Epistle to the Romans," in *Perspectives on Paul*, 60–78. The essay is intended as a critique of Krister Stendahl, who offers a response in *Paul Among Jews and Gentiles* (Philadelphia: Fortress Press, 1976), 129–33.

26. Walter Künneth, *The Theology of the Resurrection,* trans. James W. Leitch (London: SCM Press, 1965), 151–52. Künneth adds, "The 'word of the cross' is at the bottom no other than 'word of the resurrection.'"

tology and from the failure to embrace the "not-yetness" of the Christian experience. "Before Paul, the cross of Jesus formed the question which was answered by the message of the resurrection. The apostle decisively reversed this way of looking at things. In his controversy with the enthusiasts it was precisely the interpretation of the resurrection which turned out to be a problem, a problem which could only be answered in the light of the cross" (57).[27]

Thus Käsemann vigorously opposes any position that would relegate the cross to a mere chapter in a broader treatment of the resurrection. Rather, "the theology of the resurrection is a chapter in the theology of the cross, not the excelling of it. Since Paul, all theological controversy has radiated ultimately from one central point and can hence only be decided at that point: *crux sola nostra theologia*" (59).

A final word in the essay is addressed to those within the *Evangelische Kirche* who have argued the "facts" of redemption and have placed a high premium on the historicity and objectivity of Jesus' death and resurrection.[28] Such an emphasis, Käsemann argues, unfortunately severs the "facts" from their proclamation and ignores the Pauline affirmation that faith comes from preaching (Rom. 10:14, 17). Mere historical remembrances of the events always remain ambiguous and can never be a proper basis for evangelical faith. In fact, to build a faith on historical "facts" as such is to invite all manner of uncertainty and doubt. One is left to the mercy of the historians and insecure about the

---

27. For Käsemann's further treatment of Paul's encounter with the enthusiasts, see "For and Against a Theology of the Resurrection," in *Jesus Means Freedom,* trans. Frank Clarke (Philadelphia: Fortress Press; London: SCM Press, 1969), 59–84; idem, "On the Subject of Primitive Christian Apocalyptic," in *New Testament Questions of Today,* trans. W. J. Montague (Philadelphia: Fortress Press; London: SCM Press, 1969), 103–37, esp. 124–37.

28. It is interesting to note the parallel between this opposition to the "facts" of redemption and the arguments advanced by Käsemann in 1954 for a renewed quest of the historical Jesus. With the latter, the search is not for *bruta facta* but for the connection and tension between the preaching of Jesus and the preaching of the community. See "The Problem of the Historical Jesus," in *Essays on New Testament Themes,* trans. W. J. Montague (London: SCM Press, 1964), 15–47. For a recent discussion of the cross in relation to an understanding of history, see Hans Weder, *Das Kreuz Jesu bei Paulus* (Göttingen: Vandenhoeck & Ruprecht, 1981).

very salvation assuredly declared in preaching. The "theology of the cross" and the theology of the word are inextricably linked.[29]

We shall not pause here to engage in a lengthy critique of Käsemann's essay. An extensive account of his position has been given so as to provide an introduction to the fundamental issues needing to be addressed in this study and to recognize that Käsemann represents a bench mark for further discussion. No contemporary consideration of Paul's understanding can avoid the concerns he raises. We shall return to various facets of his argument, agreeing with some and expanding others, as we investigate the Pauline texts themselves. Five statements will suffice as a summary of his position.

1. The "theology of the cross" is the distinctively Pauline understanding of "the saving significance of Jesus' death," stressing (a) the scandalous crucifixion of Jesus as a criminal cursed by God, (b) through whom God justifies the ungodly.

2. This Pauline understanding of Jesus' death functions polemically to combat human arrogance and self-righteousness, particularly when clothed in the garb of piety and religion.

3. The traditional terminology that interpreted Jesus' death in its atoning significance is turned by Paul in an existential direction and is to be understood exclusively in relation to believers, who are always the ungodly whom God justifies.

4. Jesus' death has saving significance not as a historical event in itself but only in connection with the preaching of the event and the response of faith.

5. The "theology of the cross" is the center of Pauline theology, and it loses its meaning when made merely one theme among many themes.

There emerges a methodological question from the essay, however, which must be dealt with at the outset, because it markedly determines the course of our study. In making his case, Käsemann employs the discipline of redaction criticism to set in bold relief the distinctiveness of Paul's theology over against the tradi-

---

29. In this, Käsemann is in agreement with Luther, who said, "It is not enough or in any sense Christian to preach the works, life, and words of Christ as historical facts, as if the knowledge of these would suffice for the conduct of life." See "The Freedom of a Christian," *Luther's Works,* 31:357.

tion he inherits from his fellow Christians. The early church in both its Jewish and Hellenistic environments developed significant liturgical materials—creeds, hymns, baptismal and communion formulas—many of which must have been employed widely in a variety of congregations. Paul draws on this body of material, sometimes indicating that it derives from the tradition (1 Cor. 11:23; 15:3), more usually not (Phil. 2:6-11; Gal. 1:4). Since this material, its content as well as its wording, has been shaped by others than Paul, it does not carry the weight for Käsemann in defining Pauline theology as does material that Paul himself composes. The passages affirming Jesus' death as a sacrifice, as a vicarious event, and as redemption are given low priority because they, for the most part, seem to come originally from the tradition. Furthermore, Käsemann is rather clear that when Paul does cite tradition he turns it in a different direction; he radicalizes it; he corrects it. For example, Paul's distinctive "theology of the cross" causes him to give the traditional material about the atonement an anthropological or existential meaning, in essence leaving Paul without an atonement.[30] As a result, the discontinuity between Paul and the Christian tradition he inherited greatly outweighs the continuity.

Three brief questions need to be raised about this methodological issue. First, is it always possible to separate with assurance what is traditional from what is redactional? When Paul clearly states that he is citing the tradition (as he does in 1 Cor. 11:23; 15:3), that is one thing; when on metrical grounds Pauline emendations are detected in what is likely a pre-Pauline tradition (as Käsemann detects in Phil. 2:8 with the phrase "even death on a cross"), that is another.[31] The levels of certainty are not the same and need to be acknowledged, especially in moving from text to theology. No doubt there are many words, phrases, and sentences in the letters that were also a part of the common Christian vocabulary, but it is extremely difficult to isolate them. They have become so much a part of Paul's vocabulary and the

---

30. See the complaint about this by Stuhlmacher in *Reconciliation, Law, and Righteousness*, 157.
31. See Käsemann, "A Critical Analysis of Phil. 2:5-11," *JThC* 5 (1968): 45-88.

vocabulary of his churches that they cannot be easily singled out and labeled "tradition."

Second, is material taken from the pre-Pauline tradition necessarily to be given less importance than the material immediately from Paul? A creed might be quoted (as I think is the case with Phil. 2:6-11) precisely because it says what Paul wants to say and perhaps says it better. He may have intended it to be read emphatically, as if it were italicized. Or Paul may employ traditional material because it provides a common ground he shares with his audience and a basis from which to argue. In both cases, the traditional material has become "Pauline."

Third, is Paul as much of a revamper of the tradition as is suggested by Käsemann's work? A liturgical formula may be quoted for a variety of reasons. There are no doubt occasions when Paul takes over a hymnic statement (as he does with Old Testament citations) and gives it a different slant to suit the needs of the particular context he is addressing. But there are also occasions when he cites the tradition as an influential voice to which he appeals in making his own case. The use of the traditional words of institution of the Lord's Supper in 1 Cor. 11:23-25 is a good example. The nuances and authority of the citation greatly enhance the argument. The discussion surrounding the citation draws heavily on the citation to address the abuses in the Corinthian congregation (see the exegesis of the passage in chapter 4). Methodologically then, it seems unwise either to underestimate the significance of traditional material for Paul or to anticipate too quickly his alteration of it. [32]

In this study we shall not ignore the results of redaction criticism, but at the same time we shall work on the assumption that Paul is responsible for the final form of his letters. The citing of a liturgical formula makes it a piece of his own argument, unless

32. Among the conversation partners for this study there exists a divided mind on the way in which Paul is to be understood in relation to the received tradition. Luz (*"Theologia crucis,"* 119–21) and Kuhn ("Jesus als Gekreuzigter," 28–29) tend to agree with Käsemann. Stuhlmacher (*Reconciliation, Law, and Righteousness,* 157, 166), Kertelge ("Das Verständnis des Todes," 114–24), and Delling (*Die Kreuzestod Jesu,* 16–17) are less inclined to pit Paul against the tradition. Delling comments: "Paul cites the texts taken over from the tradition, or rather he works them into his presentation, because the tradition's affirmations are also his" (16).

there is some indication within the logic of the argument itself to suggest that the tradition is being redirected or opposed.[33] Undoubtedly there are more important and less important references to Jesus' death in Paul's letters, but the literary context and not redaction criticism must be the deciding factor. Our investigation, therefore, will be much more synchronic than diachronic in character, though historical issues cannot be entirely ignored.[34]

A reduced stress on redaction criticism results in a broader interpretation of the theology of the cross in the Pauline letters than that offered by Käsemann. In examining a more extensive array of texts dealing with the death of Jesus—traditional as well as redactional, texts that do not use the language of crucifixion as well as those that do[35]—we discover that the death functions in the letters not only polemically as a weapon against triumphalism and legalism but also to nurture in the readers an identification of themselves as people of the cross, people who bear in their bodies the death of Jesus. Some texts prick the bubbles of pretense and self-complacency, but others serve to instruct the churches about their unity, holiness, and calling in the world. Several texts are double-edged, judging one type of reader and comforting another. In respecting the rhetorical effect of the texts, we are left with a less neatly defined but more broadly functional theology of the cross.

PLAN OF THE BOOK

I have chosen to organize this study topically as opposed to pursuing the theme letter by letter (e.g., "The Death of Jesus in

---

33. A reevaluation of redaction criticism has certainly been taking place with regard to studies in the Synoptic Gospels. To argue "what Matthew or Luke does with the Markan source" is no longer a cogent argument apart from an appreciation of the literary integrity of each Gospel narrative.

34. We shall also seek to follow what George Kennedy calls the linear principle of reading the letters. They were no doubt written with the expectation that they would be read aloud to a group of people more often than read privately. As with a speech, the argument then is cumulative; each passage has to be grasped in terms of what has already been written. See Kennedy's *New Testament Interpretation Through Rhetorical Criticism* (Chapel Hill: University of North Carolina Press, 1984), 5–6, 146.

35. See at the end of the Introduction the excursus "The Language of Crucifixion."

Romans," "The Death of Jesus in 1 Corinthians," etc.). At the same time, I have wanted, as far as possible and in an explicit way, to deal with texts within their literary contexts, to offer "readings" of passages, in hope of avoiding an atomistic interpretation. The topical organization means that both writer and reader have to be especially sensitive to approach Paul not as a systematic theologian but as one whose theology we know only through seven occasional letters. Recent Pauline scholarship has struggled with the distinction between the theology of Paul and the theology of Paul's letters, recognizing that the theology of Paul is larger than even the accumulative theology of his letters but can be reconstructed only on the basis of the letters.[36] Though there may be no easy solution to the dilemma, a thematic investigation such as this one must proceed with care and not ignore the contingency and particularity of the genre Paul used. We are in fact primarily concerned with the theology of the letters.

Since this study has an expressed theological intent and an interest in the life and thought of the church, at various points an effort is made to engage the theological tradition of the church. The classic attributes of God (chapter 1), the historic theories of the atonement (chapter 2), and two of the marks of the church affirmed in the creed (chapter 4) are interpreted in light of our "readings" of Pauline texts. Admittedly, the engagements with the tradition are only brief and without an adequate statement of the hermeneutical issues involved. They are offered, however, out of the conviction that such theological traditions are important for the church (or should be), but must always be interpreted and reformed by the witness of Scripture.

Systematic theologians have demonstrated much interest of late in the role of God in relation to the death of Jesus, no doubt in large measure due to the intense and persistent questions arising from the Holocaust and Hiroshima. They are questions that in a variety of ways also confront pastors who seek to inter-

---

36. See in particular Leander E. Keck, *Paul and His Letters,* PC (Philadelphia: Fortress Press, 1979), who distinguishes between "the gospel Paul preached" and "what Paul fought for"; and J. Christiaan Beker, *Paul the Apostle: The Triumph of God in Life and Thought* (Philadelphia: Fortress Press, 1980), who speaks of "the coherent center" and "the contingency" of Paul's thought.

pret the ways of God in the lives of their parishioners. In the first chapter we examine three passages where Paul writes of God's intentions and actions in Jesus' death, intentions, and actions that force a rethinking of the classic attributes of God.

In the second chapter we address the issue Käsemann has so sharply raised concerning the atoning significance of the crucifixion, what the death of Jesus means with regard to human sinfulness. A number of metaphorical categories are employed to express God's saving action in Christ, each category with its own vividness and signification. Their multiformity and richness raise questions with any theory that constricts their expressiveness in an effort to make one category the interpretive key to the others.

Käsemann has shown us what is at stake in the relative importance of the cross and the resurrection of Jesus in the Pauline letters. Most modern triumphalism within the church has its roots in one understanding of the relationship, whereas Paul articulates another. In chapter 3, in examining the relation of cross to resurrection, we see how the two events belong together in the theological structure of the letters and yet how each maintains its own cutting edge.

In chapters 4 and 5 we consider several passages in which readers are reminded of their identity as people of the cross. The death of Jesus serves as the focal point of arguments that affirm the unity of Jews and gentiles in the Christian community, arguments that face the shameful disregard of poorer members of lower social standing, and address the moral sensitivity of the congregation. Furthermore, Paul brings this more sharply into view in several autobiographical passages through which he invites readers to decipher their own existence in the light of Jesus' death and resurrection. What we encounter in these texts is an exploration of the effects of the preaching of the crucified Christ for the life of the congregation, for the structure of the new life in Christ, and for a faithful witness in the world.

In the conclusion we face the "strangeness" of hearing and heeding Paul in the modern world. If the church is to move beyond triumphalism and individualism, it must from its traditions discover afresh its own individuality and discern its identity in distinction from the dominant culture. The Pauline letters with their insistence that the risen Christ is the crucified one represent a slice of the church's tradition that speaks pointedly and persuasively to that task. We seek to sketch with a broad brush at least some of the directions in which Paul's letters point.

EXCURSUS: THE LANGUAGE OF CRUCIFIXION

A variety in terminology appears in the Pauline letters to denote the death of Jesus. The pre-Pauline tradition bequeaths to Paul both specialized and general terms—cultic language like "expiation" and "blood" (Rom. 3:25) and simple language like "die" (1 Cor. 15:3). Paul exploits this received language and contributes further expressions, such as "gave himself" (Gal. 2:20) and especially "was crucified" (2 Cor. 13:4) and "cross" (1 Cor. 1:17). Since the language of crucifixion appears not to derive from the pre-Pauline store of terms, it is occasionally isolated by interpreters and made to be the foundation for a distinctively Pauline understanding of the death of Jesus. The texts using crucifixion terminology are surprisingly rare (Rom. 6:6; 1 Cor. 1:17, 18; 2:2; 2 Cor. 13:4; Gal. 2:19; 3:1, 13; 5:11; 6:12, 14; Phil. 2:8; 3:16) but often carry importance in inverse proportion to their frequency. J. C. Beker, for example, calls attention to this specialized language:

> Paul's theology of the cross is his unique contribution to the interpretation of the death and resurrection of Christ. Contrary to widespread opinion, the theology of the cross is rare in the New Testament. It must be distinguished in some ways from a theology of the death and resurrection of Christ and from that of the suffering of Christ. The interactions among these forms of reflection on the death of Christ do not permit us to fuse them, because they have distinct meanings.[37]

Though Beker does not take the isolated theology of the cross to be the center of Paul's thought, Kuhn,[38] Schrage,[39] and Luz,[40]

---

37. Beker, *Paul the Apostle,* 198.
38. Kuhn, "Jesus als Gekreuzigter," 40–46.
39. Schrage, "Das Verständnis des Todes Jesu Christi im Neuen Testament," in *Das Kreuz Jesu Christi as Grund des Heils,* ed. Viering, 67–68.
40. Luz, *"Theologia crucis,"* 116–23.

whom he otherwise follows, do make such a judgment. The small collection of texts using the crucifixion language becomes in their view the interpretive key to unlock Pauline theology.

Several questions need to be raised about the isolating of these texts specifically mentioning the cross and about claiming that they provide Paul's distinctive understanding of Jesus' death.

1. Romans, which has much to say about the significance of Jesus Christ, his death and resurrection, uses crucifixion language in only one verse: "knowing this, that our old humanity was crucified with him" (6:6). It is surprising that this epistle, speaking as frequently as it does of God's justification of sinful humanity, contains no further reference to the death as a crucifixion. If Paul's characteristic understanding of the death of Jesus is to be located exclusively in crucifixion language, then one has to say it is missing from Romans.

2. In the one occurrence of crucifixion language in Romans, it is impossible to draw a distinction between "was crucified with him ($\sigma\upsilon\nu\epsilon\sigma\tau\alpha\upsilon\rho\omega\theta\eta$)" in 6:6 and "died with Christ ($\dot{\alpha}\pi\epsilon\theta\dot{\alpha}\nu o\mu\epsilon\nu$ $\sigma\dot{\upsilon}\nu$ $X\rho\iota\sigma\tau\hat{\omega}$)" in 6:8 (cf. also 8:13). One is hard pressed to discover even a slightly nuanced variation in the phrases, suggesting that, at least in this context, they are synonymous.

3. The high proportion of the occurrences of crucifixion terminology in only two letters—1 Corinthians (and only in chapters 1 and 2) and Galatians—hardly commends it as the distinctive feature of the Pauline understanding, especially since the death of Jesus is referred to in six of the seven letters.

4. It is argued that with rare exceptions crucifixion language is never associated with the prepositions "on behalf of" or "in place of" ($\dot{\upsilon}\pi\dot{\epsilon}\rho$, $\pi\epsilon\rho\dot{\iota}$), which are regularly used with "die" and "death" to convey a vicarious or representative interpretation.[41] The rare exceptions, however, need to be taken seriously. As Beker concedes, "Was Paul crucified for you ($\dot{\upsilon}\pi\dot{\epsilon}\rho$ $\dot{\upsilon}\mu\hat{\omega}\nu$)?" (1 Cor. 1:13) no doubt connects the death of Jesus as a crucifixion with the more widely used vicarious or representative phrase. Further, in Gal. 3:13 when, with the use of a citation from Deut. 21:23, the phrase

---

41. Kuhn, "Jesus als Gekeuzigter," 28–29; Beker, *Paul the Apostle,* 199.

"hanging on a tree" appears, again we discover the preposition "on behalf of" (ὑπέρ): "Christ . . . having become a curse on your behalf." In Gal. 2:19-20 Paul can in the same sentence say "I have been crucified with Christ" and also speak of the Son of God "who gave himself on my behalf (ὑπὲρ ἐμοῦ)." These three texts (and perhaps also Gal. 6:14) suggest that the two interpretations of Jesus' death—as crucifixion and as substitution or representation—are not to be sharply separated from one another.

5. The observation has been made that crucifixion language is never combined with resurrection language (in distinction from "die" or "death," terms regularly connected to the resurrection) and that "the focus on the death of Christ in the terminology of 'the cross' is often so exclusive that in most contexts no explicit 'life' terminology relieves its darkness and judgment."[42] It is certainly true that there is no instance of a "crucified-resurrected" formula in the Pauline letters. On several occasions, however, "darkness and judgment" are in fact relieved by connected references to life, new creation, or anticipated resurrection (Gal. 2:19-20; 6:14-15; 2 Cor. 13:4; Rom. 6:6, 8; Phil. 2:8-11), raising again the question whether the death as crucifixion should be taken so exclusively.

6. Finally, the case is made that crucifixion language is distinctive in Paul because, unlike other references to the death of Jesus, it is exclusively used in polemical situations.[43] In one sense, such an observation is correct; in another sense, however, it ignores the fact that in two polemical contexts Paul refers to his previous preaching (presumably prior to the time when the polemic is made) as the proclamation of "Christ crucified" (1 Cor. 2:1-2; Gal. 3:1). One would certainly assume on the basis of 1 Cor. 2:1-2 that Paul's missionary preaching on his initial visit to Corinth as well as his later polemical argumentation included language about the cross.[44] The text certainly makes it difficult to

---

42. Beker, *Paul the Apostle,* 199.
43. Käsemann, *Perspectives on Paul,* 35–36; Kuhn, "Jesus als Gekreuzigter," 40.
44. Gerhard Friedrich, *Die Verkündigung des Todes Jesus im Neuen Testament,* BTS 6 (Neukirchen-Vluyn: Neukirchen Verlag, 1982), 133–36.

suggest that Jesus' death as a sacrifice or as a representative event is for missionary preaching, whereas Jesus' death as crucifixion is only significant polemically.

Of course texts like 1 Cor. 1:18—2:2 and Gal. 6:12-15 make an eloquent argument for the theological significance of the death of Jesus as crucifixion. The interpreter ignores the power and nuance of the language at his or her folly. It is patently obvious that expressions about the cross carry meanings different from other expressions (for example, those using cultic terms). At the same time, the language of crucifixion is employed in a variety of contexts and is drawn together with other expressions in such a way that it becomes difficult to extract a single set of terms as if it constitutes a "theology" in and of itself. While one can appreciate the peculiar power of the statements using crucifixion language, they are to be seen alongside and in tandem with other statements of Jesus' death, not in isolation from them or from their contexts.

CHAPTER 1

Jesus' Death
and God

In an age like ours, obsessed with the issue of historical and scientific causation, a natural question to raise initially about the crucifixion of Christ is: Who did it and for what reason? Was Jesus' death precipitated by Jews, who took offense at his persisting relationship with tax collectors and sinners, his apparent carelessness in observing the sacred law of Moses, or perhaps his statement about the destruction of the temple at Jerusalem? Or since Jesus was killed by crucifixion, could the Romans have been the culprits? Could Jesus have been a closet revolutionary representing a more serious threat to law and order than otherwise appears on the surface? Or could there be a sense in which Jesus was responsible for his own death? Could he have been so resolutely and recklessly obedient to his cause that he painted himself into a corner, leaving the powers that be no alternative but to kill him? Like many martyrs before and since, could he have felt that his mission was better served by death than by continued life?

It is astonishing what we discover when we put these questions to the Pauline texts. Paul appears totally uninterested in tracking down and identifying the villains responsible for Jesus' crucifixion, nor does he offer any historical reasons why they did it. To be sure, one passage speaks of "the Jews, who killed both the Lord Jesus and the prophets" (1 Thess. 2:14-15), but the problematics of the text prevent its being identified as Paul's answer to the

25

reason for Jesus' death.[1] Apart from this passage, he says nothing about the circumstances, conditions, or details of Jesus' death.

Paul's lack of interest in historical causation emerges in the apocalyptic interpretation he gives to the crucifixion in 1 Cor. 2:8. "None of the rulers of this age understood this [that is, the secret and hidden wisdom that God decreed before the ages]; for if they had, they would not have crucified the Lord of glory." The context (especially v. 6) makes it likely that "the rulers of this age" are not political figures, such as Pontius Pilate or Caiaphas, but the supernatural forces of the present evil age, "who are doomed to pass away" (2:6).[2] For Paul the death of Jesus has to be depicted on a bigger and broader canvas than that of Palestine in the third and fourth decades of the first century c.e. It is a cosmic event that in the final analysis exposes and judges the wisdom of this age and the rulers of this age.

Instead of a concern for historical causality, what dominates the texts that mention the death of Christ is the stunning news that *God* is the protagonist. Behind the drama of the self-giving Christ is the self-giving love of God. "But God shows his own love for us in that while we were yet sinners Christ died for us" (Rom. 5:8). Even in a text such as Gal. 1:4, which affirms Jesus' own initiative ("who gave himself for our sins to deliver us from the present evil age"), the initiative comes in compliance with God's intention ("according to the will of our God and Father").

---

1. Some commentators take 1 Thess. 2:13-16 to be a later interpolation, since, among other reasons, the section does not seem to fit the context well and the stance toward the Jews appears in opposition to Romans 9–11. See B. A. Pearson, "1 Thessalonians 2:13-16: A Deutero-Pauline Interpolation," *HTR* 64 (1971): 79–94; and Hendrikus Boers, "The Form Critical Study of Paul's Letters: 1 Thessalonians as a Case Study," *NTS* 22 (1975–76): 140–58. Other commentators take the verses to be part of the original letter and note that the intention in the context is a general indictment of "the Jews" for their opposition to the gospel of which the reference to the killing of Jesus is simply one incident. See G. E. Okeke, "1 Thess. 2:13-16: The Fate of the Unbelieving Jews," *NTS* 27 (1980): 127–36; I. H. Marshall, *1 and 2 Thessalonians,* NCB (Grand Rapids, Mich.: Wm. B. Eerdmans, 1983), 81; K. P. Donfried, "Paul and Judaism: 1 Thessalonians 2:13-16 as a Test Case," *Interp* 38 (1984): 242–53.

2. Cf. C. K. Barrett *The First Epistle to the Corinthians,* HNTC (New York: Harper & Row, 1967), 68–72; Hans Conzelmann, *A Commentary on the First Epistle to the Corinthians,* trans. James W. Leitch, Hermeneia (Philadelphia: Fortress Press, 1975), 61.

There is no notion of Jesus as a lonely and courageous hero, taking up the cause of humanity in its brokenness and forcing God's hand to change the course of history.[3] Nor is it that God, following the extraordinary self-sacrifice on the cross, steps in to reprieve an otherwise martyred Jesus by raising him from the dead. The hymn of Phil. 2:6-11 on the surface might suggest such a rescue operation. As is often noted, Jesus is the subject of the action in the first movement of the hymn (not counting equality with God a thing to be grasped, emptying himself, taking the form of a servant, being born in human likeness, humbling himself, being obedient unto death) and then God becomes the actor in the second movement (exalting Jesus and giving him the name "Lord"). But before the two actors are separated too sharply, the question has to be asked about Jesus' actions in the first movement: obedient unto whom? Implied is the understanding that his dramatic display of selflessness, which in some sense becomes the paradigm for the Christian community, comes in coincidence with the divine purposes, not opposed to or outside them.

The point is that Paul interprets the event of the cross *theo-logically*. His Christology makes it possible to see Jesus' action as God's action. The story of the cross relates not only the story of the Son of God "who loved me and gave himself for me" (Gal. 2:20), but at the same time the story of one "who did not spare his only Son but gave him up for us all" (Rom. 8:32).[4]

To press this divine intentionality further, we need to examine in more detail three texts of fundamental significance: 1 Cor. 1:18—2:5; Rom. 3:21-26; and Rom. 5:6-8.

GOD REVEALED IN THE CRUCIFIED CHRIST (1 COR. 1:18—2:5)

This passage is a disconcerting one in that it makes the demand that theological reflection begin with the message of the crucified Messiah. It pointedly undercuts much of our talk about God that

3. See Leander E. Keck's critique of preaching Jesus as a hero, "Biblical Preaching as Divine Wisdom," in *A New Look at Preaching,* ed. John Burke (Wilmington, Del.: Michael Glazier, 1983), 137–56.
4. The theological emphasis is forcefully argued by Wolfgang Schrage, "Das Verständnis des Todes Jesu Christi im Neuen Testament," *Das Kreuz Jesu Christi als Grund des Heils,* ed. Fritz Viering (Gütersloh: Gerd Mohn, 1967), esp. 69–77.

rests on a rationalistic or empirical base. It is true that Paul writes for the peculiar setting of the Corinthian congregation, and yet the contingency of his argument in no way lessens the force of the unexpected and exclusive statements he makes about God, about God's involvement in the death of Christ, and about God's self-revelation. In fact, the theology of the cross expressed here avoids any accusation that this is merely ivory-tower chatter precisely because its serves to illumine an actual conflict within the church and to point competing factions to the true source of authority.

The body of 1 Corinthians begins by addressing the report from Chloe's people of the divisions within the community (1:10-17). Factions have developed over particular authority figures. The strategy of Paul's response is not to pit one figure against another, but to make the whole community face the reality of schism. "Is Christ divided? Was Paul crucified for you? Or were you baptized in the name of Paul?" (1:13). With regard to his own involvement, Paul seems a bit perplexed that baptism should be an issue, since his primary mission had not been to baptize but "to preach the gospel, and not with eloquent wisdom, lest the cross of Christ be emptied of its power" (1:17).

Paul (and we) will return to the divisions in the Corinthian community later, but first he considers precisely how it is that God has used the preaching of the gospel as a critique of human wisdom. "The word of the cross is folly to those who are perishing, but to us who are being saved it is the power of God" (1:18). In one sense, such a statement represents merely an observation from experience. The preaching of the crucified Christ brings a group of hearers to a parting of the ways. Some reject it as pure foolishness; others discover in it the powerful word of salvation. The statement is documented in terms of how it works with two groups, who in a sense constitute the whole world (1:22-24). Jews look for "signs," for credentials, for verifiable proofs with which to satisfy an a priori they have as to how God *ought* to behave in a saving event. Greeks (undoubtedly to be taken generally as "gentiles," as in 1:23), on the other hand, seek "wisdom." They possess a system, a scheme (whether gnostic or not is unimportant here) for interpreting reality, and they look for confirmation or perhaps even expansion of such a system. For the former group the word of the cross is a "stumbling block," because a crucified Messiah is a contradiction in terms. For the latter group the word of the cross is "foolishness." It cannot be accommodated to the scheme; it makes no sense. At the same time, there exist both Jews and Greeks for whom the crucified Christ is both the wisdom and power of God.

But the statement of v. 18 is cast in an entirely new light by the quotation of Isa. 29:14 in v. 19 and the allusions in v. 20. "I will destroy the wisdom of the wise, and the cleverness of the clever I will thwart." The first-person language is arresting, as God's own words are cited. The division precipitated by the word of the cross then turns out to be not merely a side phenomenon Paul has observed from many occasions of preaching. The division is actually attributed to *God;* it is a part of the divine strategy to expose the wisdom of this age. The next verse explains why. "For (γάρ) since, in the wisdom of God, the world did not know God through wisdom, God was pleased through the foolishness of preaching to save those who are believing" (1:21).

Several dimensions of v. 21 are significant. First, the verse is unequivocal about the incapacity of human wisdom. The world's story of seeking God through its own wisdom is a story of failure. God may be revealed in creation, but human wisdom habitually misconstrues the knowledge of God to be found there. In the words of Romans 1:19-25, the world inevitably fails to honor or give thanks to God, but exchanges the truth about God for a lie. Like Romans, the 1 Corinthians text does not diagnose the problem as quantitative, as if to imply that up to now humanity has acted in ignorance and stupidity but some future age might achieve sufficient wisdom to transcend the gap and know God. As Leander Keck puts it, "Clearly Paul is not speaking merely of the finitude of wisdom, of its innate limitations—as in the case of a telescope not powerful enough to locate a distant galaxy. What Paul has in view is rather a distortion so profound that wisdom is judged to be folly, while folly is deemed to be wisdom."[5] Not even a wholesale reevaluation of wisdom by providing new

5. Keck, "Biblical Preaching," 149.

norms and categories will suffice, since what the preaching of the crucified Christ does is to reveal the radical discontinuity between God and the world. The gap simply cannot be bridged by more or better knowledge. The word of the cross interprets the world in such a way that God is exposed as free and thoroughly distinct from the world.[6]

Second, what are we to make in v. 21 of the prepositional phrase "in the wisdom of God" (ἐν τῇ σοφίᾳ τοῦ θεοῦ)? The word order unambiguously relates it to the causal clause, but the preposition ἐν itself is very uncertain. Does the phrase depict the cause of the world's not-knowing, or the time of its failure, or the location of the world's existence (perhaps parallel to ἐν Χριστῷ in 1:30)?[7] C. K. Barrett is probably right in taking the ἐν as instrumental and in translating the phrase "by God's wise plan."[8] The world's failure to know God through its own wisdom happens within God's wise plan.[9] The NEB puts it a bit strongly but nevertheless captures the force of the divine involvement, "As God in his wisdom ordained, the world failed to find him in its wisdom."

Third, v. 21 is a startling statement in that the main clause does not seem to fit the causal clause. One might anticipate that in the light of the world's failure to know God, some word of judgment would follow, perhaps the language of Romans, "God gave them up" (1:24, 26, 28). Instead we read, "God was pleased through the foolishness of preaching to save those who are believing."[10] God's intention in the thwarting and destroying of human wisdom is complemented by God's saving intention—both re-

6. This point is developed by Ulrich Luz. "In Paul's theology of the cross he has to do with the 'godness' of God" ("*Theologia crucis* als Mitte der Theologie im Neuen Testament," *EvTh* 34 [1974]: 124).

7. For a survey and critique of the various options, see A. J. M. Wedderburn, "ἐν τῇ σοφίᾳ τοῦ θεοῦ—in 1 Cor. 1:21," *ZNW* 64 (1973): 132–34. Wedderburn finally sides with Barrett.

8. Barrett, *First Corinthians,* 53–54.

9. Whether this is the antecedent or consequent will of God is impossible to press and a distinction really unnecessary to Paul's argument. See Robin Barbour, "Wisdom and Cross in 1 Cor 1 and 2," *Theologia Crucis—Theologia Signum: Festschrift für Erich Dinkler,* ed. C. Andresen and G. Klein (Tübingen: J. C. B. Mohr [Paul Siebeck], 1979), 63–64, 71.

10. See John Howard Schütz, *Paul and the Anatomy of Apostolic Authority,* SNTSMS 26 (Cambridge: Cambridge University Press, 1975), 195.

vealed through the word of the cross. The gap between the free, transcendent God and a not-knowing humanity is bridged by a message that does not make sense by human standards, but a message that saves. Correspondingly, responders are not described as those who understand, but as those who believe.

In the paragraphs that follow, Paul carries the discussion further by directing the readers to consider their own situation (1:26-31) and the nature of his preaching (2:1-5). The expressions that serve as the focus for 1:26-31 are: "your call" (1:26) and "God chose" (1:27 [twice], 28). Both underscore the divine initiative, the former by harking back to the language of 1:23 and the latter by its threefold emphasis. Though recent studies of the social character of the Pauline churches have shown that the community in Corinth represented a cross section of the strata of society, evidently enough poorly educated and politically weak people were among the number to appreciate Paul's stress on the divine initiative in 1:26-31.[11] Not only in the event of the crucifixion itself, but in the reception of the preached event in the lives of the readers, God's creative activity is demonstrated.

Two almost contradictory features of 1 Cor. 1:26-31 are particularly striking. For one thing Paul does *not* argue that the Corinthian Christians, though foolish and weak, are then by God's grace made to be wise and strong. The preaching of the cross does not result in a revamping of the human capacities so that heretofore weaknesses can now be overcome or that the message of the crucifixion ceases to be foolishness. Instead, by a creative act of God, Christ crucified becomes "for us" wisdom, righteousness, sanctification, and redemption (1:30). The bridging of the gap by the word of the cross does not imply that God then is less sovereign or free than before the bridging of the gap.

At the same time, seen from the vantage point of the Corinthian Christians (at least some of them), the gospel liberates the poorly educated, the politically helpless, and those of modest birth. The three groups listed in v. 26 are described in social terms. As the objects of God's election, they discover a com-

---

11. Gerd Theissen, *The Social Setting of Pauline Christianity,* trans. J. H. Schütz (Philadelphia: Fortress Press, 1982), 69–119.

pletely different way of viewing themselves that alters their otherwise inferior relationship to the seemingly wise, powerful, and mighty.[12] Reflecting on their "call" reminds them of God's disposition in the word of the cross to upset the human ordering of these social structures and categories. Hearing that the crucified Christ (and not the pretentious wisdom of the influential) is for them, "wisdom" opens a new world. They know themselves to be called by an active, creative God "who chose what is low and despised in the world, even things that are not, to bring to nothing things that are" (1:28).

In the final paragraph of the section Paul turns appropriately to his own preaching at Corinth (2:1-5), which recalls the point at which the discussion of the failure of human wisdom began (1:17). How does Paul make a case for the fact that his own ministry (both preaching and presence) is consistent with the initiative and strategy of God laid out in 1:18-25 and applied to the Corinthians in 1:26-31? Essentially, he points to three facts. First, the content of his preaching when in Corinth had been exclusively that of the crucified Christ (2:2). Such preaching happened not as an accident but as a deliberate decision on his part (ἔκρινα), presumably growing out of his understanding of the gospel and the needs of the Corinthian community. Second, his personal presence among them was characterized by weakness, fear, and trembling (2:3). Third, the manner of his preaching was not "in lofty eloquence or wisdom" (2:1; cf. 1:17) but "in demonstration of the Spirit and power" (2:4). With respect to all three, Paul intended that the resulting faith of the Corinthians be solidly based in the power of God and not in human wisdom (2:5).

We have followed the logical flow of the argument developed in 1:18—2:5. Its force, however, derives not merely from its contents but also from the highly ironical way in which the paradox of the cross is presented. The rhetoric is part and parcel of

---

12. Paul continues this concern later in the letter by addressing the way in which the table fellowship of the Corinthian community operates. See Theissen, *The Social Setting,* 121–74; Wayne Meeks, *The First Urban Christians: The Social World of the Apostle Paul* (New Haven: Yale University Press, 1983), 68–72.

the message. "The wise person," "the scribe," "the debater of this age" are those who claim to know and ought to understand, but the text exposes, even mocks, their self-confident pretensions. The foolishness of God is wiser and the weakness of God stronger than the very best that humans can muster. Furthermore, the hubris that supposes it knows better than God is undermined not by a treatise on the infinite and superior wisdom of the divine, but by the irony of God's "foolishness" and "weakness." The barbed rhetorical questions of v. 20 and the sharply stated paradox of v. 25 leave in shambles the misguided certitudes of the intellectual and religious experts.

But irony can function not only as a weapon against those who fail to see ("those who are perishing"), but also as a nurturer of those who do see ("us who are being saved"). It can create a community of kindred souls who get the point and who are drawn together by their agreement with the author.[13] This shared understanding emerges rather subtly with the inclusive pronoun "us" in 1:18, but the subtlety fades in the next two paragraphs when attention is focused on the readers and their experience (1:26-31) and on Paul and his previous preaching in their midst (2:1-5). In any case, the result fosters a community composed of readers and author united by the message of the cross and in clear distinction from the self-deceived "knowers" who balk at the message of a crucified Messiah.

This brings us back to the theme with which Paul began the body of the letter—quarreling over authority figures. It may at first appear as if this extensive treatment of human wisdom (1:18—2:5) represents an unnecessary digression in relation to the original topic of schism, except for two factors. For one thing, we discover later in the letter that human wisdom and the divisions within the community are very much connected (3:18-21; 4:6-10). The Corinthians' boasting over various leaders is taken

13. Wayne C. Booth, *The Rhetoric of Irony* (Chicago: University of Chicago Press, 1974), 28, comments: "Even irony that does imply victims, as in all ironic satire, is often much more clearly directed to more affirmative matters. And every irony inevitably builds a community of believers even as it excludes." See also the treatment of 1 Cor. 1:18-25 as a paradoxical irony by Karl A. Plank, *Paul and the Irony of Affliction* (Atlanta: Scholars Press, 1987), 55–62.

to imply a boasting of their own wisdom, with the result that when Paul deals with wisdom he is in fact addressing the problem of schism.[14] Second, the rhetoric of 1:18—2:5, with its effective irony, has already begun to address the schism by cultivating a community based not on the strength of its leaders but on the word of the cross.

But the relation needs to be probed further. How does the gospel of the crucified Christ contribute to a solution to the quarreling over leaders?[15] The struggles in the community revolve around the issue of authority. The quarreling over leadership boils down to the question as to whose authority will prevail—Paul's, Peter's, Apollos's. Paul in confronting the situation, somewhat surprisingly, neither argues his own case ("you should look to me rather than the other leaders for the following reasons . . . ") nor advocates an abandonment of all human leaders (which might be to side with "the Christ party"), but instead points to the source of all authority in the church.

Four times between 1:18 and 2:5 the word "power" occurs, and in each case, explicitly or implicitly, denoting divine power. The point is that God exercises authority through the preaching of the crucified Christ; "the word of the cross is . . . the power of God" (1:18). Since power must be understood dialectically through weakness, it becomes a complex argument to make, but for Paul a necessary one in that it explains how he understands his own authority. As Schütz puts it, "It is a restricted view of authority which calls upon the *auctor* to assert not himself and his authority, but the primary source of power. When others perceive this power correctly and act accordingly, they share in the same power with Paul and are themselves authoritative."[16] Essentially Paul sees no reason why there should be a power struggle focusing on one or another leader since the divine power that authenticates all ministries is available to the whole church in the word of the cross. Appropriately, he brings his autobiographical con-

14. Nils A. Dahl, "Paul and the Church at Corinth According to 1 Corinthians 1:10—4:21," *Christian History and Interpretation: Studies Presented to John Knox,* ed. W. R. Farmer, C. F. D. Moule, and R. R. Niebuhr (Cambridge: Cambridge University Press, 1967), 320–21.

15. John Schütz's work is particularly illuminating here; see esp. *Paul,* 187–204.

16. Schütz, *Paul,* 204.

fession to a climax by stating that his preaching and ministry were such that "*your* faith might not rest in human wisdom but in the power of God" (2:5).

The exegesis of 1 Cor. 1:18—2:5 yields a striking picture of God's purposes in the story of the crucified Christ. We can summarize by listing seven dimensions of such a picture.

1. Throughout the section it has become clear that God stands as the hidden figure behind the vivid drama of the cross. As horrifying a means of death as it was, the crucifixion is not blamed on a human source. Instead, the preaching of it is the occasion of God's self-revelation. Here God's intentions and purposes are made known.

2. The word of the cross reveals God as a free, sovereign God, not bound by human categories and expectations. Human wisdom is merely confounded by the revelation of a God like this. Its finding the message sheer folly is conclusive evidence that it honors neither the First nor the Second Commandment of the Decalogue.

3. God's self-revelation, which exposes the idolatrous nature of human wisdom, occurs in the message of the crucified one. In terms of 1:30, Christ is made for us wisdom, and as Keck puts it, this means "God made Christ the framework for our understanding of God."[17] The crucified one becomes the foundation for epistemology.

4. In this self-revelation through the preaching of the cross God is seen to be a saving God. The dissolution of human wisdom is not an end in itself, but merely the backside of God's redemptive action.

5. In the scuttling of human wisdom and the saving of those divinely called, God chooses the weak and powerless as the means of shaming the wise and the strong. At the heart of the divine revelation is a revolution of immense proportions, a thorough reversal of who is weak and who is strong. The weak find their strength not in themselves, even renewed by the gospel, but in Christ who becomes for them wisdom, righteousness, sanctification, and redemption.

---

17. Keck, "Biblical Preaching," 153.

6. Ultimate authority is exercised through the cross; it is God's power, available not to one or a few special leaders alone but to the entire community. Paul describes his own ministry primarily to illustrate precisely how God authenticates all ministries.

7. The community finds its unity in the message of the cross, whose paradox both exposes the self-deception of the wise and at the same time calls and cultivates a people who discern God's "foolishness" and "weakness."

GOD'S RIGHTEOUSNESS AND CHRIST'S FAITHFULNESS (ROM. 3:21-26)

This passage is one of the most discussed in all of the Pauline letters, and yet in asking about the role God played in the death of Jesus we bring a set of questions different from those of many exegetes.[18] Our questions in this chapter place several of the debated exegetical problems on the back burner, as it were, and push us immediately into a consideration of the entire third chapter of Romans. Recent interpreters have shown how essential the first twenty verses are to a proper understanding of the latter section and how disastrous it becomes to make too sharp a division, as is often done, between 3:20 and 3:21.[19]

In examining the initial portion of the chapter, two issues dealing with the character of God are raised, which then are addressed in 3:21-26. The first and most obvious question has to do with God's faithfulness with regard to promises made to the Jews.[20] Throughout 1:18—2:29 Paul makes the case that those

---

18. See the further treatment of Rom. 3:21-26 in the next chapter.

19. See Richard B. Hays, "Psalm 143 and the Logic of Romans 3," *JBL* 99 (1980): 107–15; Sam K. Williams, "The 'Righteousness of God' in Romans," *JBL* 99 (1980): 241–90.

20. Williams (in "The 'Righteousness of God'") argues that the primary promises under consideration in Romans 3 are the "promises to Abraham, promises which focus upon the eschatological gathering of all the nations into the people of God" (270). "I contend . . . that Paul is not thinking about all God's promises to Israel in an equal and undifferentiated way. We cannot say that he excludes any, but one set dominates and interprets all the rest" (267). Williams's case primarily rests on four exegetical points: (1) The mention that "some" (τινες, 3:3) of the Jews were unfaithful. This would imply a failure in which not all Jews participated and thus a failure more specific than their universal violation of the law. (2) The passive form of the verb (ἐπιστεύθησαν) in the phrase "are entrusted with the oracles of God" (3:2). "Israel has been

outside the law and those within the law equally stand inexcusable before God. But in concluding the case (2:25-29) he comes perilously close to obliterating the special status of the Jew. Circumcision as a rite is relativized, and the "real Jew" is characterized by secret matters of the heart, by a spiritual, not a literal, circumcision (2:28-29). To argue this way raises the serious question about God's long and involved history with the Jews. Are the special promises repeatedly made to these people now invalidated? In light of their sinfulness, has God come up with a Plan B that supplants the advantageous role of the Jews in Plan A? If so, then can God's commitments be trusted? At heart, the question concerns the reliability of God.[21] The Jews are given

and is now the trustee of the divine word that God wills the salvation of all the peoples on the basis of faith" (268). (3) The stress in Rom. 4:11-12, 17-18 on Abraham as "the father of many nations." (4) Most important, the third chapter of Galatians and especially 3:8, where the gospel preached beforehand to Abraham is identified: "that God would justify the gentiles by faith."

Williams has pointed to a neglected dimension of the promises, and yet I am inclined to think that, despite his disclaimer (267), he focuses the content of the promises to the Jews too narrowly when he stresses so exclusively the inclusion of the gentiles. With regard to (1), it is not at all clear that τινες ("some") denotes a differentiation from the universal failure of Israel. C. E. B. Cranfield is probably right in labeling it a meiosis, a slight softening of the judgment (*A Critical and Exegetical Commentary on the Epistle to the Romans,* ICC [Edinburgh: T. & T. Clark, 1975], 1: 181). With regard to (2), it is simply impossible to be precise about the Jews' entrustment with the oracles of God. Such oracles undoubtedly include the promise of God's grace to the gentiles, but would they be limited to this? With regard to (3), Romans 4 mentions the universal nature of Abraham's "fatherhood," but intriguingly says nothing about the Jews' special role (and failure) in the universalizing mission. With regard to (4), the use of Galatians 3 as the interpretive key to unlock Romans 3 is methodologically questionable. Of course, the inclusion of the gentiles in the people of God is a part of God's promise to the Jews; it is an important motif of Romans. But in light of Paul's anguish in Romans 9–11, Israel's own destiny can hardly be peripheral.

21. It becomes significant in light of the later language of 3:21-26 to notice that three expressions in these early verses of Romans 3, all designating the divine integrity under question, are virtually synonymous with each other: "the righteousness of God" (θεοῦ δικαιοσύνη, 3:5), "the faithfulness of God" (ἡ πίστις τοῦ θεοῦ, 3:3), and "the truthfulness of God" (ἡ ἀλήθεια τοῦ θεοῦ, 3:7). Their parallelism supports the case of Käsemann that the genitive in the expression "the righteousness of God" (δικαιοσύνη θεοῦ) is a subjective genitive (at least in Romans 3), designating God's own activity and nature. Käsemann's interpretation is also broad enough to include the gift-character of God's righteousness. See Ernst Käsemann, "'The Righteousness of God' in Paul," in *New Testament Questions of Today* (Philadelphia: Fortress Press, 1969), 169–72; idem, *Commentary on Romans,* trans. Geoffrey W. Bromiley (Grand Rapids, Mich.: Wm. B. Eerdmans, 1980), 78–85; Hays, "Psalm 143," 110; Williams,

"the oracles of God" (3:2) , which certainly entail divine promises.[22] "Does their faithlessness nullify the faithfulness of God?"
(3:3).

The second question has to do with what Keck has called "the
moral integrity of God."[23] Paul's preaching of radical grace, a
law-free gospel, has brought "slanderous" (but also logical)
charges that such a message inevitably undermines the basis for
morality. "And why not do evil that good may come?" (3:8). On
the one hand, it is an ethical issue, which Paul does not address
until Romans 6.[24] On the other hand, underlying the ethical issue
is a profoundly theological one. What is to be said about the
character of God if in fact "through my falsehood God's truthfulness abounds to his glory"? (3:7). Is God amoral or capricious?
If so, "how does God judge the world"? (3:6).

Before addressing these two concerns, Paul puts in slightly
different words the question with which the chapter begins
("Have we any advantage?") and in answering it reiterates a
point already forcefully made in 1:18—2:29. All humans, both
Jews and gentiles, are guilty of every kind of injustice. They are
unconditionally in the grasp of a demonic power; they are "under
sin" (3:9). With a string of citations from the Old Testament,
Paul documents the point that the law shuts every mouth and
makes the whole world accountable to God (3:19). It is not God,
but humanity, who has failed and is being judged. The reference
to Psalm 143:2 in v. 20 fittingly concludes the section by affirming the total incapacity of humans before the judgment of God,
but the psalm also anticipates the further argument. In the verse
immediately preceding the one Paul cites, the psalmist prays:
"Lord, heed my prayer; give an ear to my supplication by your

"The 'Righteousness of God,'" 268; and the review essay by Manfred Brauch,
"Perspectives on 'God's Righteousness' in Recent German Discussion" in E. P.
Sanders, *Paul and Palestinian Judaism: A Comparison of Patterns of Religion*
(Philadelphia: Fortress Press; London: SCM Press, 1977), 523–42.

22. See Franz J. Leenhardt, *The Epistle to the Romans* (London: Lutterworth,
1961), 91; and Williams, "The 'Righteousness of God,'" 266–68.

23. Leander E. Keck, *Paul and His Letters,* PC (Philadelphia: Fortress Press,
1979), 117–30.

24. In Romans 6, Paul, interestingly, points to the death of Christ (just as he
does in 3:25) to undermine antinomianism.

faithfulness; answer me by your righteousness" (from the LXX). The language of the entreaty is reminiscent of 3:21-26.[25]

Now to the two unanswered questions. First, is God trustworthy? Can God be counted on to honor commitments previously made? Or is God the sort of deity who gets so angry at a disobedient people as to say, "No more! I'm changing the plans!" Second, what about God's moral character? If the gospel announces that God forgives sinful people without the prerequisite that they first abandon their sins, then is not such a God robbed of any authority to judge? With a morally indifferent deity, the result will be antinomian anarchy, where issues of right and wrong no longer have any consequence. Unfortunately Paul's answer to these questions is fraught with exegetical complexities, but the issues are so momentous that we can neither be put off by the complexities nor get lost in trying to solve them so that we fail to hear the answer.

The expression "righteousness of God" (δικαιοσύνη θεοῦ, used in 3:5 and now the theme of 3:21-26), though difficult to handle in English, is an apt term for Paul's argument since it encompasses both God's faithfulness to promises made and God's moral integrity.[26] It designates not a static quality of God, but the nature of God as known through the way in which God has related to creation; God's faithfulness and moral integrity in action; God's "rectifying activity vis-à-vis the world."[27] The Hebrew Scriptures anticipate the revelation of God's righteousness, and it now has happened apart from the law and specifically through the faithfulness of Jesus Christ.[28] In the Christ-event,

25. Hays, "Psalm 143," 113–15.
26. The most lucid and nonsimplistic explanation of the phrase I know can be found in Keck, *Paul,* 119–21.
27. Ibid., 121.
28. I am convinced by the case made by a growing number of those who argue for the subjective genitive in the phrase "through the faith of Jesus Christ" (διὰ πίστεως Ιησοῦ Χριστοῦ) in 3:22, similarly in 3:26, and elsewhere in Paul. There is no need to repeat the arguments here, except to notice that the concern in Romans 3 is not between two human activities, obedience to the law or believing in Christ, but between a human activity and the activity of Christ. See especially George Howard, "On the 'Faith of Christ,'" *HTR* 60 (1967): 459–65; idem, "The Faith of Christ," *ExT* 85 (1974): 212–15; Markus Barth, "The Faith of the Messiah," *HeyJ* 10 (1969): 363–70; Williams, "The 'Righteousness of God,'" 272–78; idem, "Again *Pistis Christou*," *CBQ* 49

through which God graciously sets right (or rectifies) humans as a free gift, God's own righteousness is manifest.

The presence here of what is likely a traditional Jewish Christian formula, vv. 25-26a (as verses are numbered in the Nestle text), serves two purposes: to sharpen the issue (i.e., how could God have passed over previously committed sins?) and to specify Christ's role in the revelation of righteousness (i.e., as an expiation by his blood).[29] In God's forbearance previous sins had been "passed over," which might leave the impression that God takes evil lightly. But now through Christ's redemptive activity God is seen to be "in the right." The Christ-event vindicates God's dealing with previously committed sins; it shows that God's moral integrity is intact.[30]

One curious feature of this passage warrants further explanation. Romans 3:23 seems a strange redundancy that intrudes into the logic of the argument. God's rectifying power through the Christ-event becomes available to "all who believe; for there is no distinction" (v. 22). In light of the earlier section of the chap-

---

(1987): 431–47; Luke T. Johnson, "Rom. 3:21-26 and the Faith of Jesus," *CBQ* 44 (1982): 77–90; and Richard B. Hays, *The Faith of Christ: An Investigation of the Narrative Substructure of Gal. 3:1—4:11,* SBLDS 56 (Chico, Calif.: Scholars Press, 1983), 170–76. For an opposite opinion, see Arland J. Hultgren, "The *Pistis Christou* Formulations in Paul," *NovTest* 22 (1980): 248–63.

29. Käsemann argues that the traditional formula includes v. 24 as well, excepting some Pauline adaptations ("Zum Verständnis von Römer 3:24-26, *ZNW* 43 [1950–51]: 150–54; and *Romans,* 95–101), but is opposed, and rightly I think, by Peter Stuhlmacher ("Recent Exegesis on Rom. 3:24-26," in *Reconciliation, Law, and Righteousness: Essays in Biblical Theology* [Philadelphia: Fortress Press, 1986], 94–96), who cites the relevant literature. Charles H. Talbert ("A Non-Pauline Fragment at Rom. 3:24-26?" *JBL* 85 [1966]: 287–96) argues that Rom. 3:25-26 is a post-Pauline interpolation in the middle of a Pauline sentence. Arland J. Hultgren (*Paul's Gospel and Mission: The Outlook from the Letter to the Romans* [Philadelphia: Fortress Press, 1985], 62–69) takes 3:21-26 to be entirely Pauline, with 3:23-26a consisting of a portion of a homily Paul delivered in a synagogue on the day of atonement.

30. One of the perplexities of this passage is how to translate διὰ τὴν πάρεσιν in v. 25. Kümmel argues for "in the remitting of" but then pushes a forced periodization of the text: the time of God's patience versus the present time. See W. G. Kümmel, "Πάρεσις and ἔνδειξις. A Contribution to the Understanding of the Pauline Doctrine of Justification," *Distinctive Protestant and Catholic Themes Reconsidered,* ed. Robert W. Funk, JThC 3 (New York: Harper & Row, 1967), 1–15. C. K. Barrett, *A Commentary on the Epistle to the Romans,* HNTC (New York: Harper & Row, 1957), 79–80, and Cranfield, *Romans* 1: 211–12, argue for "passing over." Both translations raise the question of God's moral integrity.

ter, why is v. 23 necessary as an explanation of the inclusiveness? The point has been made repeatedly and even specifically in 3:9, 10-12, 19-20 that *all* are guilty and that *no one* is without excuse. Verse 23 makes crystal clear that the recipients of God's righteous activity are no more and no less than the ungodly, who are under divine judgment. As Käsemann comments, v. 23 "designates the solidarity of a world in guilt and need as the place of the salvation event."[31] The ethically upright and the pious are not mentioned as the ones whose relationship is set right by God, but those who have sinned and who lack God's glory, those who have absolutely no claim on God. There is no effort to water down the offensiveness of the gospel in order to vindicate the character of God. In fact, the character of God is most clearly expressed when the contours of grace are most sharply in focus. Not surprisingly, then, in 4:5 we hear God described as "the one who justifies the ungodly."

In this reminder of grace we are encountering, as we did in 1 Cor. 1:18—2:5, the sovereign freedom of God, whose gracious actions demonstrate that God's ways are simply not our ways. God is not the kind of God to be comprehended or captured by human reckoning. Grace is so radical a reality that it takes a self-revelation on God's part (3:21; cf. 1:17) to make the knowledge of God a possibility. But God's freedom turns out to be not a speculative or arbitrary independence to follow this or that whim. It is precisely known in divine trustworthiness and constancy.

The questions raised earlier in Romans 3 about the character of God have now been answered. God is a faithful promise-keeper, since just as the Hebrew Scriptures had indicated, God's righteousness is made known apart from the law—in the faithfulness of Jesus Christ. As the writer of Psalm 143 asked for in a prayer of supplication, so God's salvation is effected by divine faithfulness and righteousness. In its inclusiveness of gentiles as well as Jews, it does not annul the law but confirms it (3:30-31). Moreover, the death of Christ shows that God is not indifferent to human disobedience; the cross is the means of atoning for sin

---

31. Käsemann, *Romans,* 94.

and of setting the ungodly, who lack the divine glory, into a right relationship with God.

Our exegesis of two critical passages (1 Cor. 1:18—2:5 and Rom. 3:21-26) has indicated that the cross of Christ for Paul has indispensable significance for epistemology.[32] God is to be known precisely in the message of the cross as a shameful and scandalous event. This also means that the epistemology advocated in 1 Corinthians and Romans does not rely on an inferential method. Paul does not first reckon with the created order and inductively conclude that behind such beauty, precision, and regularity there must be a divine being to be called "God."[33] Such a cosmological argument assumes that God can be known from the divine works and that the theologian by logical inference can move from results to cause. Neither does Paul begin with a presumed understanding of justice, for example, a fair and equitable treatment of all people according to their actions, and then determine that "God" is the one who properly rewards the good and punishes the wicked. Paul would be at odds with much popular opinion today (and with Job's friends) where God is inferred from human successes or failures, from "bullish" or "bearish"

---

32. It is important in this setting also to consider 2 Cor. 5:16: "From now on, we regard no one from a human point of view (κατὰ σάρκα)." As J. Louis Martyn has shown, Paul articulates here a new epistemology appropriate to the turn of the ages, with which he has been concerned since 2:14. The death of Christ means that the way of knowing characteristic of the old age is outdated; the power and norm of the σάρξ are invalidated for the new age ushered in by the Christ-event. One might have expected Paul to contrast the old way with a new way of knowing by using the phrase "from the viewpoint of the Spirit (κατὰ πνεῦμα)," but he pointedly refrains from doing so. Life in the present is lived "at the juncture of the ages," and the implied epistemology for now is "from the viewpoint of the cross (κατὰ σταυρόν)." As Martyn puts it, "For until the *parousia,* the cross is and remains *the* epistemological crisis. The essential failure of the Corinthians consists in their inflexible determination to live either *before* the cross (the super-apostles of 2 Corinthians) or *after* the cross (the Gnostics of 1 Corinthians) rather than *in* the cross. . . . The cross is *the* epistemological crisis for the simple reason that while it is in one sense followed by the resurrection, it is not replaced by the resurrection." See J. Louis Martyn, "Epistemology at the turn of the ages: 2 Corinthians 5:16," *Christian History and Interpretation: Studies Presented to John Knox,* ed. W. R. Farmer et al., 285–86.

33. This was Luther's point in the Heidelberg disputation of 1518, where he first used the phrase *theologia crucis.* He was essentially attacking a theological epistemology based on natural theology. Paul's comments in Rom. 1:19-20 document the futility of such an epistemology.

markets, from prosperity or pain. "The God who rectifies the ungodly can no longer be regarded simply as the guarantor of distributive justice."[34]

GOD'S LOVE IN CHRIST'S DEATH (ROM. 5:6-8)

Finally, we turn to a third passage, which sheds light on the theo-logical understanding of the cross of Christ: Rom. 5:6-8. This passage more than the previous two draws the actions of God and Christ into an unusual relationship and poses for us a fundamental christological question.

In the previous section of Romans, Paul writes of the righteousness of God manifest in the faithfulness and death of Jesus and then clarifies how in the manner of Abraham the divine gift is received by faith. Genesis 15:6 is the text Paul interprets in Romans 4, concluding that the way righteousness is "reckoned" in connection with Abraham is instructive also for himself and his readers (4:23-25). Now, presupposing God's gracious action in setting people right, Paul moves on to consider the consequences of this action for human experience. Such consequences include: peace with God (5:1); access to grace (5:2); boasting in hope of the divine glory (5:2); and boasting even in afflictions, since afflictions and hope are ultimately not contradictory (5:3-4). This last consequence represents an astonishing claim, except that God's people, Paul argues, can count on the fact that hope will never disappoint or shame them. They know this because of their experience ("into our hearts") of the divine love (5:5).

Romans 5:5 represents the initial occurrence in the letter of either the noun or the verb for "love" and leads in vv. 6-8 to a remarkable affirmation of the depth of God's love, which in turn provides the grounds for hope's certainty. Neither the progression of the verses nor the flow of the syntax is smooth, but Paul's point is nevertheless clear. God's love is incredible; it exceeds the boundaries of human imagination. "While we were yet powerless, at that time Christ died for the ungodly" (5:6). Käsemann,[35] following the preferred rendering of the Bauer-Arndt-Gingrich

---

34. Keck, "Biblical Preaching," 154.
35. Käsemann, *Romans,* 137.

lexicon, is probably correct in translating κατὰ καιρὸν as "then, at that time" rather than "at the right time."[36] It was no doubt the eschatological moment of God's fulfillment (so "at the right time"), but the point of the text seems to be that insofar as all human reckoning is concerned it happened at a most *inappropriate* moment. The extraordinary feature of Christ's death was that it occurred when the unworthy were completely helpless, when they were altogether impotent to deal with their own situation.

To highlight the inconceivable depth of this love, Paul in a rather halting fashion draws a comparison to two possible occasions for self-sacrifice—for a righteous person or perhaps for a worthy or good sort of person.[37] In contrast to these, "God demonstrates his own love for us in that while we were yet sinners Christ died for us" (5:8). The awkwardness of Paul's comparison in v. 7 no doubt reveals his difficulty in discovering an analogy appropriate to the character of God's love. This becomes clear in the use of the preposition ὑπέρ four times in the passage (5:6, 7[twice], 8). We shall examine it more extensively in the next chapter, but suffice it here to say that while it can mean "for the sake of," it can also mean "in the place of." In line with other uses of the preposition in connection with Christ's death (e.g., 1 Cor. 15:3; 1 Thess. 5:10; Gal. 1:4; 2:20; 3:13; 2 Cor. 5:21; Rom. 8:32; 14:15), Paul expresses the death as at least representative, if not substitutionary. It is not just the hero (as v. 7 alone might suggest) dying for a righteous cause; it is the death of Christ "in the place of" helpless, ungodly sinners. As vv. 9-11 specify, the death is the means for setting people right (and ultimately saving them from God's wrath in the last judgment) and the means for reconciling heretofore enemies to God. It powerfully effects salvation.

---

36. Contra Barrett, *Romans*, 106; and Cranfield, *Romans*, I: 264.

37. Keck notes the problematics of Rom. 5:7 and concludes that 5:6-7 represents a post-Pauline interpolation. See Leander E. Keck, "The Post-Pauline Interpretation of Jesus' Death in Romans 5:6-7," in *Theologia Crucis—Theologia Signum: Festschrift für Erich Dinkler*, ed. C. Andresen and G. Klein, 237–48.

Before leaving this passage, we are obliged to observe the strange wording of v. 8. God, the subject, "demonstrates his own love (τὴν ἑαυτοῦ ἀγάπην) . . . in that Christ died for us." One might have anticipated that God would have been the subject of the second clause as well as the first (especially since the reflexive pronoun is used), that God's love would have been shown by *God's* having done something (as in John 3:16). Instead, Christ's death becomes the expression of God's love. The wording can partly be explained because v. 8 harks back to v. 5 and provides the reason why the love of God can keep hope from fearing disappointment and shame. The divine love experienced by humans securely anchors hope because it is the incredible love demonstrated in Christ's death for the ungodly. Still, the strangeness is not entirely removed and thus must be taken seriously.

As we shall note later, Paul's Christology is sufficiently subordinationist to prevent his thoroughly coalescing the sentiment and actions of God with those of Christ. At the same time, the wording of 5:8 suggests a striking closeness of the two. Christ's death does not merely express his own sentiment (as in 2 Cor. 5:14), but God's; or to put it the other way, God's stance toward the world is quintessentially demonstrated in the action of Christ. On the one hand, a sharply christological focus is given to the character of God; on the other hand, a decidedly theonomous accent is given to the death of Jesus. The two perspectives for Paul belong together.

PAUL AND THE CLASSIC ATTRIBUTES OF GOD

In the three passages we have examined, Paul deals with several important dimensions of God's character as expressed in the death of Christ. He writes of God's power, righteousness, wisdom, faithfulness, freedom, and love. These happen also to be among those attributes of God dealt with by traditional Christian theology. A comparison, however, between Paul's understanding of these attributes and the understanding they have often had in the history of Christian theology is very instructive.

1. Classic theology has had the tendency to begin with a general definition of the attribute and then in applying it to God to lift it

to an infinite level. *Power* implies such things as might, strength, control, domination, and authority. God's power, then, means infinite might, sovereignty, omnipotence, supreme majesty, and superiority over all other things. The impression conveyed is of a dominant deity, with ultimate control, and unlimited capacity to do whatever is wished and whose power is manifested in extraordinary events, in amazing stories of success, in tales that always have happy endings. Paul, on the other hand, talks of the power of God in terms of weakness, failure, a scandalizing death by crucifixion. In language not only the opposite of but in fact the contradiction of much of western theology, God's power is expressed in a particular event of unsuccessful and even distasteful dimensions.

2. Statements of God's *righteousness* have often had their origin in an Aristotelian understanding of justice, particularly as it was expressed in Roman law. Each person is to be given what he or she is entitled to have, with equity and fairness. Thus God is righteous in justly enforcing the law, seeing that each person receives, in this life or the life to come, exactly what is deserved. Disobedience is punished; obedience is rewarded; severity or leniency is rendered with impartiality. In Romans 3, however, we read that God's righteousness is manifested (and not compromised) in divine grace. God's people are set right not according to what they deserve but as a gift. There remains no partiality in God's relationships, because all are equally sinful and no individual or group has any more justifiable claim on God's goodness than any other. First Corinthians 1:26-31 carries this further by noting that God does exhibit a special interest in the weak and powerless, those who have few rights in terms of civil law, but who turn out to shame those who think themselves most deserving.

3. God's *wisdom,* as expressed in classic theology, has often been rooted in a Greek philosophical tradition that puts a high premium on reason as the means to knowledge. It is basically analytical and speculative in its epistemology, and God's truth is grasped by the learned and studious. In addressing the wisdom of the Corinthians, however, Paul declares precisely the opposite. God's wisdom appears foolish and contradictory to the wise.

They encounter the revelation of God and find it sheer folly. God, in fact, deliberately unmasks the arrogance of the wise in the absurdity of the word of the cross.

4. There has been a tendency in traditional theology to consider the *faithfulness* of God in terms of God's immutability. God is consistent in that God is free from change. God can be counted on precisely because God does not waver or fluctuate. In contrast, Paul expresses God's faithfulness in the certainty with which God keeps promises. It is not legal consistency or logical necessity that characterizes God, but the honoring of commitments declared. In fact, these promises and commitments may be kept in ways so unexpected that God appears to be illogical or inconsistent. Requirements of the code are overlooked; sins are "passed over"; God's faithfulness is revealed "apart from the law."

5. Much theological reflection on God's *freedom* has understood it as independence and autonomy. Often it is expressed in negative categories; freedom is the absence of limits, restrictions, or conditions. God is totally without constraints, not able to be contained in any particular action or event. God transcends the ebb and flow of human history and stands aloof from it. While "freedom" is not a word used in any of the passages considered above, Paul throughout all three describes God's prerogative as a sovereign deity in terms of the foolishness of the cross, the provision for sins' being expiated, and the astonishing death of Christ for the ungodly. It is the involved freedom of love, not autonomy, that marks Paul's understanding of God.

6. With the divine attribute of *love* classic theology has perhaps most closely approximated the texts we have considered in the Pauline letters. Classic theology and Paul both stress God's love for the unloveable. Still, many traditional treatments have begun with human analogies of love and have worked to the divine, rather than the reverse. In a sense, Paul himself shows in Rom. 5:7 how treacherous even human illustrations can be. Jesus is so easily turned into a heroic figure, in which case God becomes an important reference point for the hero (e.g., his inspiration), but is then no longer essential to the story. If Jesus is taken to be a hero, then God's love, severed from Jesus' love, fades into the

background.[38] But with Paul, Jesus' death is a revelatory event, the lens through which God's love is seen.

The terms used for God in 1 Cor. 1:18—2:5; Rom. 3:21-26; 5:6-8 are not markedly different from the terms of classic theology (though Paul includes two "heretical" attributes: God's foolishness and weakness). But given the epistemology he employs (i.e., seeing the attributes through the cross of Christ), they bear quite different meanings. They do not derive from general definitions or philosophical traditions, nor from human projections or speculation. One might even dare to ask whether the understanding of the attributes of God in much of western theology in fact represents a continuation of the thinking of the Corinthians against which Paul polemicizes. In both instances God is understood in light of human judgments as to what God must be and do if God is to be really God, and in many cases such judgments merely mask the desire for control, for moral superiority, or for the maintenance of the status quo. Paul's alternative opens the door to an entirely different way of thinking about God and about God's (and therefore also genuinely human) power, righteousness, wisdom, faithfulness, freedom, and love.

EXCURSUS: THE CRUCIFIED GOD

How far are we able to go with this Pauline alternative, with this curious reversal of the attributes of God? If the character of God is to be derived from the preaching of the crucified Jesus who died for the ungodly; if the knowledge of God begins with the word of the cross; if Christ's actions reveal God's intentions; then do we not have to go further and speak of a "crucified God"[39] or at least what a recent writer has labeled a "new orthodoxy"[40] —namely, a "suffering God"?

38. Keck, "Biblical Preaching," 147.
39. According to Jüngel, the expression "crucified God" goes back as far as Tertullian and was used by Athanasius in debate with the Arians and the Apollinarians (Eberhard Jüngel, *God as the Mystery of the World: On the Foundation of the Theology of the Crucified One in the Dispute between Theism and Atheism,* trans. D. L. Guder [Grand Rapids, Mich.: Wm. B. Eerdmans, 1983], 64–65). It occurs for the first time in Luther in 1518 in the explanation of the fifty-eighth of the "Ninety-five Theses" in a parenthetical phrase: "A theologian of the cross (that is, one who speaks of the crucified and hidden God), teaches. . . ." *Luther's Works,* (ed. Jaroslav Pelikan and Helmut T.

Before considering an answer to such a question, three important limitations need to be frankly acknowledged. First, we have available only seven letters of Paul, all occasional in nature. No doubt Paul wrote more, and no doubt his theology was "more" than what is available in the letters. Nevertheless, what we have are the letters, and the better part of wisdom is to stick close to what is written there. Second, nowhere in the letters is the issue directly addressed as to why the innocent suffer. Paul writes often about persecution received in service of the gospel and recognizes that humans are bound together with creation in groaning as they await God's ultimate fulfillment (Rom. 8:18-25). The contents of the letters provide immense resources for the innocent who suffer, but the specific questions, like those arising from the tragedies of Auschwitz, Ethiopia, and Vietnam, are not asked in the letters. Why they are not there is anybody's guess. Since the letters are generally responses to particular situations, it may be that the questions were never pointedly directed to Paul. In any case, what Paul *may* have said about a suffering God, had he written about these questions, is a moot point. Finally, it needs to be recalled that Paul's letters are pre-Nicean. Relations between Father and Son are expressed strictly on a functional level, and the letters reflect nothing of the ontological concerns at issue in the church councils of the fourth and fifth centuries. Likewise, Paul as a Jew offers no support for the doctrine of divine impassibility, which underlies the later patri-passianist controversy.

Having acknowledged the inherent limitations of an answer, we can observe that there is no unambiguous textual basis in the

---

Lehmann [Philadelphia: Fortress Press, 1975] 31:225). The hiddenness of God is a difficult notion in Luther (see B. A. Gerrish, "'To the Unknown God': Luther and Calvin on the Hiddenness of God," *JourRel* 53 [1973]: 263–92), but when the adjective "hidden" is linked with "crucified," it presumably refers to God's hiddenness *in* revelation, i.e., to the fact that some hear the word of the cross as the power of God, while others deem it foolishness. In Moltmann, the phrase "crucified God" seems to be primarily a dramatic expression for the intensity of God's suffering in Christ, particularly in forsakenness (Jürgen Moltmann, *The Crucified God: The Cross of Christ as the Foundation and Criticism of Christian Theology,* trans. R. A. Wilson and John Bowden [New York: Harper & Row; London: SCM Press, 1974], 200–90). It is Moltmann's use of the term I am reflecting here.

40. Ronald Goetz, "The Suffering God: The Rise of a New Orthodoxy," *Christian Century* 103 (April 16, 1986): 385–89.

Pauline letters for speaking of a "crucified" or "suffering God."[41] Admittedly, the text cited by Moltmann—God "did not spare his own Son but delivered him up ($\pi\alpha\rho\acute{\epsilon}\delta\omega\kappa\epsilon\nu\ \alpha\grave{\upsilon}\tau\acute{o}\nu$) for us all" (Rom. 8:32)—is but a step away. With its apparent allusion to Abraham' s offering of Isaac in Genesis 22, it certainly depicts the intense grief of the parent who suffers the loss of a child. Moltmann, however, lays great stress on the verb $\pi\alpha\rho\alpha\delta\acute{\iota}\delta\omega\mu\iota$, and in light of its use in Rom. 1:24, 26, 28 as well as in the passion narratives, claims that it carries the notion of godforsakenness. "In the forsakenness of the Son the Father also forsakes himself." It is a big jump, however, to move from Rom. 8:32 to talk about the cross as an event between Jesus and his Father, and to conclude that "God allows himself to be forced out. God suffers. God allows himself to be crucified and is crucified." It is a jump that, Moltmann acknowledges, entails a highly developed doctrine of the Trinity[42]—something anachronistic in Paul. Aside from the much contested liturgical expression in Rom. 9:5, there is no place where Paul calls Christ "God," no place where he reflects on the unity between God and Christ (as in John 10:30; 17:20-26). In fact, Paul's Christology highlights the obedience Jesus shows to God (e.g., Phil. 2:8; Rom. 5:19) and gives little support for immediately identifying the experiences of Christ with those of God or for fusing the actions of the two.[43] In any case, clearly

41. Gerhard Friedrich sees a textual basis in 1 Cor. 2:8, where the rulers of this age have crucified "the Lord of glory." The title, he argues, is used extensively for God in Ethiopic Enoch and must carry such overtones here. "Paul does not relativize the cross, but dares to speak of the crucified God" (*Die Verkündigung des Todes Jesus im Neuen Testament*, BTS 6 [Neukirchen-Vluyn: Neukirchen Verlag, 1982], 138). But it is clear that 1 Cor. 2:8 refers to Christ's crucifixion, not God's. The expression "crucified the Lord of glory" is likely aimed, as a piece of irony, at the exalted Christology of the Corinthians.

42. Moltmann, *The Crucified God*, 241–49. See the critique of Moltmann by Leonardo Boff, who accuses him of eternalizing suffering in God rather than overcoming it. Leonardo Boff, *Passion of Christ, Passion of the World: The Facts, Their Interpretation, and Their Meaning Today*, trans. Robert R. Barr (Maryknoll, N.Y.: Orbis Books, 1987), 111–15.

43. Special consideration in this context needs to be given to 2 Cor. 5:19 because of its potential as an incarnational text and because of the strongly theocentric flavor of the passage. Following the word order of the Greek text, one could translate the verse "God was in Christ, reconciling the world to himself." In such a case, the participle $\kappa\alpha\tau\alpha\lambda\lambda\acute{\alpha}\sigma\sigma\omega\nu$ is taken as attributive, separate from the main verb $\mathring{\eta}\nu$. The verse would then carry a definite incarnational emphasis and would certainly provide a basis for speaking of a

missing from Paul's letters is the vivid language of God's suffering found in the Old Testament.[44]

Though one cannot detect in the Pauline letters an unambiguous textual basis for a "crucified" or "suffering" God, the notion
is not far away. The divine purposes for the people of God are
exposed in the death of Christ. There Christ is made "the framework for our understanding of God"; there God's attributes of
power, righteousness, wisdom, faithfulness, freedom, and love
are most clearly revealed; there humanity is freed from its inevitable idolatry. How else is one to understand the strange structure of Rom. 5:8: "*God* shows *his own* love for us in that . . .
Christ died for us"?

"crucified God." It is more likely, however, in light of the context, that ἦν and
καταλλάσσων should be taken together as a periphrastic imperfect and that ἐν
Χριστῷ should be understood as equivalent to διὰ Χριστοῦ. The translation
would read, "in Christ God was reconciling the world to himself" or "it was
God who in Christ was reconciling the world to himself" (so Barrett). The
latter options provide a smoother continuation of the thrust of v. 18, rendering
Christ as the agent of God's action, and since there is no incarnational stress in
the context, they are preferred. While acknowledging the former as gram-
matically possible, Barrett, Bultmann, and Furnish also favor one of the latter
translations. C. K. Barrett, *A Commentary on the Second Epistle to the
Corinthians,* HNTC (New York: Harper & Row, 1973), 176–77; Rudolf
Bultmann, *The Second Letter to the Corinthians,* trans. Roy A. Harrisville
(Minneapolis: Augsburg, 1985), 161; V. P. Furnish, *II Corinthians,* AB (Garden
City, N.Y.: Doubleday, 1984), 318.
44. See Terence E. Fretheim, *The Suffering of God: An Old Testament
Perspective,* OBT (Philadelphia: Fortress Press, 1984).

CHAPTER 2

Jesus' Death
and Human Sinfulness

We discovered in the last chapter, somewhat surprisingly, that the Pauline letters indicate little or no interest in historical causation: Who killed Jesus, and why? Instead, they seem preoccupied with the divine involvement in Jesus' death, with the telling of the story against the background of broader issues than merely the political and religious struggles of first-century Palestine. They make it clear that Jesus was not acting "on his own," as it were, but in obedience to God's will, or put another way, that the death of Jesus is an expression of God's own love. Furthermore, the texts we examined claim a foundational role for themselves. They disclose how subversive theological reflection can be when it dares to follow the epistemology that begins with the cross (1 Cor. 1:18—2:2) and how idolatrous such reflection can be when it chooses a different starting point. They make it clear that for a theology of the Pauline letters, the death of Jesus cannot be relegated to one topic among a long list of topics, but must be perspectival, giving focus to the others.

Now we move from a consideration of the divine intentions to the human situation, from God's purposes in the death of Jesus to what the death accomplished with respect to the creatures God made. If God's love is demonstrated in the death of Jesus for weak, sinful humanity, how is anything changed or made different? Is the death primarily a God-given illustration or paradigm of the meaning of love to teach humanity its depth and breadth, and to provide a model to be followed? Are the death and the love expressed in it to be grasped along psychological lines—that is, unloveable humans are so profoundly cared for by a loving God that they can begin to accept themselves and maybe even care for others? Or could the death of Jesus function as propitiatory sacrifices do in other ancient religions, to appease the divine anger so that it is diverted from the guilty parties? Does the death do as much for God's disposition in dealing with recalcitrant and rebellious creatures as it does for the creatures themselves? These (and many more) questions propel us into the area traditionally called soteriology, and in a more limited sense, the doctrine of the atonement.[1] It is a particularly crucial area when one reads Paul's letters because for him Christology and soteriology are intimately related. What we shall do, then, in this chapter is to examine the Pauline texts in which Jesus' death is mentioned in connection with human sinfulness. So many texts make the connection that it will be necessary to select for careful consideration only a representative number and cross-reference others.

Underlying our discussion in this chapter is an issue frequently argued in contemporary Pauline studies: What conceptual category is predominant in the Pauline soteriology, and how is it interpretive of the others?[2] In a sense the issue goes back to the Reformation when particularly the Lutheran wing interpreted the letters so exclusively in terms of justification by faith. It was held to be the controlling theme of Pauline theology and the vantage point from which all else was to be understood. Since then a long line of scholars from a variety of perspectives has challenged the pride of place that justification occupied.[3] The

1. I shall use the term "atonement" throughout this chapter to designate God's activity in righting the wrongs of human sin. This is in line with C. L. Mitton's comment: "In modern usage, 'atonement' has taken on the more restricted meaning of the process by which hindrances to reconciliation are removed, rather than the end achieved by their removal. 'To atone for' a wrong is to take some action which cancels out the ill effects it has had." C. L. Mitton, "Atonement," *IDB,* 1:309.

2. E. P. Sanders says this "must be considered *the* problem of Pauline exegesis: the relation among the various soteriological terms." E. P. Sanders, *Paul and Palestinian Judaism: A Comparison of Patterns of Religion* (Philadelphia: Fortress Press; London: SCM Press, 1977), 508.

3. Outside of the history-of-religions school, which dispensed with the question by treating Paul as a religious figure rather than a theologian, Albert Schweitzer is likely the most significant name in this long list. He found the

three most prominent positions in the contemporary discussion are the following:

1. The Reformation perspective, which says that the language of justification predominates, is represented by Käsemann (among many others).[4]

2. The notion that the Pauline soteriology is primarily participationist, with the motif of dying and rising with Christ as the centerpiece, is argued by E. P. Sanders (among many others).[5]

3. That reconciliation functions as the coherent center of soteriology is posed by Ralph P. Martin (among a few).[6]

We shall propose that the search for a controlling category runs the risk of restricting the other categories and that any move toward a unified conception must respect the suggestive force of the various metaphorical terms used in connection with the Pauline soteriology.

We shall begin our investigation by taking brief note of a basic formula that Paul uses with some flexibility and frequency. It likely appears in its most basic form in the statement that "Christ died for our sins" (1 Cor. 15:3). Then we shall examine in detail three texts in Romans, treated chronologically so as to take advantage of their order in the argument of the letter (3:24-26; 4:24-25; 6:1-11). They put us in touch with the full range and variety of Pauline soteriology. Then we shall turn to the important passage in 2 Cor. 5:14—6:2, which combines a number of soteriological categories into one unified argument. Finally, in light of our exegesis, we shall consider the traditional "theories" of the

center of Paul's thought to be eschatological mysticism and became the forerunner of those who argue that Pauline soteriology is primarily participationist. See Albert Schweitzer, *The Mysticism of Paul the Apostle,* trans. William Montgomery (New York: Henry Holt, 1931), esp. 101–40.

4. See especially Ernst Käsemann, "'The Righteousness of God' in Paul," in *New Testament Questions of Today,* trans. W. J. Montague (Philadelphia: Fortress Press, 1969), 168–82, and "Justification and Salvation History in the Epistle to the Romans," in *Perspectives on Paul,* trans. Margaret Kohl (Philadelphia: Fortress Press, 1969), 60–78.

5. E. P. Sanders, *Paul and Palestinian Judaism,* 447–508. Sanders recognizes other conceptual categories in the letters but in the interest of coherence tends to subsume them under the participationist one. See also D. E. H. Whiteley, *The Theology of St. Paul* (Oxford: Basil Blackwell, 1974), 130–32.

6. Ralph P. Martin, *Reconciliation: A Study of Paul's Theology* (Atlanta: John Knox Press, 1981), esp. 90–110.

atonement, which have emerged from the church's history as ways to express the meaning of Jesus' death in relation to human sinfulness.

"CHRIST DIED FOR OUR SINS"

In a sense, this quotation from 1 Cor. 15:3 says it all. It lies at the center of the gospel Paul receives from Christians before him and which in turn he transmits in his own preaching. And yet in another sense, the citation simply raises for us the question of the atonement. In what way is Christ's death "for" our sins? The Greek preposition ($\dot{v}\pi\acute{\epsilon}\rho$) used in the statement becomes the clue for detecting a varied use of this formula in wide-ranging contexts. It appears in each of the following:

". . . the Lord Jesus Christ, who gave himself *for* our sins" (Gal. 1:4).
"Christ died *for* the ungodly" (Rom. 5:6)
"Christ died *for* us" (Rom. 5:8)
". . . our Lord Jesus Christ, who died *for* us" (1 Thess. 5:10)
"that one [Christ] has died *for* all" (2 Cor. 5:14)
". . . the Son of God, who loved me and gave himself *for* me" (Gal. 2:20)
"Christ . . . having become a curse *for* us" (Gal. 3:13)
"the one *for* whom Christ died" (Rom. 14:15)

In addition, the statement from the institution of the Lord's Supper also needs to be included, though in the shorter text it has no verb comparable to "died" or "gave": "This is my body which is *for* you" (1 Cor. 11:24).[7] Though Paul can readily use the preposition in a general sense to mean "for the good of" or "in aid of" (so Rom. 16:4; 2 Cor. 1:11; 12:15; Phil. 1:7; 4:10) and in the specific sense of "in the name of" (so 2 Cor. 5:20), when used in connection with Christ's death it seems to carry the notion of "in behalf of" or "in place of." One must of course be wary of arriving at a precise sense of the preposition in the formula in

---

7. The prepositional phrase also appears as a very doubtful reading in 1 Cor. 5:7.

abstraction and then of assuming that in every context it carries the same sense.[8] But having acknowledged the need for caution, it is appropriate to observe that in several contexts the preposition clearly denotes "in place of," a replacement of one party for another (so Gal. 3:13; 2 Cor. 5:21; probably 2 Cor. 5:14, and others) and thus a vicarious death.[9]

What emerges from investigating the various expressions of the formula is its "kerygmatic" character—that is, that it functions as a declarative announcement of something. This should not be too surprising since the formula likely comes from the preaching and credal tradition of the church; and yet immersed in Paul's letters it still does not lose its unambiguous, annunciative quality. There are no conditions set alongside the formula, no reduction of its scope to a subjective apprehension. Not even faith is given as a precondition for its validity. An event occurred in the past, once-and-for-all, which has universal dimensions. "Christ died for our sins," "for the ungodly," "for all," "for us," "for me." As Hultgren notes, "It is not said that it happened for the sake of an elect or even for those who would come to believe in the death as atoning. Instead the 'objective' and 'universal' character of the atoning death of Christ is what constitutes the gospel as being truly good news."[10] This we shall see in the texts to which we now turn.

THREE SOTERIOLOGICAL TERMS (ROM. 3:24-26)

When we examined Romans 3 in the previous chapter, we raised the question as to what role God played in the death of Jesus. From the context we discovered that in Christ's death God's righteousness is vindicated in two specific ways: God is shown to be a promise-keeping God, whose faithfulness can be

---

8. Keck, for example, notes the difficulty found in Rom. 5:7, when the preposition is used with the verb "die" but in an apparently different sense from its use in 5:6 and 5:8. See Leander E. Keck, "The Post-Pauline Interpretation of Jesus' Death in Rom. 5:6-7," *Theologia Crucis—Signum Crucis: Festschrift für Erich Dinkler*, ed. C. Andresen and G. Klein (Tübingen: J. C. B. Mohr [Paul Siebeck], 1979), 237–48.

9. On the formula, see Harald Riesenfeld, ὑπέρ, *TDNT*, VIII: 507–16.

10. Arland J. Hultgren, *Christ and His Benefits: Christology and Redemption in the New Testament* (Philadelphia: Fortress Press, 1987), 50–51.

trusted, and a God of moral integrity, who does not overlook human sinfulness. We turn now more specifically to what God does with respect to human sinfulness. How is it that Christ's death makes any difference in the situation of sinful humanity?

From 1:18 to 3:20 the text dwells on the inexcusable plight of humanity, both Jews and gentiles, who are accountable to God. While the Jews have advantages as recipients of the promise, the final verdict is that "all people are under sin," and with a chain of verses from the Old Testament the verdict is documented. Even after 3:21, when Paul turns to spell out the vindication of divine righteousness, he repeats the description of the human situation: "All have sinned and are lacking the glory of God" (3:23).

It is interesting that in vv. 9 and 23 we seem to be faced with different conceptions of the nature of sin. In the one case, sin is a dominion under which humanity exists (3:9). The failure to honor or thank God, even though God's power and deity are perceptible in the created order (1:21); the arrogance of pretentious wisdom (1:22); ridiculous idolatry (1:23); and the long and sordid story of human degradation that ensues when God's restraining hand is removed (1:24-32)—all lead to the inevitable conclusion that humanity is enslaved, helplessly and hopelessly captive to the reign of sin. In the other case, sin is a verb, something people perform. The immediate verse does not spell out the details of this action since the previous section has done it so elaborately (1:18—3:20). It is enough to say that the result of sinning is that people are left without the divine glory.[11]

A readable translation of 3:24-26 is hard to come by for several reasons, not the least of which is that a pre-Pauline tradition may have been woven into the text. Another difficulty has to do with the prepositional phrase "through faith" ($\delta\iota\grave{\alpha}$ $\pi\acute{\iota}\sigma\tau\epsilon\omega\varsigma$), which in the Greek text is sandwiched between "expiation" and "in his blood." Since the notion of "through faith in his blood" is unlikely, most English translations take the "through faith" to refer to the human response to God's action (so the RSV: "to be received by faith"). But this does not account for the awkward

---

11. The conception of sin as an act against God is of course also reflected in Rom. 3:25 in the phrase "the sins previously committed."

word order nor does it explain why the human response should be mentioned at this point in the argument.[12] Much better sense is made of the sentence if "through faith" is taken as a parallel expression (hendiadys) to "in his blood." It then denotes not the appropriate human stance for the reception of God's grace, but the faith (and faithfulness) of Jesus demonstrated in his obedience unto death.[13] Accordingly, the prepositional phrase parallels a similar expression in 3:22 (διὰ πίστεως Ἰησοῦ Χριστοῦ), where the words "Jesus Christ" seem to be a subjective genitive, else the redundancy produces a terribly clumsy sentence. In 3:25 Jesus is precisely faithful at the cost of his blood.[14] The verses convey a strong statement of the death of Jesus, appropriate to the theological freight the death must carry in the immediate argument.

Romans 3:24-26 can then be paraphrased: All are being justified undeservedly by God's grace through the redemption that is in Christ Jesus, whom God designated (or put forward) as a means of expiation, in light of Christ's faithfulness to God in the shedding of his blood. This was to demonstrate the divine righteousness, because God in his patience had passed over the previously committed sins; it was to demonstrate God's righteousness at the present time—that God is righteous and that God justifies the one who shares the faith of Jesus.[15]

12. Käsemann explains the difficult word order by saying that διὰ πίστεως in 3:25 is a Pauline insertion into the pre-Pauline formula (*Commentary on Romans,* trans. Geoffrey W. Bromiley [Grand Rapids, Mich.: Wm. B. Eerdmans, 1980], 98). In this, he is following Bultmann (*Theology of the New Testament,* trans. Kendrick Grobel [London: SCM Press, 1951], 1: 46). But one then has to ask: Why is the insertion not made after "in his blood," where it would more appropriately fit? Why does the insertion result in such a clumsy sentence?

13. Sam K. Williams, *Jesus' Death as Saving Event: The Background and Origin of a Concept,* HDR 2 (Missoula: Scholars Press, 1975), 47, 51; Luke Timothy Johnson, "Romans 3:21-26 and the Faith of Jesus," *CBQ* 44 (1982): 79–80.

14. BDF, par. 219, says that ἐν is instrumental, representing a genitive of price, on the basis of the LXX translation of the Hebrew *beth.* The prepositional phrase can then be rendered "by the shedding of his blood" or "at the cost of his blood."

15. For the translation of this concluding phrase (τὸν ἐκ πίστεως Ἰησοῦ), see Johnson, "Romans 3:21-26 and the Faith of Jesus," 80, 88; and Richard B. Hays, *The Faith of Jesus Christ: An Investigation of the Narrative Substructure of Galatians 3:1—4:11,* SBLDS 56 (Chico, Calif.: Scholars Press, 1983), 191.

Three powerful images are employed here to explicate how God effects a change with regard to the human situation. We need to investigate each in order to grasp fully what Jesus' death signifies.

1. First is the verb "justify" (δικαιούμενοι in 3:24 and δικαιοῦντα in 3:26). As we discovered in the previous chapter, the passage is strongly theocentric. The early section of Romans 3 (vv. 1-8) relates how God's righteousness is called into question. Charges have been brought against Paul's gospel of grace, that it is soft on sin and promotes libertinism. Paul answers the charges by pointing to the death of Christ as the vindication of God's character. The phrase "the righteousness of God," as we saw, does not represent a moral standard that God demands of humans, but God's own rectitude, God's faithfulness and moral integrity. Now in turning from the noun "righteousness" to the verb "justify" (both of course in the Greek language coming from the same root), we are reminded that God's righteousness is not a static quality, a divine attribute to be grasped as an abstract ideal. Rather it is "a power which brings salvation to pass. . . . God's power reaches out for the world, and the world's salvation lies in its being recaptured for the sovereignty of God."[16]

This apocalyptically based, inclusive meaning of the verb, with its world-transforming scope, is particularly evident in 3:24. As a masculine, nominative, plural, passive participle, "being justified" (δικαιούμενοι) must refer to the "all" (πάντες) in 3:23, meaning that all who have sinned (an inclusive group that can hardly be qualified) are captured by God's power for salvation.[17] Undeservedly, by a gracious gift (a double statement for emphasis), they are set right with God. The sins that have left humanity without the divine glory are forgiven in the death of Christ.

The latter translates the phrase: "the person who lives on the basis of Jesus' faith."

16. Ernst Käsemann, *New Testament Questions of Today,* trans. W. J. Montague (Philadelphia: Fortress Press, 1969), 181–82.

17. Williams says that because the participle is in the present rather than the aorist tense Paul must be stating a principle and not speaking of actual individuals who have experienced God's justifying act. The stress, he further notes, is upon the *way* God justifies—freely, by grace. See Sam K. Williams, *Jesus' Saving Death,* 15.

The second use of the verb "justify" (3:26), however, carries a less apocalyptic and more forensic cast because of its object. Now the recipient of God's action is designated not as "all" who have sinned, but "the one who shares the faith of Jesus." The phrase takes us out of the sphere of a world-encompassing act of God to a relationship to a particular type of individual. God acquits the believer, sets the one who shares the faith of Jesus into a right relationship. It appears as if "faith" has been made some sort of stipulation for justification (though not necessarily a "work" since faith, too, may be thought of as a gift of God). Does this latter statement of justification in 3:26 then condition the former statement? Should 3:23-24, in the light of 3:26, be understood to imply that "all who have sinned but have now come to faith" are being justified as a gift?

Scholars who have argued for a single understanding of justification have often found difficulty with this double-sidedness in the Pauline letters. It seems hardly possible to fit all Paul's statements into a single pattern.[18] While not solving all the exegetical difficulties, Arland J. Hultgren's recent analysis of the justification texts is instructive precisely at this point.[19] He notes that there are two types of statements of God's justifying activity in the Pauline letters.[20] One type does not mention faith but expresses or implies the justification of all humanity (e.g., Rom. 3:24; 4:5; 5:6-9). These texts are found in strongly theocentric contexts and emerge from the apocalyptic-based understanding of the revelation of God's righteousness. The christological grounding for such a cosmic interpretation can be found in Rom. 5:12-21,

18. For example, E. P. Sanders points to the unresolved dilemma in Käsemann's position. On the one hand, Käsemann stresses the cosmic character of the revelation of God's righteousness over against the intensely anthropocentric and individualistic understanding of Bultmann. On the other hand, when attacked by fellow Lutherans for deemphasizing the place of faith, Käsemann affirms that faith remains primarily a decision of the individual. See Sanders, *Paul and Palestinian Judaism,* 434–42.

19. Arland J. Hultgren, *Paul's Gospel and Mission: The Outlook from His Letter to the Romans* (Philadelphia: Fortress Press, 1985), 82–98.

20. The same phenomenon is true, as we shall see, with texts using the language of reconciliation. "In Christ God was reconciling the world to himself, not counting their trespasses against them." And yet in the next sentence Christians as ambassadors are told to urge others, "Be reconciled to God" (2 Cor. 5:19-20).

where the universality of grace in Christ is shown to surpass the universality of sin in Adam. A second type of statement explicitly mentions faith (using either the verb or the noun) and tends toward a forensic interpretation of God's justifying activity (e.g., Rom. 3:22, 26; 5:1; 10:4). These texts primarily serve an ecclesial function in defining the identity of the people of God, in answering the question as to *who* constitutes the community of the new age (and *on what basis*). Hultgren argues that the two types of statements need to be thought of as separate but obviously related topics, and that methodologically the universal statements demand prior consideration. Only in light of them should the more specialized statements of justification by faith be taken up. In turn, each type has its particular function to perform in the strategy of the letters. The repeated effort to reduce Paul's theology to the second category of statements—that is, to justification by faith—simply does not take sufficient account of all that Paul writes, even about justification itself.

Hultgren's distinction helps to make clear the point that in Rom. 3:24-26 God's action with respect to human sin is first of all cosmic and universal in scope. It is not this individual or that, not even this nation or that, but the whole created company of people, who are the object of the divine movement to set things right. The death of Jesus has an apocalyptic, world-transforming character because it effects a complete change in the situation between sinful humanity and God. This is the heart of Paul's gospel. In the context, universalism becomes essential to the argument that with God there is no distinction between Jews and gentiles. The reference to justifying "the one who shares the faith of Jesus" in 3:26 represents the second type of statement and serves as an appropriate transition to 3:27-31. There the uppermost issue (especially in vv. 29-30) concerns the people of God, that sharing the faith of Jesus, not circumcision, is the constituting characteristic of such a people.

2. The second term in the passage used to explicate what God does with respect to sin is "redemption" in 3:24 (διὰ τῆς ἀπολυτρώσεως τῆς ἐν Χριστῷ Ἰησοῦ). Its use conjures up the vivid image of a slave or prisoner released from confinement through the payment of a ransom of some sort. Since the following verse

makes reference to Jesus' blood, it is tempting to exploit the various dimensions of the image and build a soteriology based on a theory of ransom. Käsemann, however, has warned that the term has lost its vividness through repeated liturgical use and simply designates "the eschatological event."[21] Certainly neither of the two other occasions of the word "redemption" in the Pauline letters connotes any of the vividness that might be attached to its secular use (Rom. 8:23; 1 Cor. 1:30; cf. also Eph. 1:7; Col. 1:14).[22] More prominent is the simple notion of freedom or deliverance resulting from the death and resurrection of Christ (so the prepositional phrase "in Christ Jesus").

Within the context of Romans 3, however, what must be affirmed is the appropriate juxtaposition of the term "redemption" with the concept of sin expressed in 3:9. As we noted, sin is understood there as a controlling force, a dominion to which humanity is in bondage. The RSV and NEB fittingly translate the Greek phrase ὑφ' ἁμαρτίαν as "under the power of sin." In Christ Jesus comes deliverance from this dominion, escape from sin's clutches, freedom from having to march to its drumbeat. The long and dreary story of humanity's slavery is ended. Though Paul elsewhere develops more extensively this understanding of freedom from bondage and transference to a new "lord," suffice it to observe here that such language is employed alongside and in support of "justification" and cultic imagery.

3. The third term in the passage explaining the import of Jesus' death with regard to sin is ἱλαστήριον in 3:25, a Greek word to which a great deal of scholarly attention has been devoted in order to determine a proper translation. Does the word denote primarily "expiation"—that is, an action that makes amends for offenses committed?[23] Or is it to be translated "propitiation"—

---

21. Käsemann, *Romans,* 96.

22. Paul elsewhere uses with great effectiveness a similar verb in the expression "you were bought with a price" (ἠγοράσθητε τιμῆς, 1 Cor. 6:20; 7:23). In both contexts the element of price is mentioned in order to stress the resulting change of allegiance and the service of a new "lord."

23. E.g., Käsemann, *Romans,* 97–98; J. D. G. Dunn, "Paul's Understanding of the Death of Jesus," *Reconciliation and Hope: New Testament Essays on Atonement and Hope,* ed. Robert Banks (Grand Rapids, Mich.: Wm. B. Eerdmans, 1974), 137–41.

that is, as action aimed at satisfying the divine wrath?[24] Or does the word reflect a reference to the lid over the ark of the covenant (*kapporeth*), as it clearly does in Heb. 9:5, and carry an association with the day of atonement when the priest sprinkled blood on the mercy-seat (Lev. 16)?[25]

The decision is complicated by the fact that this is the only occurrence of the word or any of its cognates in the Pauline corpus. Furthermore, much of the scholarly debate has centered around the use of the Greek term (and its verbal cognate) in the Septuagint, which, while illuminating, does not solve the riddle of its use in Rom. 3:25. The immediate context (and not even its context in a pre-Pauline, Jewish Christian formula) must finally be determinative, but unfortunately the context neither dictates a particular translation nor does it ultimately preclude any of the three.[26]

One, then, has to raise the question as to whether it is wise, given the fairly broad readership this letter projects, to nail down the sense of the word too tightly. Certainly ἱλαστήριον could reflect the lid of the ark of the covenant, as it does in Heb. 9:5, but there is nothing in the context (apart from the mention of "blood") to suggest that the text has in view such specific and concrete cultic terminology. The paralleling of "by his blood" and "by the death of his Son" in Rom. 5:9-10 makes it more likely that the use of "blood" in 3:25, while not entirely free of cultic overtones, is simply a designation for Jesus' death rather than a pointed allusion to the sacrificial system.[27] "Propitiation" presents a major problem as a translation because it raises the

---

24. E.g., Leon Morris, "The Meaning of ἱλαστήριον in Romans 3:25," *NTS* 2 (1955–56): 33–43; C. E. B. Cranfield, *A Critical and Exegetical Commentary on the Epistle to the Romans,* ICC (Edinburgh: T. & T. Clark, 1975), 1: 214–18.

25. E.g., Hultgren, *Paul's Gospel and Mission,* 60–69; Peter Stuhlmacher, *Reconciliation, Law, and Righteousness: Essays in Biblical Theology* (Philadelphia: Fortress Press, 1986), 96–103.

26. John Reumann even "suspects" that ἱλαστήριον had one nuance ("mercy-seat"?) in the pre-Pauline formula and another ("expiation") in Paul. See Reumann, "The Gospel of the Righteousness of God: Pauline Reinterpretation in Romans 3:21-26," *Interp* 20 (1966): 436n.

27. The word order of the prepositional phrase "in his blood" has αὐτοῦ in the emphatic, attributive position, which favors a reference to Jesus' death rather than a sacrificial offering.

specter of the pagan deities, whose anger had to be assuaged by some sort of sacrificial gift. There is certainly no thought here that God demands or seeks appeasement because of offenses humans have perpetrated. And yet, as C. K. Barrett has noted, the idea of propitiation cannot be entirely excluded. God's response to sin is "wrath" (Rom. 1:18; 2:5, 8; 3:5). In making amends for sins in Christ, God is getting at the root of the problem and "the sin that might justly have excited God's wrath is expiated (at God's will), and therefore no longer does so."[28] The action aimed at the sin ("expiation") also has an effect with respect to God. In this sense, the propitiation is a secondary result rather than a primary cause of the atonement.

Since a choice for a translation has to be made, "expiation" or "a means of expiation" seems the simplest option, partly because it does not foreclose other possible dimensions of meaning. While essentially no different in implications from "mercy-seat," it is less technical, has the advantage of being understood by a broader readership (both original and modern), and avoids the possible misunderstandings associated with "propitiation." Having made the choice, however, one has also to recognize the fluidity of the term and the various connotations it did and does convey to readers of Romans.

How in the context are the three picture words—justify, redemption, and expiation—related? Without a doubt the dominant term of the three is the first. The passage focuses on God's righteousness, which, while revealed apart from the law, is nevertheless witnessed to by the Hebrew Scriptures and shows God to be a rectifier of sinful humanity. The devastating picture of sin painted in the previous section of the letter (1:18—3:20), which has depicted both Jew and gentile as totally corrupt, demands a world-transforming action to make things right, to rectify twisted and perverted relations. This God accomplishes out of divine

---

28. C. K. Barrett, *A Commentary on the Epistle to the Romans,* HNTC (New York: Harper and Row, 1957), 78. Dunn comments: "The wrath of God in the case of Jesus' death is not so much retributive as preventative." See J. D. G. Dunn, "Paul's Understanding of the Death of Jesus," 139. Williams also notes the connection between expiation and propitiation, but strangely dismisses mercy-seat without serious consideration. See Sam K. Williams, *Jesus' Saving Death,* 39–40.

mercy and offers as a free gift. And yet, this act of justification happens "through" (διὰ) the deliverance effected in the death of Jesus, who is then presented in the language of the cult as a means of expiation. The death, as deliverance and as sacrifice, is made the basis for God's justifying act.

Two observations need to be made about this relationship. First, the atonement—that is, God's decisive dealing with sin through the death of Jesus—is not an incidental piece of the announcement that God justifies sinful humanity. One has to take seriously George Howard's warning that Paul here does not try "to explain the atonement but rather to use it,"[29] but at the same time one cannot ignore its use. This is the complaint Stuhlmacher has repeatedly brought against Bultmann and Käsemann. By stressing that the texts about atonement come only from the tradition received from the early church, they make the case that atonement is not significant to Paul's own theology. Stuhlmacher agrees that Paul cites the tradition in the passage, but he "does not speak critically of the soteriological foundation of justification in Jesus' atoning death but in continuity and agreement with the confessional formula he received."[30] Indeed "in Paul talk about the atoning death of Jesus is no traditional relic but the condition that makes his theology of justification and of the cross possible!"[31] Our exegesis of the passage supports Stuhlmacher's position. At the same time it must be clearly recognized that the text gives little warrant for a two-staged soteriology: first what God "objectively" does in Christ and then what happens "subjectively" to change the situation of sinful people. The passage conveys a single movement of God in Christ for the salvation of humanity.

Second, the use of the atonement in the passage is nothing less than the basis for a world-embracing deed of God to rectify the human situation. What is effected is not a rearguard, clean-up action to take care only of past sins, but a thorough change in the divine-human relationship. It is not as if the human choir has

29. George Howard, "Romans 3:21-31 and the Inclusion of the Gentiles," *HTR* 63 (1970): 228.
30. Stuhlmacher, *Reconciliation,* 104.
31. Ibid., 157.

moved to another stanza of the same hymn. They now sing a brand-new song, which the psalmists long ago anticipated (e.g., Ps. 96:1; 98:1). All humanity is encompassed by the gracious, justifying act of God.[32]

Furthermore, this eschatological event by which God deals with human sin is a once-for-all act, needing no further activity, no supplement to turn a potential into an actual salvation. A number of features of the text makes this unmistakably clear. The emphasis on the present as the time of God's ultimate revelatory action is highlighted by two pointed references ("but now" in 3:21 and "at the present time" in 3:26). A new era has begun. Moreover, the use of cultic language to describe Jesus' death is a reminder that the repeated sacrifices made in the Jewish worship to secure forgiveness of sins are now rendered unnecessary. Jesus as an expiation for sin effects the full and final redemption of God's people.

A PAULINE "USE" OF THE ATONEMENT (ROM. 4:24-25)

We turn now from a passage rich in soteriological images to one in which a simple formula terminates a lengthy discussion of the significance of Abraham. And yet the two verses that conclude Romans 4 carry an import beyond their brief and lyrical affirmation of Jesus' death and resurrection. Since they contain the only reference to Jesus in the chapter, they exercise a profound effect on how the entire chapter is to be read. In fact, they illustrate how effectively statements of the atonement are used in the development of an argument. Thus we shall concentrate our investigation on the function the verses play in the Abraham story.[33]

---

32. One must also, with Howard, go further than this and say that the world-transforming deed of God is announced here in order to argue that gentiles are included with Jews in the people of God, as 3:27-30 explains. See George Howard, "Romans 3:21-31," 223–33.

33. It is very probable that Rom. 4:25 represents a pre-Pauline formula, as Bultmann (*Theology,* 1: 47, 82) and Käsemann argue (*Romans,* 128–29), though Gerhard Delling has made a case for its being a Pauline composition. See Delling, *Das Kreuzestod Jesu in der urchristlichen Verkündigung* (Göttingen: Vandenhoeck & Ruprecht, 1972), 13–14. It is insufficient, however, to do as Bultmann does and dismiss v. 25 as not containing Paul's "characteristic view" (*Theology,* 1: 296), without asking why Paul includes it in the chapter.

Both at the beginning and at the conclusion of Romans 3 the factor of circumcision is mentioned in such a way as to provide a statement of its value and limitations. At the beginning, it holds great importance because it designates the Jewish people as guardians of "the oracles of God" (3:2). Circumcision signifies the advantage they have as the chosen nation to whom God's promises have been made. At the end of the chapter, however, Paul indicates that with regard to God's justifying activity circumcision has no value at all. The movement of divine grace has nothing to do with whether the recipients are circumcised or uncircumcised (3:30). But this inevitably raises the question of Abraham, to whom circumcision was initially given. "What then shall we say about Abraham, our forefather according to the flesh?" (4:1)

Paul knew his Torah well enough to point out that it records the statement of Abraham's faith and the reckoning of righteousness to him by God *before* it records the instituting of circumcision. Genesis 15:6 precedes Genesis 17 in the order of the narrative. This precludes any notion that circumcision can be a precondition for the reckoning of righteousness; rather circumcision is "a sign or seal of the righteousness which he [i.e., Abraham] had by faith while he was still uncircumcised" (4:11). Moreover, the text moves from this historical to a theological observation. The purpose of the order was to enable Abraham to be the father of all those, whether circumcised or not, who share Abraham's faith (4:11-12). This is further documented from within Genesis 17 itself by the fact that the promise made to Abraham in the covenant renewal in 17:5 ("I have made you the father of many nations") also precedes the giving of circumcision in 17:10-14 (Rom. 4:16-17).

The theological groundwork for the inclusion of the gentiles comes, then, in a careful exegesis of the Genesis narrative. The hermeneutical key is "the faith of Abraham." The one who shares that faith (τῷ ἐκ πίστεως Ἀβραάμ, 4:16) is included in the promise and counted as a descendant. A vignette of such faith is to be found in the way Abraham and Sarah did not waver with regard to the promise that they would have an heir, but despite all the evidence to the contrary were "fully convinced that God was able to do what he had promised" (4:21). But this is not simply a matter of a historical record. Abraham's story has tremendous value for the readers of Romans. God's righteousness "will be reckoned to us who believe in the one who raised Jesus our Lord from the dead, who was put to death for our trespasses and raised for our justification" (4:24-25).[34]

Why are vv. 24-25 attached to the end of the chapter? The point that faith and not circumcision characterizes Abraham's descendants has already been eloquently made without the verses. Do they represent merely a liturgical formula that makes no contribution to the argument? Or could their function be primarily literary—to provide a transition to the beginning of Romans 5 ("for our justification. . . . Therefore, since we are justified by faith")? Two crucial connections between v. 25 and the preceding argument need to be explored in order to get at an answer. First, the phrase "was put to death for our trespasses" recalls the only other mention of sins in the chapter, the citation of Ps. 32:1-2 (LXX: 31:1-2) in vv. 7-8: "Blessed are those whose injustices are forgiven and whose sins are covered; blessed is the man against whom the Lord will not reckon sin."[35] These verses are applied to the situation of Abraham through the catchword "reckon" ($\lambda o\gamma i\zeta o\mu\alpha\iota$), which appears both in Gen. 15:6 and in Ps. 32:2. The "reckoning" of righteousness has to do with forgiveness or the nonreckoning of sins. But if the story of Abraham is to be instructive for "us" and not merely a historical record, then the move has to be made to the death of Jesus, where the final and decisive expiation takes place (3:25-26). Verse 25 serves then to "christianize" the declaration of forgiveness, an appropriate step for Paul to make in relation to his readers.

Second, the words "was raised for our justification" recall the qualifying comment about God in 4:17b: "who gives life to the dead and calls into existence the things that do not exist." This

34. There are two $\delta\iota\dot{\alpha}$ phrases in v. 25, both of which can appropriately be translated in English as "for" so as to maintain the parallelism and convey the liturgical balance in the verse. It is likely, however, that the former is causal ("because of our trespasses") and the latter purposive ("with a view to our justification").

35. The words "was put to death for our trespasses" may also carry an allusion to the LXX of Isa. 53:12 ("was put to death for their sins").

means, as Käsemann has shown, that from 4:17 to the end of the chapter Abraham's faith is a faith in the resurrection, in a God who gives life to the dead.[36] The "faith of Abraham" (4:12, 16) is a prototype for Christian faith. The mention of Jesus' resurrection in 4:25 simply underscores the fact that Abraham's trust in a God who creates ex nihilo, who gives an heir to such aged parents, is congruent with the Christian trust in the God who raised Jesus from the dead.

The two links between 4:24-25 and other points in Romans 4 thus affirm the parallels in the structure of Abraham's faith and Christian faith. Though Abraham may have initially been brought into the argument to clarify the relation between believing and circumcision, facilitating the affirmation that he is the father of all who believe, he becomes in the end a paradigm of what it means to believe, even for gentiles.[37]

But vv. 24-25 also introduce a new figure into the story—"Jesus our Lord." Without him, Abraham's faith could be understood (particularly in light of 4:12b, 18-22) in a paraenetic sense, exclusively as a model to be followed: "Be strong and claim an unwavering faith in God when faced with insurmountable odds; do not be intimidated by impossibilities, but follow the way of Abraham, who, though entirely cognizant of his physical impotence and Sarah's barrenness, did not lose faith in the divine promise. If you believe like Abraham, your faith is reckoned as righteousness." When the story is read in this exhortative fashion, Abraham is turned into a hero, and the stress falls on the persistence and quality of the human response, rather than on the divine promise. But the mention of "Jesus our Lord" prevents such a heroizing of Abraham and lifts the story above mere paraenesis. The divine promise has now been fulfilled. The God in whom both Abraham and Paul trust has given a more com-

36. Käsemann, "The Faith of Abraham in Romans 4," *Perspectives on Paul,* trans. Margaret Kohl (Philadelphia: Fortress Press, 1971), 90. The use of "give life to" (ζωοποιέω) in 4:17 rather than "raise" (ἐγείρω) as in 4:25 Käsemann attributes to the language of the Jewish liturgy, particularly the Eighteen Benedictions.

37. Leenhardt comments, "The faith of Abraham is essentially the same as our own faith, because its object is the same." See Franz J. Leenhardt, *Romans,* trans. Harold Knight (London: Lutterworth Press, 1961), 128.

plete self-revelation, has acted decisively in raising Jesus, has made final atonement for human sins, has set things right. The promise has become gospel in Jesus' death and resurrection.[38]

The "attached" liturgical formula (v. 25) specifies that it is not faith that saves, not even extraordinary faith like Abraham's, but the God who keeps promises. The statement of the atonement, which serves as the conclusion to Romans 4, then can neither be jettisoned nor accepted only as an addendum to the argument. It has a decisive role to play in allowing Abraham to function as a modern prototype of faith.[39]

PARTICIPATION IN CHRIST'S DEATH (ROM. 6:1-11)

Romans 6 is one of those chapters whose contents can hardly be overemphasized. It returns to an issue mentioned earlier in the letter (3:8), spells out the implications of Christ's triumph over the devastating results of Adam's trespass (5:20-21), and in a sense lays the foundation for all else that follows in the letter (with perhaps the exception of Romans 9–11). In view of the charges brought against Paul, that his gospel leads to libertinism and offers no help in dealing with sin (3:8), the chapter takes on considerable significance. It supplies the groundwork for ethics, for the moral life, providing a christological basis for later exhortations. The commands to be servants of righteousness (6:13), to present our bodies as a living sacrifice to God (12:1), to love one another (13:8-9), all make sense as a result of believers' death to sin in the death of Christ. In our treatment of 6:1-11, we shall first follow the "logical" flow of the argument in order to clarify the movement and development of thought, and then make some

---

38. J. C. Beker, though stressing the element of continuity in Romans 4 in contrast with Galatians 3, nevertheless warns against an omission of this "soft" christological emphasis in 4:24-25. See Beker, *Paul the Apostle: The Triumph of God in Life and Thought* (Philadelphia: Fortress Press, 1980), 103–4.

39. Stuhlmacher also calls attention to the structural order of 4:25. First is the announcement of Jesus' death, made necessary by "our trespasses," followed by God's vindication of Jesus in the resurrection with a view to "our justification." The order, Stuhlmacher argues, clearly suggests that the atonement is essential to the setting right of God's people. Stuhlmacher further critiques his own dissertation (*Gerechtigkeit Gottes bei Paulus*) by noting that "there was insufficient discussion of the atoning death of Jesus as that which made justification possible." See Peter Stuhlmacher, *Reconciliation,* 79, 91.

observations about the contributions of the passage to our theme of the death of Jesus and human sinfulness.

The question of 6:1 ("Are we to continue in sin that grace may abound?") appropriately arises from the conclusion of the Adam-Christ comparison. If the increase of sin results in a greater demonstration of grace, it is plausible to wonder whether sinning is not a good thing after all. Both Paul's detractors (3:8) as well as his own theology force him to offer an answer. The answer comes in the negative ("Rubbish!") and in the counter question, "How can we who died to sin still live in it?" (6:2). But how have we "died to sin"? Heretofore in the letter, statements have been made about Christ's death with respect to sins (3:25; 4:25), which in turn leads to acquittal (5:18), but nothing has been said to suggest a death to sin by ordinary sinners. A further explanation is needed, which the remaining verses provide.

First of all, readers are invited to recall the meaning of baptism, that in being baptized into Christ one is baptized into Christ's death (6:3-4). This would hardly be new information for the projected readers, but it helps to make an important link in the argument Paul develops. Baptized persons are seen as participants in the death and resurrection of Christ; they are "buried with him" by baptism into his death. Immediately the connection to 5:12-21 reappears, in that, here as there, Christ is presented as a corporate figure. He of course dies, is buried, and is raised only once (as is later specified in 6:10 and as the aorist tense verbs throughout indicate). Baptism does not repeat that event; it rather symbolizes the baptizands' presence there with Christ. In answer to the question of the spiritual, "Were you there when they crucified my Lord?" the response is, "Yes, we were there with him."[40] Christ does what he does, then, as a corporate figure inclusive of all persons.

---

40. Robert Tannehill comments: "The believer is baptized into Christ's death and released from the old dominion not because baptism repeats Christ's death or enables it to be present in some unique way, but because in baptism the destruction of the old world and founding of the new which the cross brings about reaches its goal in the life of the individual. . . . What takes places in baptism is a manifestation of the power of the cross." See Tannehill, *Dying and Rising with Christ: A Study in Pauline Theology*, BZNW 32 (Berlin: Alfred Topelmann, 1967), 42.

In vv. 5-7 the explanation is taken a step further. The verses contain a number of difficult exegetical problems, which need not detain us here, because they do not immediately affect our investigation.[41] The verses in fact draw a connection between union with Christ and three significant, inseparable results: the assurance of a future resurrection with Christ; the crucifixion of the old humanity; and freedom from the power of sin. The εἰ clause beginning v. 5 (as well as later in v. 8) represents a fulfilled conditional clause and therefore should be translated "since" and not "if." The verses can be paraphrased, "For since we have been united with him in conformity to his death, we shall surely be united with him in the form of his resurrection. We know that our old humanity was crucified when Christ was crucified; that the body of sin was annihilated, with the result that we no longer are enslaved to sin. The one who died has been freed from sin."

Of particular importance is the logical movement in the passage from Christ's death to the death of persons with and conformity to Christ, and finally, to their death to and freedom from sin. "Our old humanity" and "the body of sin" describe the legacy of Adam that all persons share, but the terms are not to be psychologized and translated as "our old nature" and "sinful body," as if descriptive of the sinful or pre-Christian side of the individual in contrast to a spiritual and Christian side.[42] Instead, they represent the old dominion where sin and death reign, the demonic rule, which is broken only by the obedient death of the eschatological Adam. To be sure, the death of Christ accomplishes a change for individuals, but only as the cosmic power of

41. On one of those problems, I am inclined to agree with Tannehill that "in the likeness of his death" in 6:5 refers not to baptism (or, better, what happens in baptism), but to the continuing existence of baptized persons, living in the "form" of Christ's death (so Phil. 3:10). The shift to the perfect tense of the verb (γεγόναμεν) tips the scales in this direction. If so, then v. 5 does not continue the notion of baptism, but introduces the fresh idea of conformity to Christ. See Tannehill, *Dying and Rising with Christ,* 32-39; and Gunther Bornkamm, *Early Christian Experience,* trans. Paul L. Hammer (London: SCM Press, 1969), 77-78, 85-86n.
42. "The body of sin" is interpreted here as further defining "our old humanity." As Käsemann notes, the ἱνα clause is parallel to the clause that precedes it. See Käsemann, *Romans,* 169.

Adamic humanity is dethroned. When that happens, those united to Christ are freed from sin, are no longer sin's slaves.[43]

Paul, in vv. 5-7, provides a clear enough explanation of how we have "died to sin" (v. 2), which is his answer to the question, "Are we to continue in sin that grace may abound?" Before letting it go, however, he adds a christological undergirding (vv. 8-10) and draws a conclusion (v. 11). Verse 8 simply reiterates v. 5, but vv. 9-10 emphasize that the death and resurrection of Jesus (actually in reverse order) are eschatological events. God's resurrection of Jesus from the dead means that death is past for him; he no longer has to face death; it no longer has dominion over him. Likewise, his death, which, as we have seen, is a death to sin, occurs "once and for all." The dominion of sin, too, is relegated to the past, whereas the resurrection-life opens up a future to and for God. What does this, then, imply for the readers and other baptized persons? "Reckon yourselves dead to sin and alive to God" (v. 11).

Obviously Rom. 6:1-11 contributes a great deal to the under-standing of the theme of Jesus' death and human sinfulness. First, Paul consistently operates in this text with the notion of sin as a dominion, a power, an enemy. The definition of sin found in the Westminster Shorter Catechism ("Sin is any want of confor-mity to or transgression of the law of God"), though appropriate in earlier spots in Romans, "misses the mark" in Romans 6. Sin is not defined as an abrogation of the law nor is it fundamentally disobedience of God. It was that for Adam of course, but his trespass inaugurated a rule of sin, which according to the text functions to enslave all humanity.

Highly mythological in expression, such an understanding of sin is nevertheless both profound and modern. It acknowledges that sin is bigger and more ominous than the moral failings of any one individual or group. Like a tyrannical master who de-mands absolute obedience from his subjects, sin dominates to such an extent that even when the subjects know and want to do

---

43. It seems unlikely that v. 7 is to be understood christologically in line with the martyrs' deaths, as Robin Scroggs proposes. See Scroggs, "Rom. 6:7," *NTS* 10 (1963): 104–8.

differently, they cannot (7:14-24). To underestimate the potency of sin by assuming that it can be remedied or contained by a fresh burst of energy, a new determination, or the latest self-help program is to invite frustration and further despair. Though Paul cannot be turned into a twentieth-century theologian, it is only a short step from the awareness of sin's power to the realization that sin pervades the systems and institutions of our society, and it is there that persons often experience its bondage. Distorted political and economic structures become the tentacles in which individuals are caught and either enthusiastically or reluctantly are ensnared. They need nothing short of a revolution to set them free.

But this liberation from sin can be easily misunderstood. As Furnish has pointed out, the text announces the death of the sinner and release from the control of sin; it does not say that sin itself is removed from the world or that baptized persons lead sinless lives.[44] Crucifixion with Christ neither implies a perfectionism nor does it guarantee a life free from struggles with sin's dying gasps. Existence under the cross is, in fact, characterized by anguish and suffering (1 Cor. 4:9-13; 2 Cor. 4:7-12; 6:3-10), and if the writer of Ephesians has understood Paul correctly, life is a constant war against the principalities and powers (Eph. 6:10-20). What Romans 6 does pledge is that the ultimacy of sin's threat is removed and the outcome of the struggle is no longer in doubt.[45]

Second, Rom. 6:1-11 expresses the meaning of Jesus' death not as a vicarious substitution (Jesus in place of us) but as a participatory event (we were crucified with Christ). The change in soteriological categories in Romans appropriately parallels the change in the concepts of sin (from trespasses to ruling power). What also can be observed with these changes is the presence now of the language of transference, the movement from one

44. Victor Paul Furnish, *Theology and Ethics in Paul* (Nashville: Abingdon Press, 1968), 173–74.

45. Beker in this context says that sin has become "an impossible possibility— impossible, because of the victory of Christ over sin, which is mediated to us through the Spirit, and possible because the Christian life remains threatened and liable to *Anfechtung* (attack or temptation)." See Beker, *Paul the Apostle*, 215–18.

allegiance to another. It is not as if persons are liberated from the clutches of sin so as to become independent or autonomous; they are to live "to God" (6:10) or, as the remainder of Romans 6 stresses, they are to serve righteousness.

Two other texts in Romans are important in the way in which they exploit this notion of a change of allegiance. In 7:1-6 a complex analogy illustrates how death breaks the loyalty to one party and establishes it with another. "Therefore, you died to the law through the body of Christ, so that you may belong to another, to the one who was raised from the dead, in order that we may bear fruit for God" (7:6). Participation in the crucified body of Christ brings freedom from the oppression of the law and a liberating service "in the new life of the Spirit." In 14:7-9, in the midst of a discussion of the pastoral issue involving the weak and the strong, readers are reminded that their ultimate loyalty is to Christ, not to themselves. "For to this end Christ died and lived again, that he might be the Lord both of the dead and of the living" (14:9). One can see how such a soteriology involving a change of allegiance becomes the foundation for pastoral advice and for ethics.

The word "freedom" appears in contemporary discussions in a variety of ways. For example, some define "freedom" as the removal of political, economic, or social oppression, when an otherwise enslaved racial, sexual, or national group achieves self-determination and the chance to chart its own future. Or a psychotherapist may speak of a patient's "freedom" in the sense that the patient has come to grasp something of the dynamics of his or her own history, has developed a bit of leverage on that history, and has moved to a point of personal responsibility for the present and the future. In both cases, the essence of "freedom" is autonomy, the capacity to make at least relatively uncontrolled choices. While the Christian community by its very nature must be implicated in the struggle against all forms of oppression, whether political, economic, social, or personal, the affirmation of Christian liberty in the Pauline letters moves beyond the removal of restraint, beyond autonomy and the freedom to choose. At its center is not only a deliverance "from" but a service "to," a change of allegiance, a loyalty to a God in whose company is perfect freedom. Nowhere is that clearer than in Romans 6.

RECONCILIATION THROUGH CHRIST'S DEATH (2 COR. 5:14—6:2)

The passages from Romans have presented us with a variety of categories and expressions in articulating how Jesus' death changes the plight of sinful humanity. Some are cultic and juridical, announcing that Jesus' death expiates sin and is an event of a vicarious or representative character, bringing about a new relationship to God in the present and good hope in the final judgment. Other categories in Romans express the modus operandi of salvation as a participation in Jesus' death, involving an accompanying transfer of allegiance from sin's dominion to the rule of grace. Now in turning to 2 Cor. 5:14—6:2 we find a variety of categories intertwined in the same passage, each supportive and explanatory of the other. Our plan will be first to trace the flow of the argument in the text and then to note the significance of the category of reconciliation.

Beginning at 2 Cor. 2:14, Paul reflects on the message and direction of his apostolic ministry, which is under serious attack at Corinth. The reflection gives the readers ammunition to use in answering Paul's detractors (5:12). Neither a record of success stories nor the authorization of ecclesiastical authorities has controlled his ministry, but rather "the love of Christ compels us" (5:14),[46] a love made concrete in the fact that "one died for all."[47] The shift from the first-person pronoun ("we," "us") to "all" is striking, in that it serves to democratize the nature of ministry. What compels and impels Paul's own ministry compels and impels "all." His authorizing claim is not exclusive, but inclusive.[48]

46. The Greek verb συνέχει covers a wide spectrum—restraint, compulsion, impulsion. Furnish has changed from an earlier preference for "sustains" to "lays claim to." See Victor Paul Furnish, *II Corinthians*, AB (Garden City, N.Y.: Doubleday, 1984), 309–10.

47. The NEB links the "love of Christ" and the death for all in an interesting translation: "For the love of Christ leaves us no choice, when once we have reached the conclusion that one man died for all. . . ."

48. This democratization of power is a step also taken in 1 Cor. 1:18—2:5, as we noted in chapter 2.

The death for all is immediately elaborated in two statements: "all have died" and "those who live are no longer to live for themselves but for the one who for them died and was raised" (5:14c and 15). The language is reminiscent of Rom. 6:1-11 both in the notion of the corporate Christ in whose obedient death all persons are made participants and in the change of allegiance from "themselves" to the crucified and risen one. Tannehill is no doubt correct is saying that 2 Cor. 5:14 is "merely a different formulation of the motif of dying with Christ."[49] And yet one has to take seriously that the preposition here is not σύν ("with") but ὑπέρ ("for"). The "different formulation" involves the juridical notion of Christ's being a representative or perhaps even a substitute for "all," a slightly different conception from believers' being participants with Christ in his death. It is frankly difficult to know how much weight the preposition ὑπέρ can bear in this context. Is the preposition to be construed as "for the sake of" or "in place of"? It is likely that v. 21, with its clear notion of exchange, tips the scales toward the latter—that is, Christ "in place of all"; but it would be foolish to isolate this verse and build a theory of the atonement on the preposition alone. Too many other texts and contexts need to be taken into account in constructing such a theory.[50]

From this statement of the inclusive character of Jesus' death, four consequences are drawn.[51]

1. "From now on, we regard no one from a human point of view" (5:16). The cross opens up a new way of knowing appropriate to the new eschatological order.

2. "If anyone is in Christ, there is a new creation" (5:17). To stand at the juncture of the ages and to see with the eyes of the cross is to behold a brand-new world.

---

49. Tannehill, *Dying and Rising with Christ*, 66.

50. See Bultmann, *Theology of the New Testament*, I: 296–97; C. K. Barrett, *A Commentary on the Second Epistle to the Corinthians*, HNTC (New York: Harper & Row, 1973), 168–69; Dunn, "Paul's Understanding of the Death of Jesus," 131–41; Furnish, *II Corinthians*, 310, 326–27; Hultgren, *Christ and His Benefits*, 48–49. Martin makes the interesting proposal of "proxy" rather than "substitute" or "representative" for Jesus' function. See Ralph P. Martin, *2 Corinthians*, WBC (Waco: Word Books, 1986), 130–31.

51. The conjunction "therefore" (ὥστε) at the beginning of both 5:16 and 5:17 highlights the consequential nature of the argument.

3. "All things are from God, who reconcilied us to himself through Christ" (5:18). God's action in the death of Christ transforms and renews the divine-human relationship.

4. "All things are from God . . . who gave us the ministry of reconciliation" (5:18). In the very act in which God breaks through hostility, God gathers up the reconciled into the service of reconciliation.

The latter two of these four consequences are given still further clarity in the remaining verses of the section. Particularly in 5:19, reconciliation takes on a cosmic scope and is linked to forgiveness. Then with the use of "therefore," v. 20 begins a new section continuing through 6:2, as the appeals are laid out and the ministry of reconciliation is more deliberately defined. In light of the death of Christ for "all," announcing the present day of salvation and urging hearers to be reconciled to God are no longer features of Paul's private mission but a task given to the whole Christian community. But before Paul moves too far with this elaboration of the mission, he pauses to provide a reflection on the previous discussion, as if to add to or explain a point not entirely clear. God "made the one not knowing sin to be sin in our behalf, that we might become in him the righteousness of God" (5:21).[52]

A greal deal of attention has been devoted to the question whether the notion of a sin offering (Leviticus 4) or portions of Isaiah 53 lie behind the construction of v. 21.[53] In both cases the language of the LXX is similar to 5:21, though not exact, suggesting perhaps loose allusions rather than tight parallels. More significant, however, is the clear exchange affirmed in the verse.

52. Though Käsemann sees 5:21 as traditional primarily because the ideas stand "in sharp contrast to what we find elsewhere in Paul," Stuhlmacher argues that Paul has woven the formulation into his argument "with no reduction of content; in fact, by putting it at the end of his argument, he actually gives it special emphasis." See Käsemann, "The Doctrine of Reconciliation," 52–53; and Stuhlmacher, Reconciliation, 74. Compare also Hofius's view that the entire verse is unquestionably Pauline. See Ortfried Hofius, "Erwägungen zur Gestalt und Herkunft des paulinischen Versöhnungsgedankens," ZThK 77 (1980): 186–99.

53. Stuhlmacher argues that 5:21 becomes intelligible only in the light of Isaiah 53 and the technical cultic language of Leviticus 4. See Stuhlmacher, Reconciliation, 59–60, 175. Thrall, however, lists cogent reasons why the verse does not reflect the sacrificial offering. See Margaret E. Thrall, "Salvation Proclaimed: V. 2 Corinthians 5:18-21," ExT 93 (1982): 230.

The sinless one is made sin in behalf of or in place of us (ὑπὲρ ἡμῶν), while we who are in need of reconciliation become the righteousness of God. The pattern parallels Gal. 3:13, where the innocent one takes the curse of the law upon himself so that those accursed can be redeemed. The two verses represent the most unambiguous instances of the substitutionary motif in Paul's expression of the atonement, and yet, interestingly, in neither case is the divine wrath explicitly an issue.[54] Both verses clearly announce a substitutionary death, but without the penal dimension.[55] That is to say, Paul in depicting Christ as a replacement for sinful men and women does not go on to say that he accepts their punishment so as to appease the otherwise unsatisfied anger of God, an observation that leads many simply to avoid the use of the term "substitution" altogether. For example, D. E. H. Whiteley's comments, "For St. Paul, the death of Christ was certainly vicarious: if He had not died on the cross, we should have perished eternally. Our death would have been due to our own sin, and could therefore have been described as penal. But the death which Christ died to save us from a penal death was not itself penal."[56] As is clear throughout 2 Cor. 5:18–21, God functions as the primary actor and does not become the recipient of a propitiatory offering made by Christ. For this reason, Morna Hooker's label of "interchange" may more accurately describe what the verse in fact declares.[57]

---

54. An opposite position is taken by I. Howard Marshall, who in light of 2 Maccabees sees God as offended by sins and as acting in wrath and judgment against sinners, even though God's anger is not specifically mentioned in 2 Corinthians 5. What the dying Christ does is to exhaust the divine ire. There may be some justification for this in Rom. 3:24-26, but not in 2 Cor. 5:21. See Marshall, "The Meaning of 'Reconciliation,'" *Unity and Diversity in New Testament Theology: Essays in Honor of George E. Ladd,* ed. R. A. Guelich (Grand Rapids, Mich.: Wm. B. Eerdmans, 1978), 123–30.

55. Another verse to consider alongside 2 Cor. 5:21 is Rom. 8:3. There the "sending" formula is used, and though the prepositional phrase περὶ ἁμαρτίας may also be read in light of the sin offering (so Käsemann, *Romans,* 217), God's role is clearly that of an active judge condemning sin, not of a deity being propitiated by a sacrifice.

56. D. E. H. Whiteley, *The Theology of St. Paul,* 130.

57. Morna D. Hooker, "Interchange in Christ," *JTS* 22 (1971): 349–61. Hooker wants to broaden the expression "made sin" in 5:21 to encompass the incarnation as well as the cross. See also Hooker, "Interchange and Atonement," *BJRL* 60 (1978): 462–81.

But the question arises in connection with the interchange of v. 21: How does God's making Christ to be sin result in our becoming God's righteousness? The interchange certainly does not suggest that the sinful are transformed into being morally upright people, forever living without sinning. Rather the sinful are brought into a right relationship with God, into the place where God's power effects salvation. And this is accomplished precisely in that trespasses are no longer reckoned by God. The language of 5:19 recalls Ps. 32:2 (LXX: 31:2), which is cited in full in Rom. 4:7-8.[58] As Bultmann put it, "The righteousness which God adjudicates to man . . . is not 'sinlessness' in the sense of ethical perfection, but is 'sinlessness' in the sense that God does not 'count' man's sin against him."[59] It is not just that sins "previously committed" are dealt with by God (so Rom. 3:25-26). The present participle in 5:19 (μὴ λογιζόμενος) suggests that in light of the Christ-event this now becomes God's attitude toward human sinfulness. Unlike everyone else, God keeps no account of sins. It is a pointed way of insisting that the reconciled can count on forgiveness. It stands at the heart of their new life; it characterizes the day of salvation.

In reflecting on 2 Cor. 5:14—6:2 in terms of the topic of how the death of Jesus deals with human sinfulness, several things become obvious. So many categories are employed in describing the meaning of Jesus' death that it becomes difficult to disentangle them. Though the passage flows smoothly and is marked by an orderly use of conjunctions, the soteriological terms themselves are mingled in an unusual manner. There is no progression or shift, as we noticed in the Romans passages. In 5:14-15 Jesus is

---

58. Since Paul quotes this Psalm elsewhere, its reflection here raises questions as to how much of 2 Cor. 5:19 should be thought of as a pre-Pauline formula. The tendency has been to take at least 5:19 as traditional, if not the whole of 5:19-21. See Ernst Käsemann, "Some Thoughts on the Theme 'The Doctrine of Reconciliation in the New Testament,'" *The Future of Our Religious Past: Essays in Honour of Rudolf Bultmann,* ed. James M. Robinson, trans. Charles E. Carlston and Robert P. Scharlemann (London: SCM Press, 1971), 52–53; Furnish, *II Corinthians,* 334–35. But notice the objections raised by Margaret E. Thrall, "2 Corinthians 5:18-21," 229. Both Gerhard Delling, *Der Kreuzestod Jesu in der urchristlichen Verkündigung,* 21; and Martin, *2 Corinthians,* 142, take the phrase "not reckoning their trespasses against them" to be Pauline.

59. Bultmann, *Theology of the New Testament,* 1: 276.

a representative figure in whose death "all" are incorporated and on the basis of which a transference of allegiance takes place. And yet instead of the consistently participatory categories found in Rom. 6:1-11, one discovers a vicarious phrase ("for all"). Later the death of Christ is developed in terms of a stark interchange between the sinless Jesus and guilty men and women (5:21). While the language of reconciliation dominates the passage as a whole, the phrase "the righteousness of God" appears, as does a statement of forgiveness, expressed by a commercial term, no doubt reflecting a psalm ("not reckoning against them their trespasses").

This mixing of categories serves as a healthy warning to the interpreter who is eager to draw fine lines in delineating Paul's understanding of Jesus' death. Paul is a sophisticated writer. His use of language is not careless or slovenly, but neither does he always observe the neat, discrete distinctions that modern scholarship occasionally tends to lay on him. Though employing words drawn at times from the courtroom and though defending himself in the face of accusers, Paul does not write as an attorney preparing a legal brief. Rather, he seeks, as a pastor, to persuade his people, drawing on the common language of the church, using terms that express and evoke feeling, resting his case ultimately on a gospel he knows to be "foolishness" (1 Cor. 1:18, 23).

Käsemann attributes this mixture of categories to a rather uneven blending of traditional materials with Paul's own theology and concludes that the language of reconciliation is used to "set in sharp relief the radical and universal nature of the message of justification."[60] But reconciliation, admittedly rare in Paul, cannot be so easily dismissed. Its function is more than supportive. As word pictures depicting the one salvation achieved in Christ, justification and reconciliation share much in common. For example, repeatedly in 5:18-21 Paul pictures God as the acting subject. Reconciliation functions not as a reciprocal activity in the sense that two friends who have become estranged agree to sit down and talk out their differences. Reconciliation is not equated with "making up." It describes God's saving a lost

---

60. Käsemann, "The Doctrine of Reconciliation," 52–53, 63.

and disoriented world, which is in no position to negotiate a truce. In this stress on the divine initiative, reconciliation parallels justification. And yet the two also carry varying nuances. Justification, as a forensic term, speaks of the action by which people are set in proper relation to God and God's saving power. Reconciliation, however, as a social term, primarily denotes the consequences of that action—the restored relationship, the bridged chasm, the resolution of hostility.[61] In the overall scope of the Pauline letters neither term needs to be swallowed up by the other. Given the contentious situation of the Corinthian community, the prevailing use of reconciliation in this passage seems highly appropriate and more than merely a backdrop for justification.

Moreover, contemporary Christians, aware of the depth of estrangement marking the human situation, find reconciliation to be an immediately relevant way to express the meaning of Christ's death. The language of relationships—brokenness, separation, wholeness, reunion—strikes a responsive chord.[62] Out of the chaos of alienation God fashions a new creation, marked by a sure and lasting peace. It is not surprising that the notion of reconciliation has taken a far more prominent place in later theological discussions than might have been anticipated from its infrequent use in the New Testament.

PAUL AND THE HISTORIC VIEWS OF THE ATONEMENT

When one contemplates the notion of Jesus' death and human sinfulness, the various theories of the atonement known from the church's history immediately come to mind. They have emerged as efforts to provide an answer to the question as to why Jesus had to die. Though there are obviously many variations of each theory, the three types cited by Gustaf Aulén remain the most prominent.[63] The "objective" view, associated with Anselm of Canterbury, operates on the fundamental idea that the demands

---

61. Furnish, *II Corinthians,* 351–52.
62. A glance at the contemporary lectionary of one Protestant church indicates that some part of 2 Cor. 5:14-21 appears no less than four times in the three-year cycle, a frequency paralleled only by Isaiah 53 and John 1:1-18.
63. Gustaf Aulén, *Christus Victor: An Historical Study of the Three Main Types of the Idea of the Atonement,* trans. A. G. Hebert (London: S. P. C. K., 1950).

of divine justice have to be satisfied before forgiveness can take place. Sin is so heinous that only God can pay the debt, and yet the debt has to be paid from the human side because humans are the debtors. Thus Christ, the God-man, comes as a propitiatory offering and in his death suffers the divine punishment. By Christ's death God is enabled to forgive sins without compromising the divine justice. Since humans have no part in the atonement (an action primarily between God and Christ), their justification is a second and separate act, in which God imputes to them the merits of Christ. As an explanation, the Anselmian theory has the strength of taking very seriously the nature of human sin and the inability of humanity to provide a remedy.

The "subjective" view, posed most forcefully by Anselm's near contemporary Abelard, affirms that Jesus' death is fundamentally a demonstration of God's love, which in turn evokes repentance. Contemplation of such an astounding expression of divine love as displayed in the cross is bound to breed in men and women a responding love, leading to forgiveness and a fresh obedience to God's will. "Love so amazing, so divine, Demands my life, my soul, my all." What needs to be changed is not God, but humans. In avoiding many of the pitfalls of the "objective" view, in seeing the need for a change in people, and in stressing the character of God as love, Abelard's theory held great appeal for the liberals of the nineteenth and early twentieth centuries. And it proves particularly congenial to a grass-roots, psychological rendering of the atonement, whereby God's love is seen as the power that creates in the unloveable the capacity for responding love.

The third type, advocated by Aulén himself, but with roots in Irenaeus and Luther, is usually labeled the "classic" or "*Christus victor*" view. It sees the cross as the decisive moment in a cosmic drama between good and evil, in which the victory over the hostile powers results in a new and reconciled relation between God and the world. Jesus' death is "victorious" in that it liberates sinful humanity from the clutches of the devil.[64] In what Aulén describes as "the double-sidedness of the drama of the atone-

---

64. One of the ambiguities of the "classic" view concerns exactly how the "victory" is accomplished, whether or not a ransom is paid to free enslaved humanity, and if so, to whom it is paid—to the devil or to God.

ment," God turns out to be both the author and the object of the reconciliation. From first to last it is God's work, and yet a change is also effected in God in the sense that the very act in which God reconciles the world to himself becomes itself a reconciling of God (i.e., in addition to being an agent of God, Jesus is also an offering made to God).[65]

Proponents of each of these historic views of the atonement have claimed Paul as support (though Anselm himself actually made no attempt to supply a scriptural basis for his proposal). The results of our study of the key Pauline passages, however, indicate similarities and differences between Paul and each of the three. Perhaps, as Aulén claims, the "classic" view, with its stress on the enslaving character of sin and the initiative taken by God in breaking sin's control, most closely reflects Paul's letters, though it is not at all clear that one can find such a "double-sidedness" as is essential to the view. In any case, it seeks to hold together the atonement and God's justification of sinners, as Paul does, treating them as if they were two sides of a single coin.

There is, however, a more fundamental problem involved in comparing Paul and the historical views of the atonement. The letters of Paul do not read like the Synoptic Gospels. They are not constructed as extended narratives in the usual sense of the term, with a plot and a story line; they include very few passages that are themselves narratives. They contain nothing similar to the imaginative power of Jesus' parables or the richness of his similes. Nevertheless, Paul's language, like the language of the Synoptics, is metaphorical and indirect.[66] He speaks about the un-

---

65. For a description of the atonement theories, see, among others, F. W. Dillistone, *The Christian Understanding of the Atonement* (Digswell Place: James Nisbet, 1968); Frances M. Young, *Sacrifice and the Death of Christ* (London: S. P. C. K., 1975), 85–100. For an interesting critique of the theories from the perspective of liberation theology, see Leonardo Boff, *Passion of Christ, Passion of the World: The Facts, Their Interpretation, and Their Meaning Yesterday and Today,* trans. Robert R. Barr (Maryknoll, N.Y.: Orbis Books, 1987), 86–101.

66. Paul's language also differs from the language of Jesus. Funk comments: "The parable is creating a tradition, founding a 'world'; the letter is reviewing the destiny of that foundational language in relation to other 'worlds,' the world of the apostle, the world of his readers." See Robert W. Funk, *Language, Hermeneutic, and Word of God: The Problem of Language in the New Testament and Contemporary Theology* (New York: Harper & Row, 1966), 233. Ricoeur classifies Paul's language as one of the "semi-conceptual modes of discourse" or as "translation-language." See Paul Ricoeur, "Biblical Hermen-

speakable and confesses that God and God's ways transcend his own capacity to describe and proclaim them in human language. "O the depth of the riches and wisdom and knowledge of God! How unsearchable are his judgments and how inscrutable his ways!" (Rom. 11:33). Nowhere is this more evident than in Paul's soteriological language, about what God did in regard to human sin, about why Christ died. Paul employs a whole host of images, some drawn from the Scriptures, some from the early Christian tradition, some from the common language of the day, to express what is ultimately unexpressable. The powerful and mysterious significance of Jesus' death is articulated carefully but indirectly in terms of what is known (setting relationships right, reconciling alienated people, not keeping a record of the trespasses of the guilty, expiating for sins, paying debts, triumphing over enemies, liberating the enslaved, etc.). In the course of this chapter we have detected a number of allusions, a variety of categories, some cultic, some juridical, some participatory, on occasion used in a single context, seemingly supportive of each other, all giving voice to at least one dimension of God's saving action, an action that itself cannot be related directly.

In recognizing the metaphorical nature of Paul's language, we confess to two basic quarrels with all three theories of the atonement. First is the tendency of the theories to treat imagistic language as if it were literal, to deny that Paul speaks indirectly about God's ways. I say "tendency" because it is certainly not true that every theologian who has proposed or espoused one or another of the theories has understood it literally.[67] Sallie McFague, however, has noted that for a variety of reasons literalism does run rampant in our time.[68] Religious literature is read with a positivistic scientism, and for that reason the theories, as interpretations of the biblical text, are often taken as exact descriptions of what God "had to do" in order to save a lost world.

---

eutics," *Paul Ricoeur on Biblical Hermeneutics,* Semeia 4, ed. John Dominic Crossan (Missoula: Scholars Press, 1975), 135–38.

67. For example, Aulén speaks of the classic "idea" or "motif" of the atonement and claims that "it has never been shaped into a rational theory." See Aulén, *Christus Victor,* 175.

68. Sallie McFague, *Metaphorical Theology: Models of God in Religious Language* (Philadelphia: Fortress Press, 1982), 4–7.

But more important than the potential for literalism is whether Paul's discussions can be reduced to a "theory" (or even "theories") in which one apparently dominating metaphor or category is extracted from the context and the others are given little or no play. In another setting Sallie McFague comments:

> Serious attention to metaphorical language as the way to fund theology ought to change the way theological reflection is carried on. It ought, for instance, to make theological discussions of the person of Jesus and the resurrection less anxious about logical precision, clarity, and definiteness. This is not a call for fuzzy or sentimental thinking (or for saying nothing about difficult matters); on the contrary, to take metaphorical thinking seriously is a demand for precision and clarity, though not of the logical sort. As we have seen, metaphor is the poet's way to try and define something for which there is no dictionary meaning; it is his or her attempt to be precise and clear about something for which ordinary language has no way of talking. The poet mounts many metaphors, many ways of seeing "this" as "that," many attempts to "say" what cannot be said directly. The poet sets one metaphor against another and hopes that the sparks set off by the juxtaposition will ignite something in the mind as well.[69]

Aulén, apparently to avoid some of the excessive interpretations of the past, downplays the power of metaphors used in connection with Jesus' death. He writes: "The images are but popular helps for the understanding of the idea. It is the idea that is primary."[70] The metaphor for Aulén becomes no more than an illustration to clarify the thought that lies behind the metaphor, making the metaphor dispensable once the hearer or reader has grasped the idea. Such a view fails to recognize the generative power of the metaphor. It misses the point of the maxim Paul Ricoeur finds so appealing: "Symbol gives rise to thought." The symbol gives the meaning precisely by giving something to think about, to reflect on, something that leads to ideas.[71] An effective metaphor evokes a broad range of possibilities and opens new doors of understanding. Rather than being dispensed with or substituted for, the metaphor becomes the source of thought.

69. Sallie McFague TeSelle, *Speaking in Parables: A Study in Metaphor and Theology* (Philadelphia: Fortress Press, 1975), 39.

70. Gustaf Aulén, *Christus Victor,* 175.

71. Paul Ricoeur, *The Conflict of Interpretations: Essays in Hermeneutics,* ed. Don Hide (Evanston: Northwestern University Press, 1974), 288.

Of course the interpretive process cannot merely stop with the text; the theologian has to move from Paul's metaphorical language to conceptual structures. But the demand must be for concepts that respect the richness and variety of the metaphors in the text and that resist the temptation to reduce them in the name of logical consistency. The interplay of the differing metaphors, as for example in 2 Cor. 5:14—6:2, simply must not be sacrificed for "the idea" or for a precise theory, which in itself is orderly and intelligible but not really "big" enough to encompass the less orderly but expressive categories of the text. The problem is that the Pauline language for the atonement is so diverse that it is well nigh impossible for a single theory to account for its variety.[72]

What is said here about the theories of the atonement is appropriate also for the discussion in Pauline studies about the broader issue of soteriology. The search for coherence in the theology of Paul must not do violence to the richness of the language of the letters themselves. A recent description of Paul as "a rhetorical poet" is apt.[73] His language is vivid and suggestive. Unfortunately, when the terminology of justification is determined to be the dominant category and the key to coherence in soteriology, then the other categories are likely to be constricted to make them cohere. Likewise, when the soteriology is judged to be primarily participatory, then the judicial, sacrificial, and social categories are truncated in the name of theological appropriateness. The vitality and expressiveness of the metaphorical language need to be protected against the pressure for logical precision and given full space to function evocatively with readers.[74]

72. Dillistone's book is remarkable in its capacity to allow each of the biblical images the freedom to be expressive. See F. W. Dillistone, *The Christian Understanding of Atonement.*

73. Karl Plank, *Paul and the Irony of Affliction* (Atlanta: Scholars Press, 1987), 1–2.

74. I have made no effort beyond particular passages to address Sanders's concern to relate the various soteriological terms. The most promising proposal for relating the juridical and participationist categories derives from Gal. 2:17, where the phrase "to be justified in Christ" combines the two. Hays comments: "To be justified ἐκ πίστεως Χριστοῦ is the same thing as being justified ἐν Χριστῷ. Thus 'justification' and 'participation' do not belong to divergent theological spheres; for Paul, they belong together because he understands salvation to mean our participation in *Christ's* justification." Richard Hays, *The Faith of Jesus Christ,* 251. The observation is important because it recognizes that the terms are theologically consistent even though their metaphorical impact differs.

CHAPTER 3

Jesus' Death
and Resurrection

A BBC series examined various expressions of religious life. The program presented with typical British fairness the success story of a popular, American television preacher. The camera showed us the extravagant church he had built and the throngs that came weekly to hear his positive and affirming sermons. The preacher himself came across as a warm, engaging person, who had dared to dream dreams of what God could accomplish through him and who wanted others to dream dreams about themselves.

The interviewer, a modest English woman, finally raised the critical question. "What do you think about Jesus?"

"Jesus," the preacher replied, "was the most successful religious figure of all time. Just consider it. He began in obscure surroundings amid poverty and despair; and today his followers outnumber those of any other of the world's religions. That's astounding!"

"But I thought he ended up on a cross," the interviewer said.

"Oh, no! He was raised from the dead. The cross was something he had to endure, as any successful person must endure hardships. But he arose from the dead. He overcame the cross and put all that behind him." And the camera pulled away.

From his thriving ministry, offering large numbers of American viewers a positive attitude to life and its challenges, the television preacher declares an unambiguous gospel, whose model, Jesus, has conquered sin and death in the triumphant, unparalleled victory of Easter morning. The conquest of the negative forces operative in the crucifixion presages the many small but decisive victories to be achieved in the lives of individuals who will only believe. However one may evaluate the preacher's theology and strategy, he certainly raises for us a critical question: How are the crucifixion and resurrection related to each other?

Using the Apostles' Creed, Christians recite the events in sequence, along with Jesus' conception, birth, suffering, burial, ascension, enthronement, and expected return as Judge of the world. But does God's raising of Jesus from the dead qualify our understanding of his crucifixion? And, conversely, does the fact that Jesus was crucified (as opposed to dying a natural death) impact our understanding of his resurrection? Are they simply events in sequence that have no substantial relationship to one another, each with its independent theological role to play? Or are they to be taken as a linked pair, so that when either is mentioned the other is always implied? To take two options offered in contemporary theology, is the resurrection exclusively an event of noetic significance—that is, an event that functions only to enable the church to grasp the saving character of Jesus' death, an expression of the meaningfulness of the cross?[1] Or does the resurrection represent an autonomous, new act of God, the divine vindication of the Son's obedience?[2] Or beyond these two options, could the television preacher be right, that the crucifixion poses the question that the resurrection answers, the problem for which the resurrection is the solution? In such a case, one could say that the resurrection is primarily the tangible proof of Jesus' having overcome hardship and rejection, and thus a pattern to be followed by "successful" people.

---

1. This is Bultmann's position. "For us the cross cannot disclose its own meaning; it is an event of the past. We cannot recover it as an event in our lives." But, "Jesus is not proclaimed merely as the crucified; he is also risen from the dead. The cross and the resurrection form an inseparable unity. . . . Indeed, faith in the resurrection is really the same thing as faith in the saving efficacy of the cross." Rudolf Bultmann, "New Testament and Mythology," in *Kerygma and Myth: A Theological Debate,* ed. H. W. Bartsch, trans. R. H. Fuller (London: S. P. C. K., 1957), 38, 41.

2. This is Barth's position. See Karl Barth, *Church Dogmatics,* trans. G. W. Bromiley (New York: Charles Scribner's Sons, 1956), 4/1: 304.

These questions that swirl about the connection between Jesus' death and God's raising him from the dead are both complex and important. From a theologian's perspective, Douglas John Hall goes so far as to say that "the question of the relationship between cross and resurrection is the most difficult one in Christian theology."[3] Moreover, from the perspective of the New Testament, the issue is complicated even further by the fact that the ancient witnesses carry varying nuances that make it difficult to draw them together into a consistent pattern. To cite one example, the apostolic speeches recorded in the early chapters of Acts contain a definite accusatory element in connection with the crucifixion, which is followed by a statement of God's vindication in the resurrection. "This Jesus . . . you crucified and killed by the hands of lawless men. But God raised him up" (Acts 2:23-24; cf. 2:36; 3:13-15; 10:39-40; 13:28-30). The pattern is repeated often enough for the reader to discern a major concern of the text. The letters of Paul, however, nowhere indicate a set of charges for Jesus' death, followed by a statement of divine vindication. The pattern so prominent in Acts has no place in Paul at all. This makes a discrete judgment about the overall New Testament perspective hard to come by.

But despite the complexity, the connection between cross and resurrection looms as a decisive issue.[4] At stake is nothing less than the Christian faith itself, how it interprets human existence and distinguishes ultimate from penultimate values, how it orders church life and pastoral ministry. Consider the extremes. A theology that rings loudly the joyful note of Easter without the sobering, dissonant sounds of Good Friday inevitably tends toward triumphalism. The earthly, crucified Jesus gives way to the risen, exalted Lord. The cries of human pain, rejection, and death exposed in Jesus' passion are modulated by the exuberance of "he is risen!" As with the television preacher, negative experi-

3. Douglas John Hall, *Lighten Our Darkness: Toward an Indigenous Theology of the Cross* (Philadelphia: Westminster Press, 1976), 122.

4. Paul Meyer's comment is on target: "In short, the crucial issue in our understanding of the resurrection is what it means in relation to the one whom all the world knows to have been crucified." Paul W. Meyer, "The This-Worldliness of the New Testament," *Princeton Seminary Bulletin* 2 (1979): 226.

ences are often viewed as no more than obstacles to be overcome in the journey to something more—to success and positive living. Evangelism becomes church growth; "what works" becomes the church's operational mode. "God loves you" buttons and happy smiles identify Christians.

At the other extreme, a Good Friday divorced from Easter ceases to be good. The gloom and darkness that surround Jesus' death loom heavy without a transcendent power. Even the divine embrace of suffering and defeat, which the cross represents, results in no more than continued despair, because God's suffering has no resolution, no redemptive force. There can be little or no anticipation of change in the status quo nor hope for the ultimate overthrow of the despotic rule of the principalities and powers. The church's ministry becomes exclusively presence; its mission to help people cope. The superficiality of buttons and smiles yields to the perpetually furrowed brow.

The task then comes in querying the letters of Paul to determine exactly how Jesus' cross and resurrection are to be related. Käsemann puts the question like this: Is the cross a chapter in the theology of the resurrection, or is the resurrection a chapter in the theology of the cross?[5] Since we have already given attention to passages highlighting Jesus' death, it behooves us now to turn to a selection of those dealing with his resurrection and to discern how in the nature of the various theological arguments the resurrection functions. We begin with 1 Corinthians 15 and from it move to consider three ways in which Jesus' resurrection is taken up in the letters: as God's saving event, as promise of the future, and as operative in the life of believers. This provides us an exegetical base for drawing conclusions about both the connection and separateness of cross and resurrection.

CHRIST THE FIRSTFRUITS (1 CORINTHIANS 15)

It is appropriate to begin the investigation with this important chapter, because nowhere else is the resurrection elaborated so

---

5. Ernst Käsemann, *Perspectives on Paul,* trans. Margaret Kohl (Philadelphia: Fortress Press, 1971), 59.

fully, nor are connections drawn so precisely as they are here. By no means is there agreement among interpreters about every exegetical issue in the text, but the argument laid out by the author is sufficiently clear to enable us to arrive at certain conclusions. We follow it section by section.

1. 15:1-11. The chapter begins with an announcement of the gospel that Paul has previously preached among his readers and that they have accepted: "that Christ died for our sins according to the scriptures, that he was buried, that he was raised on the third day according to the scriptures, and that he appeared to Cephas" and to other groups, concluding with Paul himself. Two observations are appropriate about the manner in which this statement of the gospel is made.

First, it is clear that this is not just Paul's personal interpretation, but a commonly shared gospel. The expression of the gospel is, in fact, a tradition that predates Paul, and the list of witnesses to the risen Christ includes a wide spectrum of authorities. Since this received tradition becomes the foundation on which the argument of the chapter is built, it is highly significant that the base is neither idiosyncratic nor controversial. "Whether it was I or they, so we preach and so you believed" (15:11).

Second, the readers are reminded that they have already accepted this message ("in which you stand, by which you are saved," 15:1-2), and yet a disturbing caveat is placed alongside the reminder: "if you hold it fast—unless you believed it in vain" (15:2). How is it that the readers might not hold fast the gospel or might believe it in vain? Rhetorically, the caveat prepares readers for the cruciality of the argument to follow, an argument not being offered merely as a possible implication of the gospel, which at one's pleasure may or may not be accepted, but as an interpretation essential to the saving character of the gospel itself (so 15:14-18). If readers can agree with the notion that the resurrection of Jesus ensures a future resurrection of all believers, then they will have held fast to the gospel and believed it to a good end. If they reject the argument and persist in saying there is no resurrection of the dead, then their believing will have been "in vain." What is at stake, then, is the gospel itself and the salvation of the readers.

2. 15:12-19. The issue is immediately enjoined in v. 12. Some of the anticipated readers, who have accepted the preaching of Jesus' resurrection from the dead, neverthless argue "that there is no resurrection of the dead." With a two-directional logic, Paul attacks such a position. On the one hand, in the question of v. 12 he moves from Jesus' resurrection to affirm a resurrection of the dead. On the other hand, in vv. 13 and 16 he argues that a denial of the resurrection of the dead necessarily implies a denial of Jesus' resurrection. In either case, the two resurrections cannot be isolated in such a way that one can be accepted and the other denied.[6]

6. Why is the resurrection of the dead denied in Corinth? Most scholars argue that the primary problem among the readers derives from an enthusiasm that has led people to assume that they have already reached the goal of salvation. In baptism they have been endowed with a heavenly, spiritual body; they speak with "the tongues of angels" (13:1); they thus have no anticipation of what is not yet. "Already you are filled! Already you have become rich!" (4:8). The readers' position evidently approximates that of Hymenaeus and Philetus "who have swerved from the truth by holding that the resurrection is past already" (2 Tim. 2:17-18). In short, they embrace a "realized resurrection." So Hans von Soden, "Sakrament und Ethik bei Paulus: Zur Frage der literarischen und theologischen Einheitlichkeit von 1 Kor. 8-10," reprinted in *Das Paulusbild in der Neueren Deutschen Forschung,* ed. K. H. Rengstorf, WF 24 (Darmstadt: Wissenschaftliche Buchgesellschaft, 1964), 338-79; Ernst Käsemann, "On the Subject of Primitive Christian Apologetic," in *New Testament Questions of Today,* trans. W. J. Montague (Philadelphia: Fortress Press, 1969), esp. 124-237; idem, *Jesus Means Freedom,* trans. Frank Clarke (Philadelphia: Fortress Press, 1969), 59-84; C. K. Barrett, *The First Epistle to the Corinthians,* HNTC (New York: Harper & Row, 1967), 348; and John H. Schütz, *Paul and the Anatomy of Apostolic Authority,* SNTSMS 26 (Cambridge: Cambridge University Press, 1975), 84-113. Two articles that survey the various positions and cite the relevant literature are J. H. Wilson, "The Corinthians Who Say There is No Resurrection of the Dead," *ZNW* 59 (1968): 90-107; and Karl A. Plank, "Resurrection Theology: The Corinthian Controversary Reexamined," *PerspRelStud* 8 (1981): 41-54. For an opposing position, see Darrell J. Doughty, "The Presence and Future of Salvation in Corinth," *ZNW* 66 (1975): 61-90. Though the majority position helps to highlight the repeated "not yet" element in Paul's argument, it may be inadequate to label the Corinthians' position as simply "realized resurrection," as if the only problem in Corinth were a wrongheaded eschatology. The readers no doubt also espouse a dualism prevalent throughout the Hellenistic world, which makes it difficult for them to embrace a "bodily" resurrection. See, for example, the reconstruction of Paul's argument in Leander E. Keck, *Paul and His Letters,* PC (Philadelphia: Fortress Press, 1979), 108-11; and in J. Christiaan Beker, *Paul the Apostle: The Triumph of God in Life and Thought* (Philadelphia: Fortress Press, 1980), 163-73. Beker comments that for the Corinthians the resurrection of the dead "is both disgusting (because the body is inimical to salvation) and unnecessary (because our spiritual union with Christ is the redemption of our true self)" (166).

Again, the argument being offered takes on considerable force when the consequences of denying the resurrection are laid out. If there is no resurrection of the dead, then:

"Christ has not been raised" (vv. 13, 16);

"our preaching is in vain" (v. 14);

"your faith is in vain" (vv. 14, 17);

God is being misrepresented (v. 15);

"you are still in your sins" (v. 17);

"we are most to be pitied" (v. 18).

Though the gospel announces that Christ died "for our sins" (v. 3), a denial of Jesus' resurrection (which is denied if the resurrection of the dead is denied) prohibits forgiveness from being actualized (v. 17). To stay in one's sins means that the sting of death remains and death retains its victory (15:56). Thus Jesus' resurrection obviously carries saving significance. As Gerhard Delling concludes from his exegesis of this passage, "the cross of Christ is not a real saving act without the resurrection."[7]

3. 15:20-28. But of course "Christ has been raised from the dead," as the apostolic gospel announces, and his resurrection carries positive consequences. These are developed both in apocalyptic and christological directions. First, in terms of the apocalyptic order this means that Christ is "the firstfruits," the first installment, which inaugurates and pledges the ultimate offering of the total crop.[8] The term signifies both something incomplete and yet something hopeful. Christ's resurrection is *only* the firstfruits, but as firstfruits it assures the whole; and thereby the two resurrections are seen as only one, revealed in two temporal stages. In the Parousia, then, those who belong to Christ will join him, at which time the final enemy, death, will be destroyed and the divine rule turned over to the Father. For the present, Christ reigns, and the powers of various enemies are being contested and made subservient to his rule.[9] In addition to this apocalyptic ordering, Paul draws on the Adam-Christ contrast in an effective

---

7. Gerhard Delling, "The Significance of the Resurrection of Jesus for Faith in Jesus Christ," in *The Significance of the Message of the Resurrection for Faith in Jesus Christ,* ed. C. F. D. Moule, trans. R. A. Wilson, SBT (Naperville, Ill.: Alec R. Allenson, 1968), 98.

8. In addition to 1 Cor. 15:20, 23, ἀπαρχή ("firstfruits") appears in Rom. 8:23; 11:16; 16:5; and 1 Cor. 16:5, but only here is it used christologically.

9. The language of Ps. 110:1 and Ps. 8:6 adds force to the argument.

manner to undergird his case. While Adam brought death (cf. Rom. 5:18-21), Christ now has brought resurrection. But, significantly, the future tense of the verb prevails: "all *shall be made alive*" (15:22). What has happened to Christ has not yet happened but will happen to "all."

4. 15:29-34. Using a series of rhetorical questions, Paul turns the argument away from the gospel to the readers and himself. Apparently the Corinthians were practising a vicarious baptism for deceased persons who had not been baptized. What meaning, Paul asks, would such baptism have if there were no resurrection to be anticipated? What meaning would his own apostolic labors have? How would anyone justify a moral life-style? Much rests on an acknowledgment of and hope in the resurrection of the dead.

5. 15:35-58. To the query, "How are the dead raised?" Paul offers a two-stage answer.[10] First, people have to die. There is no way to avoid the stark reality of death. "What you sow does not come to life unless it dies" (15:36). There can obviously be no resurrection without a death. The fact that the reader is addressed as "you foolish one!" suggests that among his projected audience are those who in taking on the heavenly, spiritual body deny death's lingering power, an enemy that, from the perspective of the text, is yet to be finally subjected. But beyond the necessity of dying is the transformation. "We shall all be changed" (15:51). The perishable must put on the imperishable; the mortal must put on immortality. While with the use of the word "body" (15:44) an important continuity is acknowledged between the "now" and the "then," more prominent is the discontinuity, since for Paul (and perhaps also for the readers) "flesh and blood cannot inherit the kingdom of God" (15:50). The healthy plant, which produces an abundant harvest, can hardly be compared to the original seed planted in the ground. Resurrection means transformation to a form appropriate to the new life.

---

10. These two features are noted by a number of interpreters. See, for example, Hans Conzelmann, *A Commentary on the First Epistle to the Corinthians,* trans. James W. Leitch, Hermeneia (Philadelphia: Fortress Press, 1975), 281.

Strikingly, 1 Corinthians 15 concludes with an injunction about the present. "Therefore, be steadfast, immovable, always abounding in the work of the Lord, since you know that in the Lord your labor is not in vain" (15:58). A resurrection faith, open to God's future consummation, is depicted (through the imperatives) as an existence that is, paradoxically, durable amid the winds of change yet growing. The final clause seems to anticipate that the readers' faith will not continue to be rooted in a "realized resurrection," which depends on the vicissitudes of present experience and is sure to turn up empty, to no avail, "in vain," but will eventually trust the certainty of God's future.[11]

What unfolds in 1 Corinthians 15 is an argument for the futurity of the resurrection of the dead based on the received gospel, which Paul had previously declared to the readers and in which they had put their trust. Two crucial moves in the argument warrant highlighting, since, as we shall see, they are not peculiar to this chapter alone but occur in other Pauline letters as well. First, the resurrection of Jesus is a constituent event in the saving action of God. The juxtaposition between "Christ died for our sins" (15:3) and "if Christ has not been raised, you are still in your sins" (15:17) leaves no doubt about the indispensable role of both crucifixion and resurrection for salvation.[12] The received gospel reports the events in sequence (15:3-4), but the argument that ensues calls attention to their soteriological significance.

Second, the resurrection of Jesus is presented in the chapter as opening and assuring God's future consummation. While it is connected to the crucifixion, Jesus' resurrection primarily functions in the argument in relation to the resurrection of the dead. It is apocalyptically oriented and set as the beginning of the end.

---

11. The use of two Greek words, εἰκῇ and κενός, both translatable as "in vain," uncover the author's underlying concern for the readers in 1 Corinthians 15. In v. 2 the absoluteness of their faith is questioned: "unless you believed it [i.e., the gospel] in vain (εἰκῇ)." As for Paul himself, God's grace had not turned out to be "in vain (κενός)" (15:10), but if they persist in denying the future resurrection, then both his preaching and their faith will be "in vain (κενός)" (15:14). Finally, the concluding exhortation contains an encouraging reminder, "since you know that your labor is not in vain (κενός) in the Lord" (15:58; taking the participle εἰδότες as causal).

12. This is especially notable since the plural "sins" is not a regular Pauline usage.

"But each in his own order: Christ the firstfruits, then at his coming those who belong to Christ. Then comes the end" (15:23-24a). As Käsemann puts it, "Christ is God's representative over against a world which is not yet fully subject to God, although its eschatological subordination is in train since Easter and its end is in sight."[13] Paul insists that one believe in the resurrection, because to deny it is to deny the power of God.

We need now to explore these two moves in more detail as they appear in other contexts and to consider a third feature of the Pauline view of the resurrection—its place in the life of believers.

JESUS' RESURRECTION AS GOD'S SAVING EVENT

In addition to 1 Corinthians 15, there are several isolated verses in the Pauline letters that reflect the soteriological aspect of Jesus' resurrection. The most obvious occurs as a confessional statement in Rom. 10:9, where Deut. 30:11-14 is interpreted christologically via a midrash-pesher style, reminiscent of the Qumran literature. The decisive word that is "near you" is not the Torah (as Deut. 30:14 declares), but "the word of faith which we preach" (10:8). And the word contains substantive content: "If you confess with your lips that Jesus is Lord and believe in your heart that God raised him from the dead, you will be saved" (10:9). In this statement of the confessional formula necessary for salvation (perhaps a pre-Pauline baptismal creed), nothing is affirmed about the crucifixion; instead Jesus' lordship is paralleled by God's raising him from the dead.

In a similar fashion, 1 Thess. 1:9-10 mentions God's raising of Jesus from the dead in connection with salvation. The difference from Rom. 10:9-10, however, lies in the fact that the salvation referred to is more explicitly linked to the Parousia: "you turned from idols, to serve a living and true God, and to await his Son from heaven, whom he raised from the dead, Jesus who delivers us from the wrath to come." Furthermore, in several texts one discovers the resurrection linked with the crucifixion as an integral part of Pauline soteriology:

---

13. Ernst Käsemann, *New Testament Questions of Today,* 133.

> And he died for all, that those who live might live no longer for themselves but for him who for their sake ($\dot{\upsilon}\pi\dot{\epsilon}\rho$ $\alpha\dot{\upsilon}\tau\hat{\omega}\nu$) died and was raised.   (2 Cor. 5:15)

> Who is to condemn? Is it Christ Jesus, who died, yes, who was raised from the dead, who is at the right hand of God, who indeed intercedes for us?.   (Rom. 8:34)

> It will be reckoned to us who believe in him that raised from the dead Jesus our Lord, who was put to death for our trespasses and raised for our justification.   (Rom. 4:24-25)

One is left with the profound impression that Jesus' resurrection, alongside the crucifixion, plays a decisive role in the drama of salvation. Bertold Klappert, who has surveyed the contemporary discussion on this issue, points to Karl Barth as the theologian who most clearly understands and articulates this soteriological function of the resurrection.[14] For Barth, "The resurrection of Jesus Christ is the great verdict of God, the fulfilment and proclamation of God's decision concerning the event of the cross. . . . The positive connection between the death and resurrection of Jesus Christ consists in the fact that these two acts of God with and after one another are the two basic events of the one history of God with a sinful and corrupt world."[15]

JESUS' RESURRECTION AS THE PROMISE OF THE FUTURE

First Corinthians 15 also makes the point that God's raising Jesus from the dead is linked to the future resurrection of the dead. Actually, this is to put the issue too weakly. Jesus' resurrection *opens the door to* and *assures* the resurrection of the dead.

---

14. Klappert himself stresses the soteriological character of the resurrection. After listing the Pauline texts, he comments: "The resurrection is thus for the New Testament not only the noetic access to the cross, so that from the vantage of the resurrection it can be confessed who the Crucified is; but the resurrection is also the ontic ground of reconciliation, because it basically goes with reconciliation." *Diskussion um Kreuz und Auferstehung: Zur gegenwärtigen Auseinandersetzung in Theologie und Gemeinde,* ed. Bertold Klappert (Wuppertal: Aussaat Verlag, 1967), 25. The noetic function (which Bultmann has stressed) seems much more prominent in Luke and Acts than in the Pauline letters.

15. Karl Barth, *Church Dogmatics,* 4/1: 309-10.

The sequence being stressed in the argument is not so much crucifixion and resurrection (as in the received tradition cited in vv.
3ff.) but Jesus' resurrection and the future resurrection of the
dead. As Beker has argued forcefully, in 1 Corinthians 15 Jesus'
resurrection is not the closure event on the incarnation but the
inauguration of the new and final day.[16] It anchors the promise of
God's future.

This apocalyptic understanding of Jesus' resurrection is not
unique to 1 Corinthians 15. It appears in a variety of literary
settings in the letters and undergirds a number of different arguments.[17] The argument in 1 Thessalonians 4 is an offering of hope
to those who are grieving deceased members of the community.
They have reason to hope, Paul writes, "since we believe that
Jesus died and rose again, even so, through Jesus, God will bring
with him those who have fallen asleep" (4:14). The dead first and
then the living are to be united with the returning Lord. Earlier in
1 Thessalonians, readers have learned about the Thessalonians'
faith (which unlike the Corinthians' theology anticipates Jesus'
Parousia and does not bask in the rays of a supposed fulfillment):
"how you turned to God from idols, to serve a living and true
God, and to wait for his Son from heaven, whom he raised from
the dead, Jesus who delivers us from the wrath to come" (1:9-10).
In both cases, it is not specifically the resurrection of the dead
that is assured by Jesus' resurrection, but the Parousia.

Two texts express this link between Jesus' resurrection and the
future in contexts dealing with the "body" (also like 1 Corinthians 15). First, in 1 Corinthians 6 the issue of immorality is
enjoined in terms of the sanctity of the "body." "The body is not
meant for immorality, but for the Lord, and the Lord for the
body" (6:13). One of the reasons why the body is so important
and thus not to be defiled by prostitution is because it will be
raised. "And God raised the Lord and will also raise us up
by his power" (6:14). This eschatological anticipation, based on
Jesus' resurrection, provides one of the pillars for Paul's "body-

---

16. J. C. Beker, *Paul the Apostle,* 156.
17. In addition to the passages discussed here, see also Phil. 3:10-11, where
"the power of his resurrection" leads to "the resurrection of the dead."

ethics."[18] The second text appears in a setting more theological and less ethical. The presence of the Spirit serves as pledge of the future. Though it is acknowledged that in the present sin renders the body dead, it nevertheless will be resurrected from the dead. "If the Spirit of the one who raised Jesus from the dead dwells in you, the one who raised Christ Jesus from the dead will give life to your mortal bodies also through his Spirit which dwells in you" (Rom. 8:11). Readers, then, are exhorted to live in line with the Spirit.

Since Jesus' resurrection as a foretaste of the general resurrection plays such a prominent role in connection with the "body," it is not surprising that it also occurs when Paul reflects on the character of his ministry. In 2 Corinthians 4 we read of the physical frailties and bodily afflictions surrounding his missionary activity, resulting in his "always being given up to death for Jesus' sake" (4:11). But this activity rests on a hopeful premise; there is a source for his boldness as an apostle: "knowing that he who raised the Lord Jesus will raise us also with Jesus and bring us with you into his presence" (4:14).

Depending on the readers and the literary context, Jesus' resurrection as anticipatory of the future resurrection can thus be aimed in four different directions. First, it is aimed at an unbounded enthusiasm and can function to put on a brake, to say, "Hold on! Not yet!" The future, then, is juxtaposed to the present to stress what is unfulfilled, incomplete, only for the time being. To the triumphalism projected among the readers of 1 Corinthians, who relish living a kind of heavenly existence and who feel they transcend the earthiness of life in the community, Paul's message is hard to accept. To such readers it has a shattering effect. It directs the community's attention away from a preoccupation with speaking in the tongues of angels to the struggle against rulers, authorities, and powers throughout the world, which must be contested before the end. It puts space between now and the consummation, during which time the community of faith awaits its transformation. To the purveyors of the message of success and positive thinking who abound on every tele-

18. Leander E. Keck, *Paul and His Letters,* 111–16.

vision set, promising an abundant life in the here and now, the "not-yetness" of the resurrection is certain to appear as a sour and negative word. It spoils the dream of limitless fulfillment and puts a damper on the pious achievements of those who might be labeled "spiritual giants."

But Jesus' resurrection as anticipatory of the future resurrection is aimed at a second group, at the fatigued, who border on hopelessness, whose weariness with ministry or even with life itself leaves them at the edge of their resources and void of vision. To discover that Jesus has been raised from the dead and is the "firstfruits" of the entire harvest is to be given a promise. The assurance that there is something more, even though the "more" defies description, not only supplies a well-founded reason to continue but also provides fresh energy for the task. This Paul declares out of his own experience (2 Cor. 4:14). Even the projected readers of 1 Corinthians 15, who are preoccupied with the present and disdainful of a future resurrection, are called by the text to a hopeful present—steady, growing, confident (15:58) —because of the promise available through Jesus' resurrection. The same persons who are reminded of the "not yet" and whose enthusiasm is to be curbed are nevertheless offered hope, a sober and realistic hope.

Third, there are those who grieve and are perplexed. They wonder at the delay of Jesus' return and why things happen the way they do. The graves of their deceased friends cause them to doubt the future so that their grief closely resembles the grief of those "who have no hope" (1 Thess. 4:13). The word that Jesus' resurrection guarantees "we shall always be with the Lord" (4:17) relieves a great deal of anxiety and anguish. The message is meant to be a source of mutual comfort and support within the community (4:18).

Finally, this apocalyptically oriented theology of the resurrection is aimed at those who disdain the physical nature of life. Either they think the body is the source of evil and something to be suppressed, resulting in an ascetic style of life, or they think it of no consequence in light of the Spirit and thus embrace a misguided freedom. Jesus' resurrection, however, signals not a release of the spirit from the body, but a future resurrection of the body, thus giving dignity to the body and its activities. It is "the temple of the Holy Spirit" and the arena in and through which one glorifies God (1 Cor. 6:19-20). The effect is to confer immense significance on the whole of human behavior, especially if one understands the body not in merely individualistic terms but as "that piece of the world which we ourselves are and for which we bear responsibility."[19] The "this-worldliness" of the Pauline ethic is confirmed, somewhat ironically, by the apocalyptic character of Jesus' resurrection.

JESUS' RESURRECTION IN THE LIFE OF BELIEVERS

One of the most prominent ways in which the relation between cross and resurrection can be discerned in the Pauline letters (though not explicitly in 1 Corinthians 15) occurs in the depiction of the life and experience of believers. In the previous chapter we investigated the motif of participation with Christ developed in Romans 6:1-11 and noted that the argument against libertinism unfolds in terms of baptism and believers' union with the crucified Christ. Three times (6:4, 5, 8-9) Christ's resurrection from the dead is mentioned in the passage as an event in sequence with his death, but in each case the text carefully avoids stating that baptized persons are participants with Christ in the resurrection as they are participants with him in his death. On two of the occasions future tense verbs express what Käsemann has aptly labeled "a remarkable caveat in the shape of an eschatological reservation."[20] "We *shall be* united in the form of his resurrection" (6:5), and "we *shall live* with him" (6:8).[21] In the

---

19. Ernst Käsemann, *New Testament Questions of Today,* 135.

20. Ibid., 132.

21. Franz J. Leenhardt, *The Epistle to the Romans,* trans. Harold Knight (London: Lutterworth Press, 1961), 161; and C. E. B. Cranfield, *A Critical and Exegetical Commentary on the Epistle to the Romans,* ICC (Edinburgh: T. & T. Clark, 1975), 1: 308, 312, both take these two future tenses as pointing to the present existence of Christians and as essentially without eschatological significance. In the case of Leenhardt, this interpretation seems in part due to the fact that he accepts Colossians as one of Paul's own letters and uses Col. 2:12 as the key to Rom. 6:5, 8. There is, however, no indication in the undisputed letters of Paul that rising with Christ is anything other than an eschatological expectation.

third instance, Christ's resurrection serves as the encouragement to believers to "walk in newness of life" (6:4).

Baptism, as depicted in Romans 6, is the occasion whereby believers are united with Christ in his death and acknowledge their own death to sin and new life in the Spirit. Baptism, however, is not a gateway into a heavenly existence, where one communes immediately with the exalted Christ, removed from the trials and anguish of earthly life. On the one hand, from the passage one may sense an antitriumphalistic trace in the argument, as evidenced by the "eschatological reservation" (as in 1 Corinthians 15). On the other hand, one must not miss the positive role played by Christ's resurrection. As the pledge that God's people will in the future share his risen existence, he undergirds their present existence. The phrase "newness of life" itself (6:4) contains an eschatological quality, albeit proleptically, denoting the extraordinary vitality of union with Christ. The future so impinges on the present as to give it a distinctive buoyancy. Instead of libertinism, which makes one a slave of sin and leads to death, union with Christ leads to the service of righteousness, sanctification, and its end, eternal life (6:22-23).

THE RELATION OF CROSS AND RESURRECTION

Having looked at the more prominent themes of the resurrection as they unfold in the Pauline letters, we need now to put again the question with which we began: In what way or ways are the cross and resurrection of Jesus related to one another? First, we have to say that the cross and the resurrection belong together. They are events in sequence in the pre-Pauline tradition, in turn cited by Paul (1 Cor. 15:3ff.), and both are constituent of God's saving action. Neither overshadows the prominence of the other. Saying they "belong together" does not mean that they always appear together in literary contexts, but that Paul does not talk about one as if the other had not happened or were not true. The "Christ crucified" of Gal. 3:1 and 1 Cor. 2:2 is not a pre-resurrected Christ, nor is the risen Christ of 1 Corinthians 15 a Christ who has not been crucified. One might say that there is a presumption in the text that when the one is mentioned or discussed the other is implied. To put it a slightly different way, what makes the message of the crucified Christ offensive is not simply the manner of his death once, but that through the resurrection Christ is still known to the church as the crucified one.[22]

This "belonging together" undergirds the tacks repeatedly taken in the letters where the word of the cross turns out to be the manifestation of God's power (1 Cor. 1:18) and where in human experience such power is hidden under the mask of weakness (2 Cor. 4:10-11; 13:4). Power and crucifixion can be spoken of together only as one interprets the death of Jesus from the perspective afforded by the resurrection.

This tight linking of death and resurrection can be appreciated when one compares it with frequent discussions that assume their separation and issue a call for their mutual need for each other. For example, Paul is clearly one step ahead of Ulrich Wilckens in his treatment of the cross and resurrection as "love" and "power." He already knew what Wilckens calls for. For Wilckens, the cross is the event "in which God showed his *justice and righteousness as love.*" As such, it "requires" the resurrection, "for in the resurrection of Christ the question has been answered as to the *power* of the love of the Crucified One and its ability to *effectuate* the redeeming intention of that love towards the person loved." At the same time, the power demonstrated in the resurrection is not pure, undefined power. The cross gives it specificity as "the power of *love.*" "Belief in the Resurrected One would be robbed of its decisive criterion if it were not expressly the Crucified One, whose resurrection was being spoken of."[23]

A liberation theologian like Jon Sobrino makes this dialectic between love and power even more pointed in the context of oppression. Raw power will be mistrusted, because it inevitably

---

22. A case for the "belonging together" of cross and resurrection is made by Dan Via, basically on structuralist grounds. Among other things, he argues that thinking in binary oppositions (such as death/resurrection), while not *the* structure of the human mind, "is certainly widespread enough to be regarded as one fundamental mode of human thought." A symbol at the semantic or mythological level is always the reverse side of a larger symbolism, because it seeks a unifying totality. Dan O. Via, Jr., *Kerygma and Comedy in the New Testament: A Structuralist Approach to Hermeneutic* (Philadelphia: Fortress Press, 1975), 40.

23. Ulrich Wilckens, *Resurrection: Biblical Testimony to the Resurrection,* trans. A. M. Stewart (Atlanta: John Knox Press, 1978), 26–27.

shows itself unfavorable to marginalized, disenfranchised people. But God's presence in the cross lends credibility to God's
power in the resurrection.

> The cross says, in human language, that nothing in history has set
> limits to God's nearness to human beings. Without that nearness,
> God's power in the resurrection would remain pure otherness and
> therefore ambiguous, and, for the crucified, historically threaten-
> ing. But with that nearness, the crucified [of this world] can really
> believe that God's power is good news, for it is love. . . . Once God's
> loving presence on Jesus' cross has been grasped, God's presence in
> the resurrection is no longer pure power without love, pure other-
> ness without nearness, a *deus ex machina* without history.[24]

The connection that Wilckens and Sobrino are calling for is
already evident and in a more dynamic fashion in the Pauline
letters.

But while the cross and resurrection belong together, it is clear
that in the Pauline letters one can become the focal point of
theological reflection without the other being mentioned. On the
one hand, the unfolding of the theology of the cross in 1 Cor.
1:18—2:5 (as we saw in chapter 1) seems notably exclusive. "I
decided to know nothing among you except Christ and him crucified" (1 Cor. 2:2). The readers projected in the text have placed
their trust in human wisdom and divided themselves by aligning
with various powerful figures in the early church. In response, the
preaching of Christ crucified is affirmed as God's wisdom and
God's power. On the other hand, in 1 Corinthians 15 the resurrection serves as the focal point of the argument. Once the
received tradition is cited at the beginning of the chapter,
nothing more is said about Jesus' death on the cross. Numbered
among the readers are those who say there is no resurrection of
the dead, and thus the lines drawn from the tradition are exclusively in terms of the resurrection. The argument concerns the
indispensable promise of the future resurrection inherent in
Jesus' resurrection.

The only conclusion to be drawn from these two passages in 1
Corinthians is that each (i.e., the cross and the resurrection) has a

---

24. Jon Sobrino, *Jesus in Latin America* (Maryknoll, N.Y.: Orbis Books,
1987), 153.

distinctive function to play in the overall argument. Each has a theological cutting edge, which is appropriated without the worry of being one-sided or exclusive. What is striking is that the readership of both these passages is the same. It is not that the theology of the cross found in 1 Cor. 1:18—2:5 is directed at one group and the theology of the resurrection in 1 Corinthians 15 is directed at another. At heart, the two passages are not opposed to one another; both serve to illumine and critique the spiritual triumphalism and misguided eschatology of readers. Believers live in the power of the cross and proclaim Jesus' death, confident that God's power will prevail because it already has prevailed in Christ's resurrection. For this reason, Moltmann prefers to label Paul's position here as an *"eschatologia crucis"*:

> The future of the resurrection comes to it [i.e., faith] as it takes upon itself the cross. Thus the eschatology of the future and the theology of the cross are interwoven. It is neither that futuristic eschatology is isolated, as in late Jewish apocalyptic, nor does the cross become the mark of the paradoxical presence of eternity in every moment, as in Kierkegaard. The eschatological expectation of the all-embracing lordship of Christ for the corporeal, earthly world brings the clear perception and acceptance of the distinction of the cross and the resurrection.[25]

What is finally to be said about Käsemann's oft-quoted option —either the cross is a chapter in a book on the theology of the resurrection or the resurrection is a chapter in the theology of the cross?[26] Käsemann of course opts for the latter, because he rightly sees that for Paul the crucifixion cannot be relegated to being merely an antiquated fact or a transition point on the way to heavenly glory. Easter does not erase or eclipse the godforsakenness of Good Friday. In one sense our reading of the Pauline letters supports Käsemann's conclusion. While it matters both that the one who is risen is the crucified one *and* that the crucified has been raised, it is clear that the accent falls on the

25. Jürgen Moltmann, *Theology of Hope: On the Ground and the Implications of a Christian Eschatology*, trans. James W. Leitch (New York: Harper & Row, 1967), 160, 164.

26. Ernst Käsemann, *Perspectives on Paul*, 55, 59; idem, *Jesus Means Freedom*, trans. Frank Clarke (Philadelphia: Fortress Press, 1969), 68. The chapter title in the latter helps to mitigate against the otherwise sharpness of Käsemann's alternative: "For and Against a Theology of the Resurrection."

former, not the latter. In another sense, however, the sharp way Käsemann has posed the options must not be allowed to eclipse the positive role the resurrection plays in the letters. The reality of the resurrection both grounds a realistic hope in God's future and expresses itself in the cruciformed life of believers (2 Cor. 4:10-11; 13:4). As such, the resurrection has its own cutting edge.

Beyond the alternative Käsemann poses, a more promising way to consider the relationship is offered by those who recognize in the Pauline letters repeated elements of a narrative Christology.[27] The narrative, isolated not *behind* but *in* the text, depicts the preexistence, incarnation, crucifixion, and resurrection of Jesus Christ as God's redemptive event. This "story" becomes the lens through which Paul the pastoral theologian views the particular congregations under his care. The nuances of this story vary from letter to letter. When the letters as a whole are considered, undeniably the most prominent aspect of the story to emerge is Christ's faithful obedience unto death, freeing humanity from the bondage to sin and its consequences. The crucifixion is repeatedly appealed to as the foundation and norm of the Christian life. And yet whenever one feature of the story is argued or even alluded to, the whole story is assumed. Both writer and readers know the complete story, how it turns out, and though the readers' attention may be immediately drawn to Jesus' death, they are not unaware of his resurrection.

But how in reading the Pauline letters in a contemporary setting are the respective "cutting edges" of cross and resurrection to be treated? Douglas John Hall helpfully calls attention to the situational character of the church's theology and notes that there are historical times and places when the "cutting edge" of one or the other is more needed. Karl Barth's persistent sounding

---

27. See Richard B. Hays, *The Faith of Jesus Christ: An Investigation of the Narrative Substructure of Galatians 3:1—4:11,* SBLDS 56 (Chico, Calif.: Scholars Press, 1982). Hays analyzes the narrative formulations in Gal. 3:13-14; 4:3-6 through the use of Greimas's model. He shows how "in Galatians the kerygma of the cross (3:1, 13) is united in an organic fashion with the motifs of pre-existence and incarnation (4:4-5); these elements are joined within the structure of a single continuous story. Thus, already present in Paul is a basic narrative pattern similar to that which informs the canonical gospels, particularly Luke and John" (256). Though the resurrection of Jesus is explicit in Galatians only in the salutation (1:1), it is obviously assumed elsewhere—in 2:20 ("Christ lives in me") and in 2:20; 3:1; 6:14 where the perfect tense of the verb "crucify" makes sense only in light of the resurrection.

of the unconditional "yes" of Easter came upon receptive ears in the postwar era, when many Europeans struggled with defeat and pessimism that occasionally bordered on fatalism. It is not surprising that his message found a ready and positive response from the depressed and disillusioned. But, Hall argues, modern-day North Americans too eagerly welcome a risen, triumphant Jesus and employ such a message merely to protect themselves from facing the cross of their own experience. "It is time now that North Americans in their churches and on their billboards and television screens should meet the Crucified. . . . Until such a mutilated, sorrowful, forsaken Christ can be met in the churches of suburbia, there will be no facing up to the mutilation, sorrow, and forsakenness that this continent and its European satellites visit upon millions of the poor, including our own poor."[28]

What Hall argues is fundamentally true to Paul. He fears the phoniness of a bright and happy message "that has all the depth of a singing commercial," especially when sung in the presence of poor and disenfranchised people. The theology of the "realized resurrection" espoused by the Corinthians would (and does) ring hollow in the presence of such folk. It is essentially the gospel of the television preacher, who describes the cross as Jesus' "hardships" and his resurrection as a victory over them.

And yet one has to recognize that it is not the resurrection of Christ itself that feeds triumphalism, but a misguided theology of the resurrection. Paul's strategy in confronting the zealousness at Corinth is not to avoid or apologize for Jesus' resurrection, but to direct attention to the crucified Christ *and* to assert unequivocally that Jesus' resurrection is a promise (*only* a promise, but a *real* promise) of the future. The latter is important even for an overoptimistic church like the one in North America, which lives in a culture where the cracks in the wall are only too visible. A shattering of triumphalism has to be complemented by an alternate vision, which more clearly interprets the present and the future. As the church learns to forsake its imperialistic struggle and to bear its cross, it must do so in the promise of the resurrection, else it will not be able to bear the cross for long.

28. Douglas John Hall, *Lighten Our Darkness,* 140–41.

CHAPTER 4

| Jesus' Death
| and the People of God

We began our study of the death of Jesus in the Pauline letters by raising the question of historical causation: Who killed Jesus, and why? What we discovered was frankly a lack of interest in the question as it is traditionally posed, no attempt to isolate the culprits of the crime, and no effort to attribute the death to political, social, or economic causes. Instead, the issue is reoriented so as to declare that God is the primary actor in the drama of the crucifixion. There is nothing to suggest that Jesus' death is to be attributed to God in the sense that God killed Jesus; nothing in the nature of God demanded the death of the Son. Rather, the Pauline letters persist in viewing the death theonomously and as an event of revelation. In and through it God's character as a righteous and loving God is displayed. God is no more fully known than in the crucifixion. The horrible manner of Jesus' death makes the message of this revelation scandalous, sheer foolishness when judged by human canons of perception, but nevertheless the wisdom and power of God.

Since the Pauline letters understand sin not merely as an accumulation of violations of the moral law but as a demonic force, a controlling power in whose grasp men and women are rendered helpless, we turned next to consider what effects Jesus' death has on the plight of sinful humanity. We found the letters rich in soteriological imagery, replete with picture words drawn from a variety of language fields depicting the liberating power of the gospel and the world-transforming scope of Jesus' death. Not only does the cross effect an atonement with God, but believers gain a share in the event through baptism, where their participation in Christ's once-and-for-all death is signified and where the break of sin's fatal stranglehold is celebrated.

The relationship between Jesus' death and resurrection has always been a complex problem for the church to unscramble, precisely because it touches the lives of people and influences the way human experience is interpreted. Our examination of the Pauline letters revealed that the death and resurrection theologically belong together in the sense that there is never any reflection on a noncrucified or unresurrected Christ. To put it in christological terms, in the understanding of the resurrection it matters that the risen Lord was crucified, and in the understanding of the death it is important that the cross was not the end. At the same time, it is transparent in the letters that we encounter God's presence in the weak, humiliated, scandalously crucified Jesus or we do not encounter him at all. Paul can declare to the Corinthians that in his preaching he "decided to know nothing among you except Jesus Christ and him crucified" (1 Cor. 2:2).

There remains for our consideration one major dimension of the importance of the cross in the theology of the Pauline letters. The crucifixion shapes the identity of the people of God and functions as the basis for their communal and individual self-understanding. As the Jews are the people of the Torah, molded by the story it contains and distinguished from others by the circumcision it demands, so the Christian community is a people of the cross. In the story of Jesus' death preached in their assemblies and celebrated at the Lord's Supper, they announce who they are and discover how they are to live.

In the present chapter and the one following, we turn to this question of the identity of the Christian community as proposed in the Pauline letters. We examine three passages that in slightly differing ways reflect the communal self-understanding of the church. Galatians 3 faces head-on the admission and attenuating problems of gentiles within a community that maintains deep roots in the Jewish tradition. The question confronting Paul is simple: Must non-Jews be circumcised in order to be full-fledged members of God's family? To answer it, Paul provides a redefinition of the people of God based on the significance of Jesus' death. First Corinthians 11:17-34 addresses the abusive practices of certain participants in the Lord's Supper and demonstrates how the crucified body of Jesus celebrated at the table shapes the social behavior of the community as it gathers to worship. In 1 Cor. 5:1-13 we see how the congregation's misunderstanding of itself, revealed in the way it treats a case of immorality in its midst, is confronted by a reference to the sacrifice of Christ, the passover Lamb. In the following chapter, we look at how Paul's own apostolic vocation is expressed in terms of Jesus' death and argue that it projects also the identity of the community of faith.

REDEFINING THE PEOPLE OF GOD (GALATIANS 3)

The literary context of Galatians 3 is decisive. An awareness of it keeps the reader reminded of the social character of Paul's argument, that he contends for the proper place for the gentiles in the Christian community. Galatians 3 comes immediately after the report of the intriguing conflict between Peter and Paul at Antioch over the issue of table fellowship with gentile Christians (2:11-14), and the theological affirmations that follow in 2:15-21 stand at a critical juncture. On the one hand, they interpret from Paul's perspective the conflict with Peter and present a theological reason why the action of Peter and his colleagues does not "square with the truth of the gospel" (2:14, NEB). On the other hand, the affirmations lay out the major proposition to be developed in the following two chapters of the letter.[1] The proposition can be briefly summarized: Jesus Christ, his faithfulness and death, effects for sinful humanity a right relationship with God, negating any notion that "works of law" are the grounds for such a relationship. Whatever Peter's reason for withdrawing from eating with the gentile Christians at Antioch, his action in doing so de facto makes "works of law"—that is, dietary rules and circumcision—the basis for the community, leaving gentile

---

1. H. D. Betz, *Galatians: A Commentary on Paul's Letter to the Churches of Galatia,* Hermeneia (Philadelphia: Fortress Press, 1979), 113–14, discusses the function of the *propositio* in terms of the manuals of ancient rhetoricians. One, however, must avoid a sharp separation between the report of the conflict (2:11-14) and the theological reflection on the conflict (2:15-21), else the social character of justification so evident in the context is obscured. See C. B. Cousar, *Galatians,* Interpretation (Atlanta: John Knox Press, 1982), 56–62.

Christians as no more than second-class members of God's family.[2] But Paul's proposition, alternative to Peter's action, needs further grounding and elaboration, and for that we move to Galatians 3.

The first phase of the argument appeals directly to the readers, in whose presence the crucified Christ has been publicly preached (3:1-5).[3] By means of a series of rhetorical queries, readers are forced to reflect on their Christian experience as evidence for validating the basic proposition. Paul's initial probing question asks, "Did you receive the Spirit by 'works of law' or by the message of faith?" (3:2).[4] What is signified by the phrase "works of law"? How could it have been the grounds for or the means of the Galatians' reception of the Spirit? Traditionally, the phrase has been interpreted as shorthand for the attempt to earn one's status with God by keeping faithfully the moral strictures of the law, a salvation by works.[5] The difficulty with this explanation, however, is that nothing in the text suggests that Peter in abandoning the gentiles at Antioch is trying to earn his justification (2:16) or that Paul's opponents at Galatia are arguing that God had to be won over by so many good deeds.[6] What Peter advocates de facto by his actions and what the Pauline opponents are preaching in Galatia are that dietary rules and circumcision (respectively) must be observed if one is to be numbered among the people of God. The law for both Peter and the

---

2. Presumably Peter *had* a serious reason and was not merely wishy-washy, else why would Barnabas and the other Jewish Christians have joined him?

3. Richard B. Hays, *The Faith of Jesus Christ: An Investigation of the Narrative Substructure of Galatians 3:1—4:11,* SBLDS 56 (Chico, Calif.: Scholars Press, 1983), 197, rightly comments: "Thus Gal. 3:1—4:11 may be read as an extended explication of the implications of the gospel story within which the phrase 'Christ crucified' finds its meaning."

4. The Greek phrase ἐξ ἀκοῆς πίστεως, rendered by the RSV as "by hearing with faith," is perhaps better translated as "by [the] proclamation of [the] faith" (so Betz, *Galatians,* 128) or "by [the] message that evokes faith" (so Hays, *The Faith of Jesus Christ,* 148).

5. This is the position, e.g., of Betz, *Galatians,* 116–17; and Franz Mussner, *Der Galaterbrief,* HTK (Freiburg: Herder, 1974), 170–71.

6. The opponents in fact do *not* keep the law (6:13) and could hardly be advocates of a salvation by works. Furthermore, Jews themselves did not think they were saved by their works. See E. P. Sanders, *Paul and Palestinian Judaism: A Comparison of Patterns of Religion* (London: SCM Press, 1977).

Pauline opponents functions as a line of demarcation, a boundary marker, distinguishing the people of God from all others. For them the law is not a moral mountain one must climb in order to be saved, but a Berlin wall separating one group from another.

The phrase "works of law," then, designates the obligations stipulated by the law or "the religious system determined by the law."[7] Paul's question of v. 2 might be paraphrased, "Did you receive the Spirit by accepting circumcision and taking on the religious system of Judaism or by the message of the crucified Christ?" Twice, these same mutually exclusive options are set before the readers (vv. 2 and 5).

Immediately following the last of the rhetorical questions comes the complex paragraph comprised of vv. 6-9, which introduces Abraham into the discussion for the first time.[8] Through a linking of Gen. 15:6 ("Abraham believed God, and it was reckoned to him as righteousness") with a composite of Gen. 12:3 and 18:8 ("In you shall all the nations [$\tau \grave{\alpha}$ ἔθνη] be blessed"), Paul is able to make three points:

1. "Those of faith" (and by implication from 3:1-5, *not* those who are characterized by "works of law") are children of Abraham.

2. The Scriptures declared that God in faithfulness to the promise would justify the gentiles ($\tau \grave{\alpha}$ ἔθνη).[9]

---

7. James D. G. Dunn, "Works of the Law and the Curse of the Law (Galatians 3:10-14)," *NTS* 31 (1985): 527. Dunn stresses the social function of the law and drawing on the work of Hans Mol and Mary Douglas elaborates on the sociological categories of "identity" and "boundary." "'Works of law' denote all that the law requires of the devout Jew, but precisely because it is the law as identity and boundary marker which is in view, the law as Israel's law focuses on these rites which express Jewish distinctiveness most clearly" (531). See also J. B. Tyson, "'Works of Law' in Galatians," *JBL* 92 (1973): 423–31, who translates "works of law" as "nomistic service."

8. George Howard (*Paul: Crisis in Galatia*, SNTSMS [Cambridge: Cambridge University Press, 1979], 55); Hays (*The Faith of Jesus Christ*, 199–200); and Sam K. Williams ("Justification and the Spirit in Galatians," *JSNT* 29 [1987]: 92–93, handle the καθώς in 3:6 differently, but agree that v. 6 is closely related to v. 5. The God who supplies the Spirit and works miracles is the same God who reckons righteousness to Abraham.

9. It seems clear that the phrase ἐκ πίστεως in 3:8 does not designate the condition by which gentiles are received into the blessing of Abraham, but rather the way God functions in justifying them. As Howard notes, there are

3. "Those of faith" (among whom are now numbered gentiles) are included in God's blessing of Abraham.[10]

The inclusion of the gentiles, then, turns out not to be a second-thought on God's part, but to be bound up with the promise originally given to Abraham.

In vv. 10-12 Paul turns the argument directly toward those who find security in the religious system determined by the law and who from Paul's perspective are "under a curse." The reference to "blessing" mentioned in the previous verse no doubt triggers its opposite and leads to the explanatory quote from Deut. 27:26: "Cursed is everyone who does not abide by all the things written in the book of the law to do them." In this choice between the religious system of the law and the message of the crucified Christ, one cannot simply opt for circumcision and dietary rules alone. To opt for circumcision and dietary rules, the readers are reminded, is to opt for the whole law: "*all the things* written in the book of the law" (also 5:3). And why in the final analysis is the option of the law (together of course with the cultic system, which allows for repentance and forgiveness) not possible? Verses 10 and 11, citing Lev. 18:5 and Hab. 2:4, answer, "Because God does not justify people by the option of the law ($\dot{\epsilon}\nu$ $\nu\acute{o}\mu\wp$), but by faith ($\dot{\epsilon}\kappa$ $\pi\acute{\iota}\sigma\tau\epsilon\omega\varsigma$)."[11] Paul's rationale is not that people will find it impossible to keep the whole law and therefore must seek another way,[12] but that the way of faith excludes the way of law.[13]

---

aspects of faith that are "temporally and causally antecedent to the Christian's faith," namely God's faithfulness to the promise, Abraham's faith, and the faith of Christ. See George Howard, *Paul: Crisis in Galatia,* 58.

10. The term $\tau\grave{\alpha}$ $\ddot{\epsilon}\theta\nu\eta$ is variously translated "nations" or "gentiles," but there is no reason why both should not be encompassed by the term. See Arland J. Hultgren, *Paul's Gospel and Mission: The Outlook from His Letter to the Romans* (Philadelphia: Fortress Press, 1985), 125–28.

11. Hays (*The Faith of Jesus Christ,* 150–57), following the suggestion of A. T. Hanson (*Studies in Paul's Technique and Theology* [London: S.P.C.K., 1974], 42–45), may be correct in taking "the righteous one" ($\acute{o}$ $\delta\acute{\iota}\kappa\alpha\iota\varsigma$) in 3:11 to be the Messiah and not as a collective signifying "the righteous ones," in which case the argument takes on even more of a christological focus.

12. So, e.g., Mussner, *Galaterbrief,* 226.

13. This is a point made in varying ways by Howard, *Paul: Crisis in Galatia,* 63–64; E. P. Sanders, *Paul and Palestinian Judaism,* 482–84; Hays, *The Faith of Jesus Christ,* 205–7; T. L. Donaldson, "The 'Curse of the Law' and the Inclusion of the Gentiles: Galatians 3:13-14," *NTS* 32 (1986): 101.

Or to put it in other terms, Paul's argument, beginning with the death of Christ, rejects any soteriological option that may make the death superfluous (so 2:21). The opponents' advocacy of circumcision in the Galatian communities, then, is totally incompatible with a gospel of the crucified Christ and thus a false option.

In vv. 13-14 the argument moves toward a climax in becoming more explicitly christological. First is the affirmation that Christ, by becoming a curse "for us" ($\dot{v}\pi\dot{\epsilon}\rho$ $\dot{\eta}\mu\hat{\omega}\nu$), "redeemed us from the curse of the law." The structure of interchange, as we have noted earlier, parallels that of 2 Cor. 5:21 and, with the preposition $\dot{v}\pi\acute{\epsilon}\rho$, presents Christ's death as vicarious (rather than participatory).[14] The citation from Deut. 21:23 links the manner of Christ's death with the actuality of the curse. It is as if the law has done its job, performed its condemning function at the cross, and has exhausted itself so that it ceases to be effective. The curse of the law is removed. Thus the chapter, which begins with a recalling of the preaching of "Christ crucified" (3:1), in v. 13 arrives at a statement of the atoning character of Christ's death.[15]

One thorny exegetical problem appears in connection with the affirmation of 3:13 and demands careful consideration. Who are the "us" who are redeemed from the curse of the law? Interpeters differ sharply as to whether the "us" refers to only Jewish Christians or whether it can be taken more broadly to include gentile Christians as well.[16] The limiting of the pronoun to Jewish Christians initially seems the better choice. It is generally more characteristic of the Pauline usage and would be continuous with the first-person pronoun found in 2:15-16 ("We ourselves who are Jews by birth and not gentile sinners"). Furthermore, one is otherwise faced with the difficulty of explaining how the gentiles might be considered "under the curse of the law," since they presumably had no prior association with the law. If, however,

14. In Gal. 4:4-5 another occasion of interchange occurs, though the structure is modified somewhat by the "sending" formula.

15. Though the verb "crucify" is not used in 3:13, the manner of Jesus' death is obviously underscored through the citation of Deut. 21:23. As in 1 Cor. 1:18—2:5, the scandalous means of Jesus' death becomes the explicit occasion for something positive, for blessing and liberation.

16. See the list of interpreters on both sides of this question in Donaldson, "The 'Curse of the Law' and the Inclusion of the Gentiles," 95–99.

the limited definition is chosen, one must explain how the redemption of Israel becomes a step in the move toward the inclusion of the gentiles. Why would Christ have to redeem *Jews* from the curse of the law in order for the blessing of Abraham to come to the *gentiles?* T. J. Donaldson (unlike many other interpreters) has faced this question and concludes that Paul is struggling here with seemingly divergent concerns—namely, with the concern that salvation is through Christ crucified and with the concern that the law is the gift of God. The two concerns result in an affirmation of the redemption of Israel as an intermediate step in the route from the "Christ crucified" of v.1 to the inclusion of the gentiles in v. 14. Passages such as Tobit 14:5-7 are cited as evidence of a Jewish anticipation of the establishment of Jerusalem just preceding the eschatological inclusion of the gentiles.[17]

The problem with Donaldson's solution, however, is that Galatians offers little or no concern for the salvation of the Jews qua Jews. Their plight is simply not the burning passion of this letter. If the author were seeking to present an order of salvation along the lines of the expectations of Jewish literature (i.e., first the redemption of the Jews, then the inclusion of the gentiles), he would certainly have used a less ambiguous word as the direct object of the verb—perhaps "Israel" or "the Jews."[18] The shadow of the Epistle to the Romans ("to the Jew first and also to the Greek," Rom. 1:16) seems to hang heavy over Donaldson's interpretation.

The flow of the argument throughout Galatians 3, however, seems much better served if "us" ($\dot{\eta}\mu\hat{\alpha}\varsigma$) in v. 13 is taken to include gentiles as well as Jews. The movement of the immediate paragraph is to the end that "in Christ Jesus the blessing of Abraham might come upon the gentiles, that we [now certainly inclusive of Jewish and gentile Christians] might receive the promised Spirit through faith" (3:14).[19] The entire chapter reaches its climax with the confession that in Christ "all" are

---

17. Ibid., 94–112.
18. On several occasions Paul uses the first- and second-person pronouns in the same passage, including both Jews and gentiles. See Rom. 7:4-6; Gal. 4:4-7.
19. Along with the majority of commentators, I am taking the two $\acute{\iota}\nu\alpha$ clauses in 3:14 as parallel to one another and dependent on the main clause, rather than as sequential. For a contrary opinion, see Betz, *Galatians,* 132–33.

children of God, without distinctions such as Jew and Greek
(3:26-28).

But how, then, can it be said that gentiles were "under the curse
of the law"? The text suggests that the curse of the law affects
them as well as Jews precisely because the law excludes them.
They are isolated by the wall that the law erects and are thus
rejected, unless of course they choose to accept the religious
system of Judaism and come "under the law." As Paul put it, "the
scripture consigns all things to sin" (3:22). It is not just that the
law is a problem for Jews; it is equally a problem for non-Jews in
its demand that they put themselves under its sway. And from
"the curse of the law" Christ has redeemed both.[20]

In v. 14 the result of the vicarious death of Christ is made
explicit in two parallel clauses, tying together the complex argument of 3:1-14. First, Christ's redemption of Jews and gentiles
from the curse of the law results in "the blessing of Abraham,"
announced in Gen. 12:3, reaching its fulfillment. The gentiles are
numbered among its recipients—that is, God in faithfulness to
the promise justifies the gentiles (3:8).[21] But Christ's redemption
leads also to the experience of the Spirit, which the readers have
been urged to recall in vv. 1-5, termed now "the promised
Spirit." As Dahl and Williams have pointed out, it is unlikely
that a separation is to be understood between the parallel clauses,
between God's justifying of the gentiles and God's giving of the
Spirit. Instead, "the gift of the Spirit is evidentiary proof of God's
acceptance."[22]

Before moving to the remainder of Galatians 3, we pause to
note that the statement of the atonement made in 3:13, like so
many other such statements in the Pauline letters, is made not as
an end in itself but as the means to an end. The chapter contains
no implied debate about *how* it is that Christ's crucifixion

---

20. See the treatment of this "thorny problem" by Howard, *Paul: Crisis in
Galatia,* 58–61; Dunn, "Works of the Law and Curse of the Law," 536, 542n.;
and Williams, "Justification and the Spirit in Galatians," 91–92.

21. The conceptual categories have switched between v. 13 and v. 14 from a
vicarious death stated in terms of an interchange to a category of inclusiveness
and participation—"in Christ Jesus." This is not unlike the switches in 2 Cor.
5:14-21.

22. Nils A. Dahl, *Studies in Paul* (Minneapolis: Augsburg, 1977), 133;
Williams, "Justification and the Spirit in Galatians," 91–100.

redeemed Jews and non-Jews from the curse of the law, no instruction as to particulars of the atonement beyond the notion of an interchange. If sacrificial ideas are present in the verse, they are certainly not spelled out.[23] It is rather the results of the death in terms of its meaning for the people of God that come to expression.

Having said this, however, we also note that the atonement is (in terms of the logic of the argument) the *necessary* means to the end. It is not that some other event in biblical history could be substituted for the role of the crucifixion. Even if Abraham's offering of Isaac is reflected in "the blessing of Abraham" (so Gen. 22:18), in itself it only foreshadows but does not effect what Galatians 3 affirms. The death of Christ becomes the indispensable grounds for arguing that gentiles are rightfully to take their place among the people of God. E. P. Sanders, for example, has argued that 3:10-13, containing a chain of proof texts, is basically subsidiary in the argument to 3:8, where the blessing to Abraham is elaborated in terms of God's justification of the gentiles.[24] Our observation that the statement of the atonement serves as a means to an end in a sense supports Sanders's conclusion. And yet such a conclusion is possible only if one presupposes the christological substructure of the chapter, even before 3:13. The preaching of "Jesus Christ crucified," with which the chapter begins, underlies and in a sense controls the flow of thought up to 3:13-14, where the function of Christ's death is specifically related to the fulfillment of the promise.

Three times in the remainder of Galatians 3 this christological emphasis emerges. First, in 3:16 Abraham's "seed" is identified not in terms of a nation of people descending from him, but solely (and pointedly) as "Christ." Surprisingly, even a collective interpretation, which one might have anticipated from both the Greek and Hebrew words for "seed," is ruled out. Christ alone is

---

23. Betz, *Galatians,* 150–51. Dahl finds allusions in 3:13 to the story of Abraham's offering of Isaac and draws a parallel between the sacrifice of the ram "caught in a thicket" and the sacrifice of Christ "on a tree." But the connection here seems a bit farfetched. See Dahl, *Studies in Paul,* 132.

24. E. P. Sanders, *Paul, the Law, and the Jewish People* (Philadelphia: Fortress Press, 1983), 22.

Abraham's "seed." But then in the concluding verse of the chapter we discover what we have suspected all along: "If you are Christ's, then you are Abraham's seed" (3:29). The one way to be a part of Abraham's lineage, an heir to the promise, is to belong to Christ.

Second, in 3:22 "the faith of Jesus Christ" is stated as the grounds on which the promise (presumably referring to "the promise of the Spirit" in 3:14) is given to those who believe.[25] Exactly what is encompassed in Christ's "faith" is not immediately spelled out, though "faith" appears to be used as a near synonym for "Christ" in v. 23. In light of the flow of the argument, however, it likely serves as shorthand for the death mentioned in 3:13. Just as God is faithful to the promise made to Abraham (3:8), so Christ is faithful to God in becoming himself "cursed," hanging on a tree, so as to redeem humanity from the curse of the law and make possible the gentiles' reception of the blessing and the experience of the promised Spirit. As Hays has argued, there is a narrative structure to 3:13-14, which then is alluded to by the expression in 3:22, "the faith of Jesus Christ."[26] The step between the promise made and the promise received is the soteriological activity of Christ.

The third christological emphasis in the latter half of Galatians 3 actually comes with the repeated use of Christ as a representative figure in whose actions and destiny the people of God participate. Employing baptismal language (and perhaps even a traditional baptismal liturgy),[27] Paul speaks of being "in Christ Jesus" (3:26, 28), of baptism "into Christ" (3:27), of "putting on Christ" (3:27), of "belonging to Christ" (3:29).[28] It is this participatory

---

25. It is not necessary to repeat the reasons why Ιησου Χριστου in 3:22 should be taken as a subjective, rather than an objective, genitive. See Hays, *The Faith of Jesus Christ,* 157–67.

26. Ibid., 110–15; and idem, "Jesus' Faith and Ours: A Re-reading of Galatians 3," *TSF Bulletin* 7 (1983): 2–6.

27. Wayne A. Meeks, "The Image of the Androgyne: Some Uses of a Symbol in Earliest Christianity," *HR* 13 (1974): 165–208; Betz, *Galatians,* 181–85; Elisabeth Schüssler Fiorenza, *In Memory of Her: A Feminist Reconstruction of Christian Origins* (London: SCM Press, 1983), 208–9.

28. Though Christ's death is not mentioned in the last paragraph of Galatians 3, it is clearly assumed. The baptismal flavor of the text recalls Rom. 6:3, where the participation is expressly grounded in the crucifixion. "Do you not

stress that enables the shift from Christ as the lone "seed" of Abraham (3:16) to the readers' being "Abraham's seed" (3:29).

What becomes even more significant for the overall reading of Galatians is the effect of such a participation in Christ. The characterizing features and, with them, the parameters of the people of God are redefined. "There is neither Jew nor Greek, there is neither slave nor free, there is no 'male and female'; for you are all one in Christ Jesus" (3:28). We have come full circle from Peter who at Antioch observes just such a distinction between Jew and gentile by withdrawing from the table fellowship with gentiles now to the affirmation that in baptism such distinctions are no longer valid. The law, which drives a wedge between Jew and non-Jew and sets a curse upon both, has completed its custodial function and thus no longer characterizes the people of God. In place of the law is Christ; in place of circumcision and the rules of the Jewish system is the faithful death of Christ in whom believers are incorporated; in place of divisions—ethnic, social, and gender—is unity.

Throughout the consideration of Galatians 3 we have repeatedly spoken of the faithfulness of God to. the promise made to Abraham and the faithfulness of Jesus Christ to God in the execution of the promise. Such a preoccupation with the divine activity (i.e., the faithfulness of God and the faithfulness of Christ) becomes essential to the proper grasp of what Paul is about in the argument in redefining the people of God. The redefinition does not entail some new activity humans perform (believing) that now replaces another activity humans have unsuccessfully tried to perform (doing the law). And yet the stress on the divine faithfulness does not eliminate but rather establishes the human response of faith. Believing for humans assumes a new dimension in that at a particular moment in the fullness of time Jesus trusted and obeyed God in such a way that his faith and obedience took the shape of a shameful death. There is now "the pioneering faith of Christ,"[29] not so much as a model

---

know that all of us who have been baptized into Christ Jesus were baptized into his death?"

29. Sam K. Williams, "Again *Pistis Christou*," *CBQ* 49 (1987): 447.

to be followed (though there is something of that) but as one in whose faithfulness humans are incorporated. Believers are those who gratefully accept their place in the faithful activity of Christ and whose lives then are molded by and conformed to that faithfulness.

At heart it is a question of identity. Believers express who they are not by telling their own individual stories, but by telling the story of God's faithfulness to the promise and of Jesus' faithfulness in the cross. It is the divine story, which then functions to shape their individual stories. As a people of faith, they seek to display a community in which the categories of Jew-gentile, slave-free, male-female no longer count, in which power is shared, in which no other distinguishing feature diminishes that of belonging to Christ.

PROCLAIMING THE LORD'S DEATH (1 COR. 11:17-34)

Galatians 3 declares that the people of God are reconstituted and redefined by Jesus Christ, his faithfulness to God even in death. Non-Jewish, as well as Jewish, believers discover their inclusion in the chosen family precisely in that faithfulness. The Corinthian passage, to which we now turn, sheds further light on how the death of Jesus has a continuing function in the life and discipline of the people of God. The text speaks of repeatedly observing the sacrament of the Lord's Supper, a remembrance of the Lord's death, which is to shape the character of the community of faith, providing pointed directions not only for its interior life (i.e., how it is to behave at the meal) but also for its dilemmas in dealing with the world (i.e., participating in pagan feasts).

Actually 11:17-34 is not the first mention of the Lord's Supper in 1 Corinthians. In 10:1-13 the ancient Israelites, baptized into Moses and partakers of the supernatural food and drink, are cited as an example to the Corinthians. The Israelites had their "sacraments," but God was not pleased with them and they were overthrown in the wilderness (10:5). They ate and drank, but also engaged in immorality and "put the Lord to the test," until disaster struck. This, then, is to be a warning to the readers (10:6,11). Sacraments are not insurance policies that either protect their participants against trials or guarantee immortality. God will assist in times of trials, but "let anyone who thinks that he stands take heed lest he fall" (10:12).

In the following section (10:14-22), the historical allusion to the Israelites is applied to the specific situation of the readers— namely, to the practise of eating at table in an idol's temple.[30] They are to avoid the worship of idols, because a participation in the Lord's Supper rules out a concomitant participation in idol worship. Even though the idol is nothing and the food eaten at the pagan banquet is harmless, the participation (κοινωνία) involved violates the participation in the sacrament.[31]

In the specifics of Paul's argument, an important linguistic and theological move is made, which becomes decisive in relating the sacrament to the life of the community. In 10:16 two rhetorical questions are posed in such a way as to anticipate positive responses. "The cup of blessing which we bless, is it not a participation in the blood of Christ? The bread which we break, is it not a participation in the body of Christ?" The author assumes that he and the readers agree that to share in the elements of the Lord's Supper is to share in the death of Christ. But in the following verse we read, "Because there is one loaf, we who are many are one body, for we all partake of the same loaf" (v. 17). The subtle turn comes in the use of "body" (σῶμα), which shifts from being the crucified body of Jesus (v. 16) to being the ecclesial body (v. 17). Partaking of one loaf makes the partakers to be one body, producing a linked relationship: sacramental bread, crucified body of Jesus, ecclesial body. What results is that "participation in Jesus and his body becomes identical with incorporation into the church as the body of Christ."[32] The connection enables Paul later to condemn the behavior of the

---

30. Charles H. Talbert, *Reading Corinthians: A Literary and Theological Commentary on 1 and 2 Corinthians* (New York: Crossroad, 1987), 56–57, provides helpful historical material that distinguishes the two separate issues dealt with in 1 Corinthians: eating meat, originally sacrificed in a pagan temple, and participating in a banquet in a pagan temple.

31. We do not have an English term adequate to convey the intensity encompassed in κοινωνία. One might note that it is a favorite term for marriage as the most intimate of human relations.

32. Ernst Käsemann, "The Pauline Doctrine of the Lord's Supper," in *Essays on New Testament Themes*, trans. W. J. Montague, SBT (London: SCM Press, 1964), 110.

Corinthians who become drunk at the sacramental table but leave others hungry (11:17-22, 29).

Following a consideration of eating food offered to idols' (10:23—11:1) and of the wearing of veils by the Corinthian women at worship (11:2-16), the topic comes back to the Lord's Supper. Paul finds the practice of the Corinthians so intolerable that they would do better not to gather, for they deceive themselves in thinking that what they are doing is celebrating the Lord's Supper. "For in eating, each goes ahead with his own meal, and one is hungry and another is drunk" (11:21). Evidently the custom practised at other social events was prevailing also at the meal at which the community observed the sacrament. The custom allowed the host to serve the largest portions and the best food to his friends and social peers, leaving the less fortunate to be humiliated and latecomers to get little or nothing to eat. The host no doubt justified this preferential service on the grounds that the sacrament was separate from the meal, that the traditional liturgy of the Lord's Supper applied only to the bread and cup, and not to the accompanying meal. He and his peers may well have felt more comfortable in a fellowship regulated by the conventional social customs than by one where such observances are forsaken in favor of an egalitarian etiquette.[33] With a series of barbed questions, Paul suggests that those who are so hungry that they cannot wait on others should eat at their homes ahead of time before coming to the community meal (11:22, 33-34).[34] As is, they are treating the church of God with contempt (11:22).

This initial analysis of the Corinthians' practice is followed by a recitation of the liturgy of the Lord's Supper (11:23-25), not new information to the readers but a basis for common reflection. Two features of the received tradition are particularly significant for our consideration. First, the emphasis throughout the

33. For a description of this social custom, see Gerd Theissen, *The Social Setting of Pauline Christianity,* trans. J. H. Schütz (Philadelphia: Fortress Press, 1982), 145–74; Wayne Meeks, *The First Urban Christians: The Social World of the Apostle Paul* (New Haven: Yale University Press, 1983), 68–72; and Charles H. Talbert, *Reading Corinthians,* 74–75.

34. Paul's counsel to the hungry to eat before coming should be taken at face value as simply practical advice. There is nothing in the text to suggest that Paul was arguing that the meal should be separated from the sacrament.

liturgy falls on the death of Christ. From the setting ("on the night in which he was betrayed"), through both the bread-word ("my body which is for you") and the cup-word ("new covenant in my blood"), finally to Paul's addition in v. 26 ("you proclaim the Lord's death"), the allusions to the crucifixion give unity to the whole. No explicit mention is made of the incarnation or the resurrection, only of the death. Not surprisingly (in light of 10:16), we hear again of the connection between participation in the sacrament and participation in the crucified body of Jesus. Verse 26, not itself a part of the liturgy,[35] gives focus to the sacrament by anchoring the institution itself ("Do this in remembrance of me") in "the Lord's death" and by orienting the sacrament to the Parousia.[36] The point is that whenever the Lord's Supper is celebrated it becomes an announcement of the saving character of the crucifixion, a declaration that the death is both vicarious ("for you") and inaugurates a new eschatological order where the exalted one reigns ("the new covenant in my blood").[37]

Second, the single christological title used in the liturgy (and in Paul's addition in v. 26) is "Lord." It facilitates the link between the crucified one who gives up his body in death and the exalted one who reigns. Furthermore, it is precisely the christological nuance exploited in the following paragraph (11:27-32), when Paul warns the community that they stand under judgment "by the Lord," by the exalted one who instituted the meal "on the night when he was betrayed." Käsemann's comment is apt:

35. The separation of 11:26 is of course due to the change from the first person pronoun in the liturgy to the third person in the Pauline "addition."

36. The mention of the Parousia seems to carry a double-sided effect. On the one hand, it speaks to the situation of the readers who understand the Lord's Supper as the heavenly banquet and who in eating it celebrate their transference out of this earthly existence. The phrase "until he comes" puts a damper on an overrealized eschatology and reminds the Corinthians that the life of the present is a life under the cross. On the other hand, the eschatological reference also gives a positive cast to the observance. The sacrament is celebrated in anticipation of and hope in God's final triumph.

37. Beverly Roberts Gaventa, "'You Proclaim the Lord's Death': 1 Corinthians 11:26 and Paul's Understanding of Worship," *RevExp* 80 (1983): 377–87, makes a strong case for the fact that the observance of the sacrament itself, with its liturgy, is a proclamation of the Lord's death and does not imply an accompanying sermon or homily.

> The Lord's supper sets us in the Body of Christ, in the presence of the Exalted One who, having passed through death, now reigns: it therefore places us under the lordship of this Kyrios. Thus our encounter with the Kyrios in the sacrament can be presented as an encounter with the Judge of all, as Paul points out in his gloss in vs. 26 on the command to repeat the actions of the Last Supper. A meeting with the exalted Kyrios means grace in the midst of judgment and judgment in the midst of grace.[38]

This is precisely the motif developed in 11:27-32, where readers are sternly warned of an unworthy or inappropriate observance of the sacrament and are exhorted to examine themselves prior to participating.[39]

But how does one participate "unworthily" or "inappropriately"? What can one do to avoid letting the elements become a poison rather than a nourishment, a curse rather than a blessing? The answer comes in v. 29 in the phrase "discerning the body." Failure to "discern the body" has already brought judgment among the readers (v. 30). What does "discerning the body" involve? With the phrase Paul is certainly not advocating a sacramentalism in which the elements take on mysterious or even magical force and the proper observance demands either a deep spiritual perception on the part of the participants or a fastidious care with the elements themselves. There is nothing in the text to suggest this. We have to look elsewhere.

In our consideration of 10:16-17 we observed how the term "body" could shift from denoting the crucified body of Jesus to denoting the ecclesial body, the congregation. This seems the best clue for our understanding of 11:29. Since eating the one loaf unites the many into one body, participants cannot ignore the life within the ecclesial body when partaking of the crucified body. "Discerning the body" (as the context also confirms), then, has to do with how members of the community treat one another,

---

38. Ernst Käsemann, *Essays on New Testament Themes,* 132.

39. First Corinthians 11:27 seems to contain the formulation of a sacral law, whose validation awaits confirmation in the final day. See Käsemann, *Essays on New Testament Themes,* 122; Gunther Bornkamm, "Lord's Supper and Church in Corinth," in *Early Christian Experience,* trans. Paul Hammer (London: SCM Press, 1969), 148.

whether they exercise patience and thoughtfulness at the meal, showing concern for the poor and the latecomers, or whether they let the prevailing social customs determine their conduct.[40] The Lord's Supper at its heart carries a call to obedience, to the forsaking of practises by which participants "despise the church of God" (11:22), to the loving ordering of life within the community where each member is honored, to an awareness that the crucified Jesus is also the exalted Lord and Judge, to a time of "grace in the midst of judgment and judgment in the midst of grace."

CHRIST'S DEATH AND THE PURITY OF THE COMMUNITY
(1 COR. 5:1-13)

One further text from 1 Corinthians warrants investigation in our consideration of the function of the death of Christ in relation to the people of God. Its importance lies in the fascinating way in which a matter of immorality is faced within the community—not moralistically or with self-righteousness, but so as to affirm the purity and holiness of the people of God.

In 5:1-13 a reported case of incest is mentioned, and directions are given for the appropriate disciplinary action to be taken by the community. The individual, who apparently is living with his stepmother, is to be excluded from the assembly in the hopes that he will repent and mend his ways.[41] Paul, absent from the community, announces not only that he is present in spirit but that "my judgment upon the man who did this thing is already given" (5:3, NEB).[42] The congregation, which hears this decision

---

40. Bornkamm, *Early Christian Experience,* 149, comments: "To discern the body, to esteem Christ's body in its particularity, means to understand that the body of Christ given for us and received in the sacrament unites the recipients in the 'body' of the congregation and makes them responsible for one another in love."

41. 1 Cor. 5:5 is a difficult verse to decipher. "Flesh" seems to signify not an evil substance within the physical body or the physical body itself, but the manner of life lived, the life in opposition to God's will. "To deliver to Satan" denotes excommunication. The purpose of the exclusion from the community is clearly remedial, not merely penal, "the repentance of the sinner (i.e., the destruction of the flesh) and God's approval of his life's orientation (spirit) at the Last Judgment" (Charles A. Talbert, *Reading Corinthians,* 16).

42. The translation of 5:3b-4 is complicated by the ambiguous location of the prepositional phrases in the sentence. For the various possibilities, see Hans

of Paul read in its midst and which has heretofore remained tolerantly (or even boastfully) passive about the case, is confronted in such a way that it can no longer remain silent.

The most striking feature of the passage, however, is the force of the argument directed not at the guilty individual but at the community. No moralizing about the individual's trangression appears in the text at all. As soon as the problem is stated (5:1), the congregation itself is addressed: "And you are arrogant! Ought you not rather to mourn?" (5:2). Then, having specified the disciplinary action to be taken (5:3-5), Paul again confronts the readers: "Your self-satisfaction ill becomes you. Have you never heard the saying, 'A little leaven leavens all the dough'?" (5:6, NEB). Modern readers are left wondering exactly why the initial readers might have exhibited arrogance and boasting with regard to this situation. Is the community openly rejoicing in the behavior of one of their number who in being freed from the strictures of the law is supposedly acting out his newly discovered liberty? Or is it a "live-and-let-live" toleration of his actions that masks their complacency and self-assurance, perhaps because in their enthusiasm they have grown indifferent to moral matters? In any case, they are told to cleanse out the old leaven (5:7) and to celebrate the festival "with the bread of sincerity and truth" (5:8).

Three reasons are given for this needed response of the community. First is the simple but practical truth of the matter, that the conduct of one can effect the life of the whole (5:6), and therefore the behavior of the one cannot be ignored. The clear implication is that the quality of life within the community, which matters greatly, cannot be assumed apart from the quality of life of the individual members. Church discipline is essential not only for the guilty party but also for the health of the Christian fellowship. Second, in purging the leaven "that you may be fresh dough," the community is being faithful to its true nature ("as you really are unleavened," 5:7). It denies its character as a people of the holy God when it remains passive regarding the sins of one of its number.

Conzelmann, *1 Corinthians: A Commentary on the First Epistle to the Corinthians,* trans. James W. Leitch, Hermeneia (Philadelphia: Fortress Press, 1975), 97.

Third, "Christ, our paschal lamb, has been sacrificed" (5:7). The shift from the imagery of leaven to the imagery of the sacrifical lamb complicates the analogy, but the point is clear. The death of Christ is a completed event, which makes the people of God truly "unleavened." Mention of it forces them to recall who in fact they really are and stimulates them to care about the purity of the community, about the life and well-being of each member.

The concluding paragraph of 1 Corinthians 5 clarifies the counsel contained in a previous letter, which apparently has been misunderstood by the readers (5:9-13). In making the clarification, Paul at the same time offers a profound reflection upon the purity and holiness of the community in relation to "this world." Christians are not to withdraw from associations with pagan society, with its immorality, greed, corruption, and idolatry. If they do so, they lose their contact with the world, which is so important to their missionary calling ("since then you would need to go out to the world," 5:10). They are not burdened with judging the world; that is God's business (5:13). Instead, while not becoming an isolated enclave, they are to exercise discipline within their own community, even to the point of excluding one whose actions violate the true nature of the fellowship.[43]

The purity of the Christian congregation is maintained not in separation but in involvement, but an involvement in which members of the community resist being conformed to the world. The text encourages their association with "immoral" people of the world but their disassociation from "immoral" people within the congregation. Why? Clearly the readers are those who have themselves left the world for the community whose purity and distinctiveness are found in the Lamb already sacrificed. When, however, they tolerate one of their number who acts like the world, they in reality forsake the identity that characterizes the people of God, cross again the boundary into the world, and in a sense reestablish their residence there. It behooves them, therefore, to be in practise who they in Christ truly are.[44]

43. See especially Paul S. Minear, "Christ and the Congregation: 1 Corinthians 5-6," *RevExp* 80 (1983): 341–50.
44. This paraenetic use of Christ's death appears also in 1 Cor. 6:19-20; 7:23; and Rom. 15:1-4 (where the citation of Ps. 69:10 links the text to the death of

CONCLUSION

SUMMARY

Having examined Galatians 3; 1 Cor. 11:17-34; and 5:1-13, we are in a position now to reflect on the nature of this communal self-understanding. At the heart of the identity of the people of God is the remembrance of Christ's death. Amid the crisis precipitated when gentiles begin to be a part of the early Christian community, Christ's death becomes *the* theological focal point for Paul's argument that converts are to be received into the fellowship without first receiving the Jewish rite of circumcision.[45] Christ in his death not only saves people from their sin; he also, in redeeming them from the curse of the law, tears down the wall that divides Jew from non-Jew, free person from slave, male from female. God's way is to unite in justifying and to justify in uniting. By finding its identity in the crucified Christ, the community of faith operates as one in which table fellowship between persons ethnically, socially, and sexually different becomes not only possible but characteristic of its life. People with differing histories and differing stories to tell belong together at the same meal.

This becomes heightened even further by 1 Cor. 11:17-34, where the Lord's Supper, the sacrament repeatedly observed in the community, results in a proclamation of the Lord's death. The people of God announce who they are by remembering. And yet the remembering becomes more than merely an anniversary, more than merely a recollection of a past event. In its proper practise it powerfully shapes the life of the community, calling into question social customs that reinforce rank and privilege at the expense of others. The Lord, whose death is remembered in the sacrament, exercises judgment, but in that judgment grace is displayed, since "we are disciplined so that we may not be condemned along with the world" (11:32). Partakers are called to a

---

Christ). See Gerhard Delling, *Das Kreuzestod Jesu in die urchristlichen Verkündigung* (Göttingen: Vandenhoeck & Ruprecht, 1972), 39–41.

45. It is interesting that the death of Christ (in distinction from the incarnation, resurrection, exaltation, and Parousia) dominates the logic of the argument within the letter to the Galatians, a letter dealing with the entrance of gentiles into the community. See Gal. 1:4; 2:20, 21; 3:1, 13, 27; 5:11, 24; 6:12, 14, 17.

new obedience, to a life appropriate to the new covenant. The bread and wine of the Lord's Supper indeed carry a numinous quality. In terms of the setting in the Corinthian letter, however, what is essential is not the transformation of the elements themselves, but the transformation of social relationships that participation in the sacrament demands. "We who are many are one body, for we all partake of the same loaf."[46]

As 1 Cor. 5:1-13 indicates, not only the liturgical and social life of the Christian community but also its discipline regarding moral matters is shaped by the recalling of the crucifixion. Because "Christ, our passover lamb, has been sacrificed," the congregation's true character can be termed "unleavened," and the Christian life is to be lived in "sincerity and truth." To be true to its character as the fellowship Christ has redeemed, the community must exercise appropriate discipline.

The Unity of the Church

What the former two of these texts point to in terms of the ongoing identity of the people of God is its unity, confessed in the creed as one of the traditional marks of the church. "I believe in *one* holy catholic and apostolic church." The texts, however, become instructive in understanding the source, the nature, and the challenge of such a unity.

First, the unity derives from Christ. The argument of Galatians hinges on the fact that there is but one gospel ("not that there is another gospel," 1:7), which consists in the message of Christ crucified. To demand circumcision for gentiles is to negate the very nature of the one gospel. The requirement of such a religious rite, which seems like a harmless addendum, turns out to be a gross contradiction. The unity of the community simply cannot derive from the Jewish (or American) affiliation of all its members, but from their being "in Christ Jesus." In terms of the Corinthian passage, the unity is first Christ's before it is the church's. Participation in the crucified body of Christ through the sacrament ("the same loaf," 10:17) unites participants in the

---

46. There is no mention of the Lord's Supper in the account of the meals at Antioch in Gal. 2:11-14; however, it may lurk behind Paul's rebuke of Peter.

one ecclesial body, which is the church. As Moltmann puts it, "the unity is an evangelical unity, not a legal one."[47] It does not emerge from a similarity in economic and social views, from a likeness in educational achievements, from a shared ethnic heritage. The unity is a "given" in Christ. There are various strategies Paul could take in the Corinthian letter to deal with the factionalism present when worshipers gather in assembly (11:18-19). What in fact he does is simply to recite the liturgy of the Lord's Supper, which in its dimensions of remembrance and proclamation powerfully calls the community to a new obedience, involving a new openness to one another. From a sociological point of view, one speaks of the sacrament as "a symbolic accomplishment of social integration."[48] From a theological point of view, one speaks of the open invitation to the liberating presence of the crucified Lord.[49]

Second, the texts point to the nature of the church's unity as basically one of mutual concern of members. The particular criticism Paul lays at the feet of the Corinthians is very instructive. The members who imbibe so freely at the community meal as to be drunk (11:21) are confronted not because their excessive imbibing might lead to shameful behavior, but because their greediness leaves some without enough to eat and drink, resulting in the embarrassment, humiliation, and exclusion of those who have nothing. "Are you so contemptuous of the church of God that you shame its poorer members?" (11:22, NEB). Disunity is exhibited in the lack of concern on the part of the congregational establishment for the less fortunate. Or to state the matter positively, unity is expressed in a form of partisanship in behalf of the poorer members, a partisanship in which social customs are disregarded in assuring both the dignity of the poor and the satisfaction of their real needs. The unity then does not "happen" when bureaucracies arrive at a common mind about organizational merger or when committees on doctrine agree on a statement about the nature of Christ's presence in the elements.

---

47. Jürgen Moltmann, *The Church in the Power of the Spirit: A Contribution to Messianic Ecclesiology,* trans. Margaret Kohl (London: SCM Press, 1977), 343.
48. Gerd Theissen, *The Social Setting,* 167.
49. Jürgen Moltmann, *The Church in the Power of the Spirit,* 244–46.

Important as these tasks may be, the nature of unity lies elsewhere, in the expressions of social and physical as well as spiritual care for one another.

Another instance of Paul's urging this sort of unity based on concern for others comes in connection with the issue of whether to eat food previously offered to idols. The "strong" member is challenged to forego the right to eat the food so as not to injure the conscience of the "weak" member, who on two occasions is characterized as "the brother for whom Christ died" (1 Cor. 8:11; Rom. 14:15). The death of Christ gives to each member a dignity and a distinction that must be honored above one's own prerogatives. Unity has to do with this mutual respect.

Third, the texts acknowledge that unity remains a challenge. While the church's oneness lies in Christ's activity, his unifying activity has to express itself concretely in the life of the church. The fact that Paul condemns Peter at Antioch because he fails to demonstrate a mutual respect for gentiles for whom Christ died, the fact that opponents in the Galatian congregations are confronted because they seek to gather the community around the rite of circumcision and not the gospel, and the fact that the Corinthian congregation allows social customs to disrupt the fellowship of its community meals reveal the brokenness of the church. The exposure in each case becomes the challenge to reform, to change, to make actual and visible the mutual care given in the unity of Christ. The creed's confession of "the one church" becomes then a statement of action as well as a statement of faith.[50] It commits the confessors to a style of life in which unity is sought as well as confessed, because it characterizes the people of God.

The Holiness of the Church

The third of the texts considered in this chapter (1 Cor. 5:1-13) points to another mark of the church affirmed in the creed—its holiness. Again, as with the mark of unity, the text is instructive in clarifying the source, the nature, and the challenge of holiness. First, it derives from Christ himself, the paschal sacrifice, in whose holiness the church is made holy. Neither the word "holy"

---

50. So Moltmann, *The Church in the Power of the Spirit,* 339–40.

nor any of its cognates appear in 1 Corinthians 5, and yet the readers will grasp the chapter's meaning in terms of what they have already read about themselves in the letter and what they will yet read. In the epistolary prescript they are addressed as "those sanctified [made holy] in Christ Jesus, called to be saints [holy ones]" (1:2), and when their calling is spelled out in the first chapter, they are reminded that their life in Christ derives from God, who made Christ "our wisdom, our righteousness and sanctification [holiness] and redemption" (1:30). Later, in contrast to the unrighteousness in the world, they are told, "but you were washed, you were sanctified [made holy], you were justified in the name of the Lord Jesus Christ and in the Spirit of our God" (6:11). As Conzelmann rightly comments, "holiness is not the goal of conduct, but its presupposition."[51]

Second, the nature of holiness has to do with the integrity of the community's life. Strikingly, the church does not demonstrate its holiness by moral perfection, by being more righteous than the sinful world around, by separation from every taint of evil. If that were the case, then Paul would have encouraged the Corinthian readers not to associate with immoral types in the world lest the world contaminate them. As a matter of fact, he assumes they will rub elbows and share life with all sorts of people (1 Cor. 5:9-10).

The imperatives in 1 Corinthians 5 are not addressed first and foremost to the individual guilty of incest, but to the community indifferent to (or perhaps even proud of) one of its number who is in the process of destroying himself. What violates its holiness is the manifestation of "arrogance" and "boasting" in the presence of a practise "not found even among the pagans" (5:1):

> This means for the church as a whole that the *communio peccatorum* it acknowledges in the confession of guilt is its past, and the *communio sanctorum* that it believes in the forgiveness of sin is its future. It testifies to the fellowship of justified sinners, which acknowledges both, in the perpetual conversion from that past to this future. In this sense the holy church is the converting church of the new beginnings. It is *ecclesia reformata et semper reformanda* . . . . In the context of the fellowship of sinners, the sanctification of

---

51. Conzelmann, *1 Corinthians,* 98.

the church lies in its justification. In the context of the coming kingdom of glory its sanctification lies in its call to service, to suffering, and to poverty.[52]

Two nouns in the Corinthian text give further definition to this holiness. The festival (now metaphorical for the Christian life) is to be celebrated with the unleavened bread, "which is sincerity and truth" (5:8, NEB). The Greek word translated as "sincerity" (εἰλικρινεία) occurs two other times in the Pauline letters, both instances instructive as to its signification. In 2 Cor. 1:12 Paul declares that he has conducted himself "with candor and sincerity befitting God," meaning by that a behavior that will be judged as genuine "on the day of the Lord Jesus."[53] In 2 Cor. 2:17 "people of sincerity" are contrasted with those who are huckstering the word of God, who treat it as cheap merchandise to be peddled from the bargain counter. In both contexts, the word depicts the quality of honesty, integrity, freedom from hypocrisy, the coincidence of word and deed. Similarly, the word "truth," more widely employed in the Pauline letters, denotes truthfulness and dependability. The opposite of "sincerity and truth" is the pretense of posing as different from who one really is. The church's holiness, given in Christ, then consists in its acknowledgment of its sinfulness and of its forgiveness, in its refusal to claim a righteousness as its own that it has only as a gift, in its persistent honesty about itself.

Finally, the situation described in 1 Corinthians 5 demonstrates the need for reform, the *challenge* of holiness. Paul's rhetorical style in vv. 3-5 brings the readers face to face with the demand for action. They must either confirm or reject the judgment Paul has already pronounced. As is, the individual is engaged in a self-destructive relationship. To exclude him from the fellowship is to open the door to a possible change in the relationship. Holiness, therefore, does not consist in the church's passive acceptance of its sinfulness and forgiveness, but entails a move to reformation, a "perpetual conversion." Its faith becomes trustworthy in its continually being conformed to the will of God.

52. Moltmann, *The Church in the Power of the Spirit,* 354–55.
53. Victor Paul Furnish, *II Corinthians,* AB (Garden City, N.Y.: Doubleday, 1984), 159.

CHAPTER 5

Jesus' Death
and the Christian Life

In the previous chapter we examined three passages in which mention of Jesus' death figures prominently in the Pauline understanding of the people of God. When Paul deals with the relationship between Jews and gentiles in the Galatian congregations, when he confronts the disturbing social customs practised at the Corinthians' observance of the Lord's Supper, and when he challenges the Corinthians' failure to exercise appropriate church discipline in connection with an obvious instance of immorality, he returns to the foundational story of the community, to the statement of the death of Jesus. That death characterizes the community, sets it apart as a distinctive people, and shapes its memory. Whenever its members gather to celebrate the sacrament that repeatedly nurtures its corporate life, they "proclaim the Lord's death."

There is another category of texts in the Pauline letters that operates in much the same fashion as these three we have just examined. It is a group of autobiographical passages, in which the apostle describes a dimension of his own life or ministry and does so precisely in connection with Jesus' death. Using the first-person pronoun, he interprets his own experiences as a preacher of the gospel in light of the very gospel he preaches. There is even a sense in which he becomes the embodiment of the gospel itself. "The 'little story' of Paul's life finds meaning by being related to the 'big story' of which the organizing center is Christ."[1] The

---

1. William Beardslee points to the distinctive way in which Paul's story is

passages provide a rather clear picture of the apostle's understanding of who he is, his identity as a Christian.

On the one hand, the experiences Paul describes are of course
his own. In their peculiarities they remain unique to him as the
apostle to the gentiles. When, for example, he relates the persecutions he received and the hardships he endured, these experiences were known in the various congregations as being special to
Paul since opponents seem on occasion to use the information as
evidence against Paul. And yet we shall take the line (and it has to
be argued in terms of the particulars of each passage) that these
autobiographical reflections are not to be understood merely as
the exclusive experiences of one unusual Christian or only as raw
data for constructing a biography of Paul. Instead, the experiences are reported and function as a paradigm, to illustrate how
the preaching of the crucified Christ is to work itself out in the life
and service of every "ordinary" Christian. In this sense, then,
these passages express, as clearly as the communal passages dealt
with in the previous chapter, what it means to be a Christian,
how the gospel is embodied in the lives of believers.[2] We shall
give special attention to four texts: Gal. 6:11-18; 2 Cor. 4:7-15;
Phil. 3:2-11; and 2 Cor. 13:1-4.[3]

subordinated to the story of Christ.

> The story which orients Paul's life, the story of Christ, is one which
> continually challenges the continuity of Paul's own life-story, by present-
> ing him with the challenge of power-in-weakness through the symbol of
> the cross. We should also note that in contrast to many modern tellers of
> their own story, Paul's ordering myth is not a personal one, but a
> universal story; his telling about himself is a way, not of inviting others to
> do their own thing, but of inviting his hearers to share this universal
> story, the story of Christ.

William A. Beardslee, "Narrative Form in the New Testament and Process
Theology," *Encounter* 36 (1975): 306–7; cited by Richard B. Hays, *The Faith
of Jesus Christ: An Investigation of the Narrative Substructure of Galatians
3:1—4:11,* SBLDS 56 (Chico, Calif.: Scholars Press, 1982), 12–13.

2. The verb "embody" is used deliberately because in two of the texts to be
considered Paul writes of the evidence of the gospel in his "body" (2 Cor. 4:10;
Gal. 6:17).

3. It could be argued that 2 Cor. 13:1-4 should not be called "autobiographical," since it provides no extensive account of Paul's personal history.
We, however, are treating the passage in connection with 2 Cor. 11:23—12:13,
the so-called fool's speech.

BOASTING IN THE CROSS (GAL. 6:11-18)

The conclusion to the Letter to the Galatians looms as an important text for our consideration for three reasons. First, it centers on the continuing meaning that Jesus' death has in the life of the apostle. Second, it is a passage in which Paul shows no hesitancy in identifying himself with God's new creation and, somewhat daringly, pits himself against his opponents. It is the sort of role that makes some commentators squirm, as they wonder whether Paul claims too much for himself.[4] And yet, as in few other places, readers are given a clear indication of Paul's apostolic identity, stated in theological language. Third, the passage takes on even greater significance when we recognize that it serves as the interpretive clue for a proper reading of the entire Epistle to the Galatians, an epistle that consists of a passionate statement of the decisive role of the gospel.[5] In Galatians sharp lines are drawn and readers are confronted with dramatic eitheror's, in a series of what J. Louis Martyn calls "apocalyptic antinomies."[6] To come to grips with the conclusion is to come to grips with the heart of the entire letter.

The passage begins with an introductory statement, in which

---

4. John Bligh, *Galatians: A Discussion of Paul's Epistle* (London: St. Paul's Publications, 1969), 492–93, says this passage exposes "a less attractive side of St. Paul's personality." Paul "describes himself as 'crucified to the world' with a note of self-approval, enhanced (unconsciously, no doubt) by the contrast he sees with others."

5. Hans Dieter Betz, *Galatians: A Commentary on Paul's Letter to the Churches in Galatia,* Hermeneia (Philadelphia: Fortress Press, 1979), 313, says: "Seen as a rhetorical feature, the *peroratio* becomes most important for the interpretation of Galatians. It contains the interpretive clues to the understanding of Paul's major concerns in the letter as a whole and should be employed as the hermeneutical key to the intentions of the Apostle." Betz analyzes 6:11-18 in terms of its rhetorical functions (as outlined primarily by Quintilian and Cicero): to recapitulate briefly the pertinent arguments of the case and to make a final appeal of an emotional nature to the audience. The latter involves both the arousing of hostility against the opposition and the arousing of pity for the speaker. See also Steven J. Kraftchick, "Ethos and Pathos Appeals in Galatians Five and Six: A Rhetorical Analysis," Ph.D. dissertation, Emory University, 1985, 260–65. As Kraftchick points out, an analysis of the passage in terms of its *ethos* and *pathos* appeals does not preclude consideration of its *logos* appeal, its cognitive character.

6. J. Louis Martyn, "Apocalyptic Antinomies in Paul's Letter to the Galatians," *NTS* 31 (1985): 410–24.

Paul's "large letters" (6:11) call attention to what he has to say.[7] The omission of conventional forms like the holy kiss, extended greetings, closing exhortations, and a doxology adds further force to the content of the epilogue. The structure of the remainder of the conclusion is distinguished by the pronounced element of contrast.[8] The adversaries described in vv. 12-13 are sharply opposed by Paul himself (vv. 14-17).[9] Specifically, they compel the gentiles to be circumcised (v. 12), while for Paul neither circumcision nor uncircumcision is of any worth (v. 15). They avoid persecution for the cross of Christ (v. 12); Paul bears in his body "the marks of Jesus" (v. 17). They aim at boasting "in your flesh" (v. 13), while Paul boasts only "in the cross of our Lord Jesus Christ" (v. 14). Fundamental to each of these contrasts is the opposition of "world" (v. 14) and "new creation" (v. 15), a contrast that interprets all the others.[10] Contrasts in the passage are set out in Table 1.

Table 1
Contrasts in Gal. 6:12-17

OPPONENTS	*PAUL*
compel you to be circumcised (v. 12)	circumcision and uncircumcision do not matter (v. 15)
avoid persecution for the cross (v. 12)	bears the marks of Jesus (v. 17)
boasts in your flesh (v. 13)	boasts in the cross of Christ alone (v. 14)
(seek to make a good showing in the flesh, v. 12)	
↑	↑
WORLD (v. 14)	NEW CREATION (v. 15)

7. E. D. Burton, *A Critical and Exegetical Commentary on the Epistle to the Galatians,* ICC (Edinburgh: T. & T. Clark, 1921), 348, compares "the large letters" to the modern practice of bold-faced type.

8. Aristotle particularly recommends this way of summing up a speech. See *The "Art" of Rhetoric,* III, 19, 6.

9. Note the prominent location of ἐμοί in 6:14 and the first-person pronoun used three times in 6:17.

10. This passage is complicated by several subcontrasts, functioning almost like subplots within a larger plot. For example, in order to expose their

While our primary interest lies in the statements Paul makes about himself, we must consider these statements in the context of what is said about the opponents. Four descriptive judgments are made about them: they wish to make a good showing in the flesh; they demand circumcision in order to avoid persecution for the cross of Christ; they do not themselves keep the law; and they want gentile Christians to be circumcised in order to "boast" about it. The judgments have to be taken seriously.

Unfortunately commentators have occasionally moved in one of two directions, both of which lessen the force of the argument. Some take the statements as indictments based simply on the insincerity of the opponents. The opponents are described as those who want "to make a pretentious display of their religion in outward ordinances"[11] or as those who have "a desire for social prestige" and enjoy boasting in Jerusalem of their conquests.[12] Other interpreters, however, warn about a mixture of objective facts and subjective opinions in the statements. For example, Betz, agreeing that Paul denounces the opponents "as morally inferior and despicable," interprets this in terms of classical rhetoric as an example of *indignatio* (a component of the conclusion that seeks to arouse great hostility against the opposition). He adds, "This looks very much like a caricature, and we must be cautious in assuming that this is really what the opponents have in mind."[13]

---

inconsistency the opponents are contrasted with themselves: they make circumcision a necessity but do not themselves keep the law (6:12-13). In 6:15 circumcision and uncircumcision are set in opposition to (ἀλλά) "new creation." The intertwining contrasts make for an intricate but not disorderly passage. Johannes Weiss long ago noted about Paul that "antithesis is perhaps the most distinctive characteristic of his style. We may say, perhaps with some exaggeration, that all his speaking and thinking has an antithetical rhythm about it." Weiss, however, attributed it not to a literary influence, but to Paul's own personality and experience. See *The History of Primitive Christianity,* trans. F. C. Grant (London: Macmillan, 1937), 1:411–14.

11. J. B. Lightfoot, *St. Paul's Epistle to the Galatians* (New York: Macmillan, 1890), 221.

12. J. Bligh, *Galatians,* 491.

13. Betz, *Galatians,* 314. George Kennedy, *New Testament Interpretation Through Rhetorical Criticism* (Chapel Hill: University of North Carolina Press, 1984), 146, feels that Betz "consistently identifies rhetoric with deceit," making Paul's disclaimers about rhetoric in 1 Thessalonians and 1 and 2 Corinthians hypocritical. Such an identification, according to Kennedy, "seems unneces-

Both positions, however, soften the primary force of the contrast drawn between the opponents and Paul, and lead modern readers to second-guess the text. In the case of the former, the antithesis is reduced to one of insincerity versus sincerity, with the result that the opponents can too readily be dismissed on the basis of selfish and hypocritical motives. In the case of the latter, the contrast is undermined if in fact the statements about the opponents represent *merely* a rhetorical tactic on Paul's part and an unwarranted caricature of their real position. It just may be that v. 12 functioned with the initial readers to arouse hostility towards the opponents, though it is hard to be certain about that since it is not at all clear what "good show in the flesh" implied: A good show with whom? To what end? On what standard of judgment? Whose flesh? The suggestion that Paul's charge is only strategical, an unwarranted caricature of the opponents, obscures the fact that the charge is significant theologically. To put the matter another way, statements in a text may serve rhetorically as *ethos* or *pathos*, but this does not preclude their force also as *logos*. The opponents, to be sure, would not have agreed with Paul's judgments, but their disagreement need not imply that the judgments are to be discounted or even taken with a grain of salt. The entire letter represents only one side of the issue—Paul's side. The point is that the comparison between the opponents and Paul, as reflected in the text, exposes *theological* differences that are profound and far-reaching.

It is when we look at the other side of the contrast, at what Paul says about himself, that we discover the significant dissimilarity in the positions. The dissimilarity is attributed to the cross of Christ, shorthand for the message of the gospel at whose center is the declaration of the crucified Christ. Several features of the passage warrant clarification as we seek to discover how the cross becomes the watershed between Paul and the opponents. First is the matter of persecution. The adversaries advocate circumci-

---

sary." In a later article, Betz addresses the question in the Pauline letters of a rhetoric that corresponds positively to the gospel and one that clashes with the gospel. See H. D. Betz, "The Problem of Rhetoric and Theology according to the Apostle Paul," in *L'Apôtre: Personnalité, Style et Conception du Ministère,* ed. A. Vanhoye (Louvain: University Press, 1986), 16–48.

sion "that they may not be persecuted because of the cross of Christ" (6:12).[14] It is interesting that Paul does not tell the reader more about this potential persecution—who initiates it, what sort of persecution it is, and in what historical context. Perhaps the Galatian readers already know; it may be information that writer and initial readers share. In any case, what seems more important in the text is its cause, not its historical source and circumstances. The same phenomenon occurs in 5:11, the other occasion in this letter where the motifs of circumcision, persecution, and cross are drawn together. "But if I still preach circumcision, why am I still persecuted? Then the offensiveness of the cross would be removed." Again, modern readers are left with unanswered questions about the historical parameters of the persecution, since Paul responds to the rhetorical question with a theological answer. The advocacy of circumcision would leave him unpersecuted, but then the cross would be devoid of its provocation. The two texts (6:12 and 5:11) agree that the preaching and advocacy of the cross issue in conflict and persecution and that the preaching and advocacy of circumcision function as a protection against conflict and persecution.[15]

In this context 6:17 is to be seen as a part of the major contrast of the passage.[16] "The marks of Jesus" that Paul bears in his body stand in sharp antithesis to the opponents who avoid persecution. The text, again, is remarkably terse; we are told nothing of the source or occasion when he received these marks. That they are designated as "the marks *of Jesus*" and serve as the basis for

14. Nearly all commentators agree that τῷ σταυρῷ in 6:12 is a dative of cause. See BDF, par. 196; Burton, *Galatians,* 350; Heinrich Schlier, *Der Brief an die Galater,* KEK (Göttingen: Vandenhoeck & Ruprecht, 1951), 207; Franz Mussner, *Der Galaterbrief,* HTK (Freiburg: Herder, 1974), 412; Betz, *Galatians,* 315.

15. This is developed by Hans Weder, *Das Kreuz Jesu bei Paulus: Ein Versuch über den Geschichtsbezug des christlichen Glaubens nachzudenken* (Göttingen: Vandenhoeck & Ruprecht, 1981), 202–5.

16. John S. Pobee, *Persecution and Martyrdom in the Theology of Paul,* JSNTSS 6 (Sheffield: JSOT Press, 1985), 94, argues that 6:17-18 should be taken as a separate paragraph and that "the marks of Jesus" play no part in relation to 6:12-16. It is true that the passage may be divided into two paragraphs, but it is impossible to ignore the connection between "the marks" and the previous material. They function not primarily in contrast to circumcision (though that is by no means excluded) but to the "mark-less" opponents.

the concluding charge ("let no one continue to hassle me") makes it likely that they signify the wounds Paul received in his missionary activities (cf. 2 Cor. 1:8-9; 4:8-11; 6:4-10).[17] The phrase functions here both as a validation of the message of the cross and, in rhetorical terms, as *ethos,* establishing the credibility of the speaker. Paul embodies the gospel and is to be accepted as a trusted advocate.

Second, the verb "boast" in 6:13-14 becomes another literary vehicle that sharpens the contrast between the opponents and Paul. While they "desire to have you circumcised that they may boast in your flesh," Paul vows never to boast, "except in the cross of our Lord Jesus Christ." The strong language of negation gives Paul's statement about himself enormous force ($\mu\dot{\eta}$ $\gamma\acute{\epsilon}\nu o\iota\tau o$ $\kappa\alpha\upsilon\chi\hat{\alpha}\sigma\theta\alpha\iota$ $\epsilon\dot{\iota}$ $\mu\acute{\eta}$). The NEB properly renders it not as a descriptive statement (as if Paul were boasting about not boasting in anything but the cross), but as an oath: "But God forbid that I should boast of anything but the cross."

"Boasting" (whether as a verb or a substantive) is a favorite Pauline theme, a flexible one used to great advantage in attacking those who rely on the law (e.g., Rom. 2:17, 23), but also employed to describe Paul's own commitments (e.g., Rom. 5:2, 11). When used in polemical contexts, such as this one, it often takes on a highly ironical tone. Opponents, very logically it seems, boast in their accomplishments, but Paul boasts in his weaknesses (cf. 2 Cor. 11:30; 12:5, 9). The irony introduces a different perspective to boasting, which the reader reconstructs (often from the context)—namely, that human weaknesses become the occasion for God's power to be operative. So in Gal. 6:14 Paul boasts in the scandalous and provocative cross. The reader is left to recognize, beyond the disreputable and offensive dimensions of the crucifixion, its positive and transforming character (e.g., its power to liberate people from the curse of the law, 3:13).

17. For a survey of the various treatments of "the marks of Jesus" and a critique of the options, see Erhardt Güttgemanns, *Der leidende Apostel und sein Herr: Studien zur paulinischen Christologie* (Göttingen: Vandenhoeck & Ruprecht, 1966), 126–35; Udo Borse, "Die Wundermale und der Todesbescheid," *BiblZeit* 14 (1970): 88–111; and A. T. Hanson, *The Paradox of the Cross in the Thought of St. Paul,* JSNTSS 17 (Sheffield: JSOT Press, 1987), 83–86.

Third, the boasting is further illumined by a statement of three crucifixions—Christ's, the world's, and Paul's.[18] The latter two are part of and yet secondary to the former. The cross of Christ entails the crucifixion of the world with respect to Paul, and Paul with respect to the world. Two details in the text help to cast these crucifixions into a clear light. The verb "has been crucified" (ἐσταύρωται) appears in the perfect tense, in line with a similar perfect tense in 2:20, indicating an action in past time that continues to effect the present. What emerges with this reference to a threefold crucifixion, then, is not its focus in baptism (as, e. g., in Rom. 6:3-4), but its continuous shaping of the life of the apostle. The crucifixion of Christ remains not merely a part of Paul's memory to which he returns now and again, but creates a new and persisting situation whereby Paul's allegiance is radically changed, his identity revamped.[19] Then, the christological designation, "our Lord Jesus Christ," is striking: the title "Lord" appears only three other times in Galatians, twice in liturgical formulas (1:3; 6:18) and once in what seems to be a title for James, "the brother of the Lord" (1:19).[20] Its use in 6:14 signals that the death of Christ and participation in it involve a change of lordship. To share in the death is not to be a party to a paper transaction, as it were, but to live in the "new creation," where the "Lord" is Jesus Christ.

In saying this, one must guard against the reduction of these derived crucifixions to the private perspective of a single believer, as if they were only a matter of subjective experience, merely an individual's change of attitude.[21] They involve a

18. Paul Minear, *To Die and To Live: Christ's Resurrection and Christian Vocation* (New York: Seabury, 1977), 66–88; and idem, "The Crucified World: The Enigma of Galatians 6:14," in *Theologia Crucis—Signum Crucis: Festschrift für Erich Dinkler,* ed. Carl Andresen and Gunther Klein (Tübingen: J. C. B. Mohr [Siebeck], 1979), 395–407.

19. This is sharply put in Gal. 2:19-20, where the aorist tense ("I died to the law") is supplemented with a perfect tense ("I have been crucified with Christ"), implying that the present life with God ("that I might live to God") is lived in the light of the cross. The "Christ who lives in me" is the Christ with whom "I have been crucified."

20. Betz, *Galatians,* 78 (206n, 209n).

21. Minear rightly notes that the ἐμοί in 6:14b cannot be construed as signifying "in my view of things." The dative has the same force as with κόσμῳ, which could hardly signify "in the world's view of things." What the text says

change that effects the ordering of the relationship between God and humans, something *extra nos,* which in Paul's case becomes also *pro me.* As Tannehill comments:

> The world has a structure which determines the life of each individual, and so human life as a whole, and man can only escape from this through an event which breaks into the all-encompassing world of sin and opens the possibility of a new existence in a new world. It is to such an eschatological event that Paul is referring when he speaks of the crucifixion of the world.[22]

Fourth, what is to be made of the contrasting terms "world" and "new creation"? Lexicons offer a whole range of possible meanings for κόσμος ("world"), but the context itself provides our best clue. "World" is that realm where the distinctions of circumcision and uncircumcision matter a great deal, where people boast in the flesh, where the avoidance of persecution is a high priority, where the cross of Christ is misunderstood. It is the "world" at odds with God and God's grace. It is "the present evil age" under "the weak and beggarly elemental spirits" (4:10), from which the self-giving Christ has brought deliverance (1:4; 2:20). This world has been and remains crucified. All it denotes can now be labeled impotent, anachronistic, and worthless.

Again, there is a strong element of irony in Paul's language. To choose "world" as a term for the advocacy of a religious practice like circumcision (not to mention the use of "flesh" in 3:3; 6:12, 13) is, as Minear points out, to use a boomerang. Both "world" and "flesh" would have been taken pejoratively by the opponents, realities against which they are unalterably opposed; and yet here the terms come back at them with a vengeance, a parody at the heart of their religion.[23]

If "world" designates the opponents' position, then "new creation" is its antithesis. The parallel argues strongly in favor of the

is that "the world's authority over me has been terminated, just as my loyalty to it has been terminated." See Paul Minear, *To Die and To Live,* 78. Stuhlmacher makes a similar case with regard to "new creation." See Peter Stuhlmacher, "Erwägungen zum ontologischen Charakter der καινὴ κτίσις," *EvTh* 27 (1967): 1–35.

22. Robert C. Tannehill, *Dying and Rising with Christ,* BZNW 32 (Berlin: Alfred Töpelmann, 1967), 64.

23. Paul Minear, "The Crucified World," 403.

translation "new creation" for καινή κτίσις and not "new crea-
ture."[24] What is affirmed is not merely the renewal of the individual, but the presence of a new world. The cross with its two
derived crucifixions has brought the end of the "world" and the
advent of a completely new age.

But what is the character of this "new creation"? Are there
clues in the letter or elsewhere in the Pauline letters that give the
phrase further clarification? Three related passages provide help.
First, Paul uses the phrase one other time. "When anyone is in
Christ, there is a new creation" (2 Cor. 5:17). The context, as we
noted earlier, describes the reconciliation accomplished by God
in Christ, in which "the human point of view" is set aside (5:16)
and the world's transgressions are discounted. For Paul no longer
does alienation mark the human community. "We are convinced
that one has died for all; therefore all have died" (5:14). To be
sure, not "all" know that God has acted so mercifully in their
behalf, and that is precisely why the readers are urged to accept
their role as ambassadors, declaring the message of reconciliation. The "new creation," then, encompasses a reconciled and
reconciling community.

Second, within Galatians there is one likely allusion to creation, which in turn helps us to interpret the "new creation." In
3:28, in what we have noted is a likely baptismal formula, an
otherwise smooth parallelism is broken in the third of three pairs
(not always evident in English translations). "There is neither
Jew nor Greek, there is neither slave nor free, there is no 'male
and female.'" The only satisfactory explanation for a shift from
the conjunction οὐδέ in the former two expressions to καί in the
third expression is that "male and female" (ἄρσεν καὶ θῆλυ) reflects the LXX of Gen. 1:27.[25] Humanity is created as "male and

---

24. It is misleading to designate a precise source for this term and from the
source to arrive at a translation. Stuhlmacher, "Erwägungen zum ontologischen
Charakter der καινὴ κτίσις," 4, though noting its Jewish heritage, calls it a
technical term for which Paul himself is responsible. Bruce Chilton, "Galatians
6:15: A Call to Freedom," *ExT* 89 (1978): 311–13, warns against tracing its
genetic origins in rabbinic literature since most of the citations come from a
time later than Paul.

25. Nils A. Dahl, *Studies in Paul* (Minneapolis: Augsburg, 1977), 133;
Elisabeth Schüssler Fiorenza, *In Memory of Her: A Feminist Reconstruction of
Christian Origins* (London: SCM Press, 1983), 211.

female," but now in baptism, in the putting on of Christ—that is, in the new creation—such social distinctions are eliminated. What is now being affirmed is an "egalitarian ethos of 'oneness in Christ.'"[26]

Third, in Gal. 5:6 we meet substantially the same formula found in 6:15, that "neither circumcision nor uncircumcision matters," but the formula is now contrasted not with "new creation" but with "faith working through love." It appears at the conclusion of a paragraph that has argued the disastrous nature of the message of circumcision. In contrast to the obligation "to do the whole law" (implied by circumcision), Paul advocates a different style of obedience. Presumably the two verses (5:6 and 6:15) inform each other, suggesting that the dynamic of the "new creation" is an active faith that reaches out in acts of mercy toward the neighbor.[27]

The three passages present us with a picture of the "new creation" as an eschatological reality, a community reconciled to God and to one another, in which the customary social distinctions are not observed and the dynamic of faithful love is operative. It is not reading too much into the context to recognize these features also in Gal. 6:15. The phrase "circumcision and uncircumcision" denotes the rite of initiation to the Jewish community and the lack of it, but it also connotes the results of the rite (and lack of it)—that is, Jews and gentiles (cf. 2:7-9). Thus 6:15 in a sense encapsulates the major thesis of the letter. While distinctions such as Jew and gentile, slave and free, male and female are determinative in the "world," they have no legitimation in the "new creation." Martyn writes:

> Perhaps in this final paragraph Paul is telling the Galatians that the whole of his epistle is not about the better of two mystagogues, or even about the better of two ways, and certainly not about the future of Judaism. He is saying rather that the letter is about the death of one world and the advent of another. With regard to the former, the death of the cosmos, perhaps Paul is telling the Gala-

---

26. Elisabeth Schüssler Fiorenza, *In Memory of Her,* 218.
27. The parallel in 1 Cor. 7:19 is a highly paradoxical statement where "keeping the commandments" is set over against "circumcision."

tians that one knows the old world to have died, because one knows that its fundamental structures are gone, that those fundamental structures of the cosmos were certain identifiable pairs, and that, given the situation among their congregations in Galatia, the pair of opposites whose departure calls for emphasis is that of circumcision and uncircumcision.[28]

Our treatment of 6:11-18 has highlighted its construction as a comparison between the opponents of Paul and Paul himself. Before we leave the passage, we need to note that its function is clearly to confront readers with a choice. The indicative nature of the contrast carries an implied imperative. As Minear has noted in connection with 6:14, the three crucifixions do not apply to every one of Paul's readers. At least, some have not recognized the two derived crucifixions. The verse (and in fact the whole section) needs to be read in terms of its intent to persuade. Readers are faced with the need to acknowledge not only Christ's death, but the world's death to them and their death to the world.[29] The daring use of the first-person singular, then, does not function to set the author apart from the readers as one who has had an extraordinary and unrepeatable experience. Rather, his experience illustrates the power and scope of the gospel. He is an example of the new creation precisely in the sense that to live in the new creation means to be crucified to the world and the world to him, to bear in his body "the marks of Jesus."[30]

Two features of 6:11-18 necessitate special comment, particularly as we move to other texts in the letters where Paul's experience is interpreted in light of the cross. First, while the decision

---

28. J. Louis Martyn, "Apocalyptic Antinomies," 414.

29. Paul Minear, "The Crucified World," 396–97.

30. Beverly R. Gaventa, "Galatians 1 and 2: Autobiography as Paradigm," *NovTest* 28 (1986): 309–26, taking some cues from the work of John H. Schütz (*Paul and the Anatomy of Apostolic Authority,* SNTSMS 26 [Cambridge: Cambridge University Press, 1975], 114–58), has analyzed the autobiographical character of Galatians 1 and 2 and concluded that these chapters function, somewhat indirectly, as a paradigm of the singularity of the gospel. Paul presents his own "biography of reversal" to document the revolutionary element of grace, confirmed by the churches of Judea, who hear "that the one who persecuted us now preaches the faith which once he tried to destroy" (1:23). The prominence of Paul in the contrasts of 6:11-18 is to be understood in the same way.

facing the readers is a clean either-or, it is not a choice between religion and irreligion, between morality and immorality, between piety and impiety. These categories often loom large in modern discussions about the difference between church and world, especially if one wishes to document the differences with quantifiable measures of religious activity. ("How many times have you been to church in the last year?" "How many times a week do you pray?" "What is the size of your financial contribution to the church?") The options with Paul, however, are different: an obsolete and powerless world or a new creation? circumcision or the cross of Christ? protection against persecution or an openness to afflictions and hardships? The issue revolves around the cross as the exclusive norm of Christian life and thought, around the singularity of the gospel of grace, around freedom as a cherished gift to which believers are called—not around religion, morality, and piety.

Second, the mention of persecution introduces a disturbing theme for most North American Christians, especially when it appears as prominently as it does in the options Paul poses. While Galatians cannot be called "persecution literature" (as, e.g., the Book of Revelation), nevertheless, the language is unsettling. One gets the impression from the text that the life of the new creation is open to such sharp conflict that inevitably its citizens are left vulnerable to abuse (see also 4:29; 5:11) and thus should not be surprised at suffering. There is a way to avoid persecution (6:12), but to follow this way is to be severed from Christ (5:4). If 6:11-18 is to be understood in a paradigmatic fashion, what is one to do with the words regarding persecution? Does this signify that persecution is of the essence of the Christian life? How integral is suffering to the experience of "boasting" in the cross of Christ?

These are important questions, requiring hermeneutical as well as exegetical reflection. Before attempting answers, we need to consider three other places where Paul reflects on his own experience in light of the cross. They provide further help in our quest to understand how Jesus' death shapes the lives of Christians.

ALWAYS CARRYING IN THE BODY THE DEATH OF JESUS (2 COR. 4:7-15)

At several places in his letters Paul recounts for readers a series of afflictions he has undergone in his missionary activities. The enumeration sometimes occurs as a simple list (2 Cor. 11:23-29; 12:10; Rom. 8:35); sometimes in the form of comparisons or antitheses (1 Cor. 4:9-13; 2 Cor. 4:8-9); and at least in one case, as a combination of a simple list and a set of antitheses (2 Cor. 6:4-10).[31] Each recounting has its own function in the particular context in which it occurs and thereby creates its own rhetorical effect. We turn now to a passage containing one of these catalogues of Pauline hardships (2 Cor. 4:7-15), a passage of special interest to our investigation because it brings the list of hardships in close relation to the death of Jesus and provides us with another picture of Paul's identity as "minister of a new covenant" (3:6).

From as early as 2:14 the Letter of 2 Corinthians focuses on Paul's ministry. Though the context is clearly not such a hostile one as is encountered in 2 Corinthians 10–13, where the author's frustration with and indignation at what is occurring among the readers are readily visible, nevertheless certain clues in the text of 2 Corinthians 1–9 reveal Paul's sensitivity to rivals in Corinth with whom he disagrees.[32] In a "guardedly optimistic mood,"[33] he expresses his apostolic commission, partly at least in response to the stance of the rivals. His broader intention, however, is not polemical, but an effort to commend the visit to Corinth of Titus, who has brought good news from a previous visit and who is now leading a deputation to see to the collection.[34]

31. For an extensive consideration of the literary and cultural background of the lists, see Robert Hodgson, "Paul the Apostle and First Century Tribulation Lists," *ZNW* 74 (1983): 59–80. Hodgson surveys the recent literature and argues that the Pauline lists represent a literary convention of the first century far more widespread than previously noted. See also John T. Fitzgerald, *Cracks in an Earthen Vessel: An Examination of the Catalogues of Hardships in the Corinthian Correspondence,* SBLDS (Atlanta: Scholars Press, 1988).

32. See 2 Cor. 2:17; 3:1-2; 4:2; 5:12.

33. V. P. Furnish, *II Corinthians,* AB (Garden City, N.Y.: Doubleday, 1984), 44.

34. See 2 Cor. 7:6-7, 13-15; 8:6, 16-24.

One of the prominent features of the statement about Paul's apostolic commission is the repeated word that God is the source and sufficiency of the ministry (2:14-17; 3:4-6). The passage we consider begins with such an affirmation. "But we have this treasure in earthen vessels, to show that the power which exceeds comparison belongs to God and not to us" (4:7).[35] The elaboration of the hardships Paul has endured, which follows in vv. 8-9, indicates that "earthen vessels" signifies not merely the normal mortality of the messengers—their human frailties, their aging, and their physical death—but specifically their vulnerability to tribulations, perplexities, and persecutions. The "treasure"— that is, the message of Jesus Christ as Lord and as bearer of the divine glory (4:5-6)—is conveyed not via supersuccessful vehicles, who encounter no opposition, but by humans who are exposed to negative reactions, sometimes violent, which the message is inclined to evoke. And this vulnerability in turn serves a greater end—namely, that people discover that the colossal power belongs to God and not to the human bearers of the message.

Two details about the list of hardships (vv. 8-9) need to be noted. First, the antithesis, stated four times ("but not," ἀλλ οὐ), is a bit unusual. It is not a contrast between two groups of messengers (as in 1 Cor. 4:8-13), but a contrast between dreadful situations that have occurred and potentially disastrous ones that have not occurred. The reader is teased by the list into wondering why the potentially disastrous situations have not followed the dreadful ones. If afflicted, why not crushed? If perplexed, why not driven to despair? If persecuted, why not forsaken? If struck down, why not destroyed? The answer, in fact, is already given: the power of God that exceeds comparison (v. 7). It is not simply that Paul has found himself in dire circumstances but somehow has managed to grit his teeth and hold on, that his courage or reason has overcome the hardships.[36] It is rather that the hard-

35. Furnish appropriately labels 4:7 the "thesis" of 4:7-15. See V. P. Furnish, *II Corinthians,* 278–80.

36. Commentators have pointed out the arresting difference between Paul's words here and the approach to hardships expressed in Stoic writers like Seneca and Epictetus. In the writings of the Stoics, wise persons are not immune to suffering, but they transcend it by a rational attitude of indiffer-

ships are seen to be the occasion for discerning the divine power of the gospel. And this amazing recognition casts afflictions in a different light. Though still dreadful (and no doubt painful), they no longer carry an ultimate threat. As Bultmann put it, "all suffering loses its desperate character."[37]

Second, the list of afflictions is preceded by the phrase "in every way" (ἐν παντί), a phrase reinforced by the use of two adverbs in the following verses: "always" (πάντοτε in v. 10) and "constantly" (ἀεί in v. 11).[38] The effect is to make the list of specific afflictions into a description of the way the whole of Paul's ministry is experienced and perceived. It is not so much particular incidents of suffering that are in view (as in 11:23-29) as the fact that such incidents characterize the preaching of the gospel, the bearing of the treasure. Being an apostle and thereby an advocate of the revelation of God's glory in Christ means facing a life marked by conflicts and hardships.

Verses 10-11 break the list of vv. 8-9 by providing an *interpretation* and an *immediate intention* for the sufferings. The interpretation comes with the references to Jesus' death, a death that is born in the body of the apostle and is offered as the reason for the afflictions. The hardships then receive not a psychological or sociological explanation, but a theological (or more accurately, a christological) one. The intention comes in the repeated affirmation, "so that the life of Jesus may be manifested in our bodies." The dialectic stated in the thesis of v. 7 is thus applied to the hardships the apostle suffers.

Perhaps the key to the interpretation is to be found in the phrase in v. 11, rather weakly translated in the RSV and NEB as "for Jesus' sake" (διὰ Ἰησοῦν). The preposition, however, carries here its less ambiguous, causative meaning when used with the accusative case, "on account of Jesus." It is not that the afflictions

---

ence, which enables them to remain unperturbed and even happy. Tribulations are to be viewed as simply unimportant. The overcoming of hardships by the wise testifies to their own indomitable virtue. See, e.g., Seneca, *Epistles* 71.26; 85.37; Epictetus, *Discourses,* 1, 25.28; 1, 30.2. How different it is with Paul!

37. Rudolf Bultmann, *The Second Letter to the Corinthians,* trans. Roy A. Harrisville (Minneapolis: Augsburg, 1985), 114.

38. The present tense participles in 4:8-9 further support this broadening interpretation of the afflictions.

endured in the line of duty are "for the benefit of Jesus." When the beneficiaries of the hardships are later mentioned, they turn out to be the Corinthians, not Jesus (4:12, 15). Instead, as Schrage explains, "Christ and his cross are the ground and cause of the suffering of the Christian."[39] A historical explanation would lay the blame for the troubles on a particular person or group of persons offended or threatened by Paul's missionary preaching. An apocalyptic explanation would attribute the cause to the hostile demonic forces arrayed against the children of light. Paul, however, sees Jesus as the reason.

But how can this be? Jesus is the cause in the sense that association with him by definition, as it were, entails "being given up to death." Identification with him results in carrying in one's body his dying. Presumably, had Jesus' own pilgrimage been different, say that of a military hero, then association with him would have implied something different. As it is, Jesus' way is the way of the cross, and identifying with him means that afflictions are simply part and parcel of the apostolic existence. The hardships, then, are not confronted as an inexplicable mystery to be unraveled or as a dark riddle to be solved. They are the not unexpected cost of life in Christ.

This positive stance is further reinforced as the intention of the afflictions is twice affirmed (vv. 10-11). The "carrying in the body the death of Jesus" results in "the life of Jesus" being manifested in the actual person of the apostle ("our bodies," "our mortal flesh"). The phrase "the life of Jesus," which functions as a correlative expression for the divine "power that exceeds all comparison" (v. 7), designates not the earthly, precrucified ministry, but the resurrection-life of Jesus. A number of commentators describe it as "a strange life" (*vita aliena*), because it does not emerge, as in the Stoic explanation, from the natural resources of the individual, an expression of either one's reason or courage. Instead, God functions as *creator ex nihilo* to bring life out of death, power out of weakness.[40] It is *Jesus'* life, the resurrection-

---

39. Wolfgang Schrage, "Leid, Kreuz und Eschaton: Der Peristasenkataloge als Merkmale paulinischer *theologia crucis* und Eschatologie," *EvTh* 34 (1974): 162.

40. See, e.g., Güttgemanns, *Der leidende Apostel und sein Herr,* 121–22; and Schrage, "Leid, Kreuz und Eschaton," 153.

power of the new creation, which amid tribulations becomes manifested in the person of the apostle.[41]

The remaining verses of the passage (vv. 12-15) provide a double horizon to Paul's reflections. On the one hand, readers are reminded of the missional context. The sufferings are not valued simply because of what Paul experiences and perceives about himself (i.e., that the life of Jesus is manifested only *in him),* but for what they mean for the outreach of the church. "Death is at work in us, but life in you" (v. 12); "it is all for your sake" (v. 15). The hardships have not been sought out in order to provide a self-validation for the apostle; rather, they have happened in the course of his passion for his parishioners, for the authenticity of *their* faith. This ministry to the Corinthians, in turn, is given both a narrower and broader focus. Its narrower focus is preaching (vv. 5 and 13), the particular aspect of ministry foremost in Paul's reflections. The broader focus makes the ministry an act of worship, oriented to God: "as grace extends to more and more people it may increase thanksgiving, to the glory of God" (v. 15).

On the other hand, these verses (4:12-15) provide another horizon to Paul's reflections on sufferings by setting them in an eschatological framework. The resurrection-power of Jesus in Paul and in his readers is a reminder that God "will raise us also with Jesus and bring us with you into his presence" (v. 14). It is not as if the world's violent opposition to the gospel goes on and on, with no resolution, no conclusion, or as if the paradoxical pattern of life manifested in death, power in weakness, remains forever. The poles of the dialectic ultimately become sequential. The hardships, afflictions, and persecutions, now the locus where life is evident, find a terminus in the eschatological resurrection. The concealment and paradox come to an end. Hope, therefore, has an anchor in the future triumph of God, a triumph promised in Jesus' resurrection.[42]

---

41. The NEB of 2 Cor. 4:10 stresses this point: "Wherever we go we carry death with us in our body, the death that Jesus died, that in this body also life may reveal itself, the life that Jesus lives."

42. Schrage, "Leid, Kreuz und Eschaton, 170. This futuristic orientation to Paul's theology is most consistently developed by J. Christiaan Beker, *Paul the Apostle: The Triumph of God in Life and Thought* (Philadelphia: Fortress Press, 1980).

As we consider the passage as a whole, several observations are in order. First, in 2 Cor. 4:7-15 the theology of the cross becomes the lens through which the apostolic ministry is viewed. What 1 Cor. 1:18—2:5 says about the scandal and foolishness of the gospel functions now to interpret the messenger of the gospel and the responses the messenger encounters in preaching the message. Precisely for this reason the perception of the ministry is turned upside down. We are surprised to discover that the extraordinary quality of God's power comes to light not via a list of successes, such as an account of the conversion of various groups or the enumeration of spiritual achievements, but by a list of hardships through which the paradoxical life-in-death of Jesus is operative.[43] There is nothing particularly heroic or glorious about the presentation of this ministry. Though Paul's rivals at Corinth are not far from view, his interpretation is straightforward, without the more sharply ironical and polemical cast of 1 Cor. 4:8-13 and 2 Corinthians 10–13. It is simply that the theology of the cross issues in a ministry like this.

Second, the message and the messenger are drawn together into a remarkably tight relationship. Terms that are unambiguously physical occur three times within two verses ("in the body," "in our bodies," and "in our mortal flesh," 4:10-11), underscoring that the locus for the manifestation of both the death and risen life is in the actual, concrete life of the apostle. It is not through an ecstatic or mystical experience but in his relatedness to this world that the reality of Jesus' life becomes evident. Paul's physical circumstances make him a living expression of grace. This coheres theologically with the fact that in the Pauline letters the gospel is not presented simply as a report of a past event (in which case message and messenger might be separated from one another) but as a continuing force, God's persisting activity, shaping the community and the messengers. Schütz comments, "Paul appropriates to his entire ministry this close relationship to the gospel. In a sense all that Paul does is a reflection of

---

43. There is a sense in which the hardships do eventuate for Paul in a certain type of "success"—namely, that grace may extend to more and more people. The grammar of 4:15, however, is not entirely clear.

what the gospel does; all that he is is a reflection of what the gospel is."[44]

Third, though the hardships and trials of ministry are realistically related, the text is intended to encourage and offer hope. When viewed in relation to the cross, the hardships become the occasion for the manifestation of Christ's risen power in Paul's life and in the life of readers. They contribute to the growth of the church and ultimately to the glory of God. The initial verse in the following section makes this intent to encourage even more obvious: "So we do not lose heart" (4:16; see 4:1). In fact, a renewal is taking place amid the afflictions, a renewal that has its source in the unseen and still future eschatological glory, and that enables afflictions to be seen as even trifling and transitory (4:16-17). Throughout the discussion of ministry in 2 Corinthians, mention is repeatedly made of an apostolic confidence and boldness (3:4, 12; 4:1, 13, 16; 5:6), indicating that the afflictions, though real and harsh, are not ultimately discouraging or intimidating. It is not a brash self-confidence nor professional arrogance but the theology of the cross that makes possible the unusual doxology that begins this section: "Thanks be to God, who continually leads us about, captives in Christ's triumphal procession" (2:14, NEB).

44. J. H. Schütz, *Paul and the Anatomy of Apostolic Authority,* 232. On the basis of this close relation between message and messenger and in light of the language used, A. T. Hanson argues that the apostolic sufferings have "atoning" or "substitutionary" significance. Like the death of Jesus, the tribulations of the apostle result in life for the Corinthians. Hanson first finds this in 1 Cor. 4:10-13, where he suggests that the text reflects Lam. 3:45. Paul would have there discovered "the description of the atoning sufferings, death, and resurrection of the Messiah, to be reproduced in the lives of the apostolic community." See A. T. Hanson, *The Paradox of the Cross,* 32–37, 47. Since Hanson attributes uniqueness to Jesus' suffering and death, it is not clear what he intends by the terms "atoning" and "substitutionary" when used of Paul and the community. If he simply means that Paul suffers in the service of others, then Lam. 3:45 is not needed to make the point. If, however, he means that Paul suffers so that the Corinthians do not have to suffer, then this flies in the face of a number of other texts where Paul's sufferings unite him with his readers' sufferings (e.g., 2 Cor. 1:6-7; Phil. 1:29-30) or where his readers are encouraged to imitate him in suffering (1 Cor. 4:16; 1 Thess. 1:6). As Schütz says, "Paul is not in Christ on behalf of others. He is in Christ with others." See J. H. Schütz, *Paul and the Anatomy of Apostolic Authority,* 245; also W. Schrage, "Suffering in the New Testament," in Erhard S. Gerstenberger and Wolfgang Schrage, *Suffering,* trans. John E. Steely (Nashville: Abingdon Press, 1977), 189–92.

Fourth, while the theme in these verses is Paul's own apostolic ministry, it is clear that the statements are not to be taken exclusively, as if the sufferings are only for apostles.[45] In the various lists of hardships, Paul of course enumerates experiences that happen to him on specific occasions and under a particular set of circumstances, and yet the hardships listed in his catalogue are typical of others mentioned in the New Testament. They presuppose situations common to early Christians.[46] The unusual prayer of thanksgiving at the beginning of 2 Corinthians conveys the mutuality of afflictions and comfort between the author and the readers (1:3-7), indicating the parallel between his troubles and theirs. In a sense there emerges an equality of sufferings not calculated on a scale of how much or how many, but on their character as Christ's sufferings. Thus 2 Cor. 4:7-15 (like Gal. 6:11-18) functions as a model for the church.

Finally, while we have reflected on the cognitive character of 4:7-15, there is a sense in which the text defies a carefully stated theological analysis.[47] There is "more" to the passage than can be captured by a few concluding observations.[48] Its rhetorical effect is immense and hard to calculate. The provocative antitheses (4:8-9) are not presented as abstract or theoretical, but as the real life experiences of the apostle. Their paradoxical structure ("but not") greatly heightens the impact on the reader. Then the apostle's experience is actually linked with the experience of Jesus by the use of two dramatic expressions: "always carrying in the body the death of Jesus" and "constantly being given up to death on account of Jesus" (4:10-11). Finally, the readers find themselves in the text as beneficiaries of the apostolic afflictions

45. The distinction between apostolic and general Christian suffering is a major point in Güttgemanns's book. See E. Güttgemanns, *Der leidende Apostel und sein Herr,* esp. 323–28. For a contrary opinion, see, among others, R. C. Tannehill, *Dying and Rising with Christ,* 86; R. Bultmann, *The Second Letter to the Corinthians,* 116, 120; W. Schrage, *Suffering,* 191; and J. Lambrecht, "The *nekrosis* of Jesus' Ministry and Suffering in 2 Cor. 4:7-15," in *L'Apôtre Paul: Personnalité, Style et Conception du Ministère,* ed. A. Vanhoye (Louvain: University Press, 1986), 128–32, 140–43, who specifically critiques Güttgemanns.

46. See the list of parallels compiled by W. Schrage, in *Suffering,* 157.

47. This could be said of Gal. 6:11-18 as well.

48. I have in mind Ricoeur's notion of "the surplus of meaning." See Paul Ricoeur, *Interpretation Theory: Discourse and the Surplus of Meaning* (Fort Worth: Texas Christian University Press, 1976), esp. 45–69.

(4:12, 15). The result is a powerful and, especially to a North American audience, unsettling text.

The passage obviously does not communicate new information. The readers know of Paul's afflictions, else he would have described them in more detail. Instead, the text reaches the readers at an affective level, prodding the imagination, questioning a carefully ordered structure of meaning, opening new and disturbing visions of life and its purposes. Readers are confronted in a way that is hardly possible had the language appealed purely to the mind or had the meaning been nailed down more precisely. The passage overflows with connotations and leaves readers to ponder the nature of a gospel so mysterious and paradoxical.[49]

CONFORMITY TO CHRIST'S DEATH (PHIL. 3:2-11)

The third autobiographical passage to be considered also makes the same type of affective appeal as does 2 Cor. 4:7-15 (and Gal. 6:11-18). At a certain point in the passage the phrases become difficult to pin down, the edges of meaning are blurred.[50] The reader wants to press Paul as to exactly what he means, to raise questions, to argue. The difficulty lies not in the failure of his expression, but precisely in its success. The text effectively creates a radical world of relationships that challenges the usual way western readers (at least) know and interpret reality. By the "gain-loss" imagery, the intimate language of "knowing Christ," and the strange order of resurrection and sufferings (v. 10) of Paul's autobiography, readers are confronted with an exceptional statement of what it means to be a Christian.

Philippians 3:2-11 begins with a caustic warning about the opposition at Philippi and with a clear-cut contrast between the opposition and the church constituted by the gospel. While the opponents are charged with being "dogs," "evil-workers," and "mutilators of the flesh," the church is characterized as "those who worship by the Spirit of God," as "those who boast in Christ Jesus," and as "those who put no confidence in the flesh" (3:2-3). Whatever one finally decides about the identity of these oppo-

---

49. See the perceptive study of the language of suffering in 1 Cor. 4:9-13 by Karl Plank, *Paul and the Irony of Affliction* (Atlanta: Scholars Press, 1987).
50. This happens particularly in Phil. 3:7-11.

nents, the text strongly suggests that they are Jewish by birth and are advocates of the necessity of circumcision for membership in the people of God.[51] The play on words between τὴν κατατομήν ("the mutilation of the flesh, concision") and ἡ περιτομή ("the circumcision"), together with the emphatic "we" (ἡμεῖς), has a powerful effect. The opponents are ridiculed for their false trust in circumcision, and the very term they cherish is snatched from them and, spiritualized, is given to the church.

At this point the opponents as specific targets drop from view until 3:18-19, and the irony shifts from "circumcision" to "flesh," as the author thrusts himself into the limelight as one who above all others might have reason "for confidence in the flesh."[52] He lists the advantages he has by birth and by parental influence (3:5a-d) and then the choices and achievements he has accomplished on his own (3:5e-6). But the encounter with Christ provokes a thorough reevaluation of this rich and commendable heritage. Items initially categorized as "gains" are abruptly shifted from the credit column to the debit column, from an asset to a liability.[53] But the "loss," in turn, is just as quickly erased in

51. The precise identification of the group or groups opposed in the text is a complex question and is intertwined with the further question as to whether Philippians contains several fragments of letters or is a literary unity. I am assuming the letter is a literary whole and that the group addressed in 3:2 is the same as "the enemies of the cross" mentioned in 3:18. In addition to the commentaries and introductions, on the question of the opposition, see Helmut Koester, "The Purpose of a Polemic in a Pauline Fragment (Phil. III)," *NTS* 8 (1961–62): 317–32. For the notion that in Philippians 3 Paul is fighting on two fronts, see Robert Jewett, "Conflicting Movements in the Early Church as Reflected in Philippians," *NovTest* 12 (1970): 362–90. On the question of literary integrity, see most recently David Garland, "The Composition and Unity of Philippians: Some Neglected Literary Factors," *NovTest* 27 (1985): 141–73; and Duane F. Watson, "A Rhetorical Analysis of Philippians and Its Implications for the Unity Question," *NovTest* 30 (1988): 57–88.

52. The term "flesh" is used ironically in the sense that it becomes the category under which *religious* prerogatives and achievements are listed.

53. The translation "I have *suffered* the loss of all things" (3:8, RSV) is potentially misleading (better, "I have sustained the loss of all things"). Some commentators speak of the "sacrifice" involved and the "heavy price" Paul has to pay. See, e.g., Ralph P. Martin, *Philippians,* NCB (Grand Rapids, Mich.: Wm. B. Eerdmans, 1976), 131. The language, however, comes from the realm of bookkeeping and hardly suggests either personal suffering or great sacrifice on Paul's part. Self-perception is the fundamental issue, since three times the verb used is ἡγέομαι ("consider, regard, count"). The "gains," which have become "loss," are valued as mere trash. The suffering for Paul comes, but it comes later in the living out of the new self-perception (3:10).

favor of a new "gain," the incomparable worth of the knowledge of Christ.

Throughout the remainder of the passage, it is this "incomparable worth of the knowledge of Christ" that Paul elaborates, giving readers a remarkably personal statement of his "Christian" identity (as valuable theologically as the biographical details of 3:4-6 are for his historical identity). Two moves are made in the text to define this knowledge of Christ. The first is spelled out in juridical language. There is the anticipation of being found in the eschatological day as one acquitted by divine grace. Paul flatly denies having a righteousness of his own and instead claims an alien righteousness, a righteousness given by God, actualized through the faithfulness of Christ, and available in the adoption of Christ's stance as his own (3:9). In light of his claiming this alien righteousness, readers can understand why Paul's rich heritage and achievements listed in 3:4-6 take a back seat. It is not that they are bad; they are simply put into a kind of eclipse "on account of Christ." The knowledge of Christ means claiming the divine acquittal.

We are more interested, however, in the second move made in the text. The knowledge of Christ is spelled out in 3:10-11: "that I may know him and the power of his resurrection and fellowship of his sufferings, being conformed to his death, if somehow I may attain the resurrection from the dead." The structure of this part of the sentence is complex and needs careful analysis.[54] The first "and" (*καί*) in 3:10 is an explanatory (epexegetic) one, making the phrase "the power of his resurrection and fellowship of his sufferings" interpretive of "him."[55] One might translate: "that I may know him, namely the power of his resurrection and fellowship of his sufferings." The two following clauses, one a participial construction ("being conformed . . . ") and the other a conditional clause ("if somehow I may attain . . . "), function adverbially to provide the circumstances for knowing Christ. Further-

---

54. Analyses of the structure similar to the one offered here are given by R. C. Tannehill, *Dying and Rising with Christ,* 119–21; and J. H. Schütz, *Paul and the Anatomy of Apostolic Authority,* 219–21.

55. There is more than sufficient text-critical evidence to omit the article (*τήν*) before "fellowship" (*κοινωνία*), thus linking the two nouns "power" and "fellowship" with one article.

more, the four expressions are structured in a chiastic fashion: a, b, b, a (resurrection, sufferings, death, resurrection).[56] The structural relationships are depicted in Diagram 1.

Diagram 1
Structural Relationships in Phil. 3:10-11

that I may *know him*

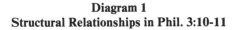

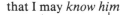

┌─power of his resurrection (a)

└the ─┤   and

└─fellowship of his sufferings (b)

┌─ being conformed to his death (b)

└─ if I somehow may attain the resurrection from the dead (a)

These last two verses answer for the readers two fundamental and inextricably related questions: "What is it to know *Christ?*" and "How does one *know* Christ?" The first question is answered by explaining that to know Christ is to know the power of his resurrection and fellowship of his sufferings. The second is answered by explaining that the knowing has to do with conformity to his death and anticipation of the resurrection from the dead. The two answers obviously reinforce one another.

At the heart of Paul's "Christian" identity is a matter of knowledge, a knowledge of Christ, the value of which exceeds all else. The way the epistemological issue is worked out indicates that "knowing" Christ is not thought of in terms of acquiring information about or of developing a proper attitude toward, as if the locus of knowledge were the brain or the emotions. Nor, as Tannehill rightly points out, is this a seer's knowledge, who may be "caught up into the third heaven" to receive visions and revelations (2 Cor. 12:3). Rather, knowing Christ is elaborated in

---

56. The chiasm makes it clear that "the sufferings" are the sufferings connected with Jesus' death. The word is appropriate (instead of "death") in the first pair of the chiasm because it is through suffering and not physical death that Paul participates in Christ.

terms of participation in Christ. "Being conformed to his death" suggests the continuous identification with Christ, begun at the cross, confirmed in baptism, lived out by "constantly bearing in the body the death of Jesus" (2 Cor. 4:10). This engages not one particular faculty of knowing, but the whole person. Though the language is at time mystical, the text does not propose a meditative reliving of the passion of Jesus, but a participation experienced amid the afflictions and trials of ministry.[57] The same epistemology connected with the theology of the cross, which we have seen operative in 1 Cor. 1:18—2:5, is expressed here.

The order of the expression "the power of his resurrection and fellowship of his sufferings" sheds further light on the knowledge of Christ. One would expect the more natural sequence—of sufferings and then resurrection, of Good Friday and then Easter, of anguish endured and then resolved. The inversion of the expected order is not only surprising but a bit disturbing. What are we to make of it? The textual sequence suggests that the power of Christ's resurrection leads to and is known in the sharing of his sufferings. Instead of discovering that sufferings may be endured for a time because the sufferers ultimately will be vindicated, we find in the text that the resurrection-power comes to expression in the very midst of tribulations. This is supported by the presence of the following participle, which declares that the knowing of Christ has to do with a continual conformity to his death.

Moreover, there is no indication of a temporal distinction between the resurrection-power and the fellowship of Christ's sufferings. The same paradox we discovered in 2 Cor. 4:7-15 (i.e., the risen life of Jesus manifested in bearing in the body Jesus' death) is operative in the Philippians text. While the two realities are not synonymous (i.e., one expression cannot be simply substituted for the other), the power of his resurrection and the fellowship of his sufferings nevertheless belong intimately together. As Karl Barth commented: "To know Easter means, for the person knowing, as stringently as may be, to be implicated in the events of Good Friday. . . . The way in which the power of

---

57. R. C. Tannehill, *Dying and Rising with Christ,* 119, comments: "Mystical language is being used to describe a participation in Christ which is of another kind than that which the individual enjoys in mystical experience."

Christ's resurrection works powerfully in the apostle is, that he is clothed with the *shame of the cross.*"[58]

As in 2 Cor. 4:7-15, the Philippians text sets the knowledge of Christ in an eschatological framework. The conformity to Christ's death is paired with the anticipation of the resurrection from the dead, but now there emerges a definite temporal distinction. The resurrection from the dead is not yet attained, rather something to be expected because "Christ Jesus has made me his own" (3:12). While the reference in 3:10 is to Christ's own resurrection, the language in 3:11 is apocalyptic and futuristic.

What does this imply with regard to conformity to Christ's death? The ensuing passage employs a cognate of the participle "being conformed to" and speaks of a transformation of the body and a conforming to Christ's glorious body, all which occurs at the Parousia (3:20-21). Clearly, then, the time of conformity to Christ's death has a terminus. The dialectic of power in sufferings is not eternal. But for the time being believers in their conformity to Christ's death live in hope. Unlike "the enemies of the cross," their present is shaped by the risen Christ, crucified and returning. The commercial terms of 3:7-8 yield to the athletic imagery of 3:12-14: "I press on to make it my own," "straining forward to what lies ahead," "I press toward the goal." The present is depicted as an active time, focused and purposeful, fraught with urgency and anticipation.

What of the rhetorical effect of this passage? How does it address the readers as we know them from the letter? More explicitly than the previous two autobiographical texts we have considered, this one sets up Paul and those who live like him as models to be followed.[59] "Let those of us who are 'mature' be thus minded" (3:15). "Join in imitating me, and mark those who live as you have an example in us" (3:17). This modeling, in turn,

---

58. Karl Barth, *The Epistle to the Philippians,* trans. James W. Leitch (Richmond: John Knox Press, 1962), 103.

59. The autobiographical material exhibits a remarkable quality as "witness," in that it points beyond the person of the "I" to the gospel that has rearranged the values and priorities of the "I." It is a narrative of what the knowledge of Christ has accomplished and does accomplish in a person. For that reason, readers are led to focus on the new life Paul confesses rather than on his virtues or sacrifices.

addresses the projected readers at two levels. First, the lure of circumcision is confronted by the gain-loss-gain movement of the autobiography. Such "confidence in the flesh," as represented by the insistence on circumcision, turns out to be incompatible with the knowledge of Christ and God's righteousness given in Christ. At one level, then, readers are confronted with a sharp choice: circumcision or knowing Christ.

But readers also are facing the prospect of persecution (1:29-30) and apparently with it the taunts of opponents.[60] In the very context in which the issue is raised for the first time in the letter, the readers are urged to remain united in striving for the gospel, not to be intimidated by the opponents (1:27-28), opponents who are, not surprisingly, labeled "enemies of the cross" (3:18). The readers are told that their suffering is a gift, on a par with faith, linking them to the apostle (1:29-30). Here in the autobiographical passage they hear of a fellowship of suffering, which is the essence of knowing Christ. And thus, while readers find themselves at one level confronted with a choice, at another level they discover a basis for interpreting their experience. Their suffering is part and parcel of their bonding to Christ, who was himself "obedient unto death, even death on a cross" (2:8).

In this chapter we have thus far examined three autobiographical passages from the letters in which Jesus' death functions as a key ingredient in the understanding of the apostle's experience. They are passages (though certainly not the only ones) in which readers are brought face to face with the apostle's statement of what it means to be a Christian and are challenged about their own lives. In two of the passages the context is Paul's ministry, and the experiences interpreted are the persecutions received in the service of the gospel (Gal. 6:11-18; 2 Cor. 4:7-15). In the third passage (Phil. 3:2-11) we hear of Paul's change from being a

---

60. It admittedly takes some "mirror-reading" (but not implausible "mirror-reading") to make the case that the opponents operated with a misguided eschatology, which led them to assume that they were already "mature" or "perfect." Koester suggests that it was this "radically spiritualized eschatology" that earned them the tag "enemies of the cross." In their already arrived state, they were unwilling to take on the realities of suffering and hardship, and could only interpret the suffering of the readers as a sign of inauthenticity. See H. Koester, "The Purpose of a Polemic," 325.

faithful Pharisee, persecuting the church, to one who delights in the knowledge of Christ. But the third passage speaks also of sufferings, not an accounting of specific incidents, but of a participation in Christ's sufferings, entailing a conformity to his death. We turn now to a final passage, which introduces for our consideration a new term, "weakness," and a variant version of the Pauline dialectic "power-in-weakness."

CRUCIFIED BUT ALIVE, WEAK BUT POWERFUL (2 COR. 13:1-4)

Second Corinthians 13:1-4 stands at a critical spot in the development of the letter and opens for us a window through which we can examine the heart of the argument of 2 Corinthians 10–13.[61] It brings to a head the difficult but forceful polemic against "the false apostles," who have launched attacks against Paul in Corinth, and immediately precedes the concluding exhortations. But more important, the passage provides the christological foundation for the motif of power-in-weakness, which so pervades Paul's defense. Having followed the flow of the argument, we shall be in a position to deal with the questions arising from this crucial Pauline paradox.

We begin with the context. Second Corinthians 10–13 presupposes a deterioration of the relationship between Paul and the Corinthian church. The text speaks of "false apostles, deceitful workmen, disguising themselves as apostles of Christ" (11:13), persons who have developed a substantial following among the Christian community and who by *argumentum ad hominem* are undermining the Corinthians' confidence in the gospel previously preached there (11:1-6). Their main strategy involves discrediting Paul's apostolic vocation by charging him with being weak (11:21). When he is away he talks big and writes strong letters, but in person he has no charisma (10:10). He is an ineffective speaker (10:10; 11:6), and apparently because he refused to accept financial support during his stay in Corinth is charged with being crafty and manipulative (12:16-17). He simply does

---

61. I am taking 2 Corinthians 10–13 to be originally a letter separate from 2 Corinthians 1–9, but a letter written to the same readers at a later stage in Paul's troubled relations with them. For a concise and judicious discussion of the various theories, see V. P. Furnish, *II Corinthians,* 30–55.

not demonstrate the spiritual qualities an apostle should demonstrate, the opponents argue.

Paul can claim that through him all the proper signs of an apostle have been performed (12:12), but his actual defense does not consist of a listing of such accomplishments. Instead, he accepts the charges that he is weak and that his ministry has been marked by hardships and even failures, but then he turns that argument on its head by the dialectic of power-in-weakness. Three items comprise the centerpiece of his argument, offered in response to the opponents (11:22-23). First is a list of hardships, longer and more detailed than the list we considered in 2 Cor. 4:7-15 and including "daily pressure" as well as physical dangers and persecutions (11:23-29). It is introduced in such a way as to provide a comparison with the opponents. Second is the brief report of the escape from Damascus, offered here not as a miraculous sign of deliverance but as an episode of withdrawal and failure (11:31-33). Instead of confronting the governor of the city eyeball-to-eyeball as any self-respecting apostle would do, Paul beats a retreat. The sentence that joins together the first two items of Paul's argument categorizes both as incidents that display his "weakness." "If I must boast, I will boast of the things that show my weakness" (11:30).

The third item in the centerpiece of the argument is the account of the thorn in the flesh, given to Paul to prevent his being overexalted by the extraordinary revelatory experience (12:1-10).[62] The interpretation (in a sense for all three items in the argument) comes in the Lord's answer to his prayer, "My grace is sufficient for you, for the power is made perfect in weakness," and in Paul's own conclusion, "I will all the more gladly boast of my weaknesses, that the power of Christ may rest upon me. For the sake of Christ, then, I am content with weaknesses, insults, hardships, persecutions, and calamities; for when I am weak, then I am strong" (12:9-10).

---

62. The mention of "visions and revelations" in 12:1 serves two subsidiary functions: to show that the extraordinary spiritual experiences are not the basis for Paul's apostleship and to provide the background for the thorn in the flesh (12:7).

Like his antagonists, Paul "boasts," but his boasting takes an ironical twist, becoming even a parody of the boasting of his rivals.[63] In a sense his boasting in weakness acknowledges the charges brought against him, but instead of disqualifying him as an apostle, the acknowledgment serves as the basis for his validation. In weakness, such as Paul exhibits, the divine power is made perfect. It is significant to note that Paul's defense is not game playing, not sophistry, not a slick effort to deceive his readers. His defense rests on a fundamental christological conviction. His "fool's speech" (11:1—12:13) succeeds precisely because his rhetoric and theology cohere.

In 13:1-4 we arrive at the christological statement. Paul looks forward to yet another visit to the Corinthians and anticipates that they will demand of him proof that Christ is speaking through him (13:3). Since the prospects with the community at Corinth suggest that he will confront a rapidly deteriorating situation (12:20-21; 13:2), Paul fears that he will be forceful in a way that the Corinthians will not want, that he will show no leniency with those who have blatantly sinned. Despite their situation, however, Paul acknowledges that Christ is not weak but powerful among them. Then he goes on to explain: "Indeed, he was crucified in weakness, but lives by the power of God. For we are weak in him, but in dealing with you we shall live with him by the power of God" (13:4).

The irony of Paul's argument throughout 2 Corinthians 10–13, as well as the strategy for dealing with his impending visit, are here grounded christologically. The Christ who acts powerfully among the Corinthians (as they have claimed [1 Cor. 4:10] and as Paul seems to agree) is the Christ crucified as a weak person.[64] The statement is double-edged: the crucified Christ now *lives by the power of God;* and the risen Christ alive by God's power is none other than *the one who was crucified in weakness.* Neither edge can be ignored. To revel in an exalted Christ, now powerfully present in the community and endowing the members with

---

63. For the parallels in Hellenistic rhetoric, see Christopher Forbes, "Comparison, Self-Praise and Irony: Paul's Boasting and the Conventions of Hellenistic Rhetoric," *NTS* 32 (1986): 1–30 and the recent literature noted there.
64. See R. Bultmann, *The Second Letter to the Corinthians,* 243, and V. P. Furnish, *II Corinthians,* 571, for this interpretation of ἐξ ἀσθενείας.

an abundance of spiritual gifts, without discerning that he bears the marks of one crucified, results in a skewed Christianity. Such a Christianity will naturally find afflictions, hardships, and other expressions of "weakness" to be either an embarrassment or evidence of inauthenticity. Throughout 1 and 2 Corinthians this seems to be the type of Christianity addressed. The sentence structure of 13:4, however, indicates that at this point in the argument the other edge of the Christology is not to be forgotten.[65] A Christ crucified in weakness is not to be construed as an impotent, pathetic victim, unable to effect change and unfit for worship. Instead, such a Christ lives and reigns by God's power.

Two immediate conclusions are drawn from this double-edged Christology, as it is applied to Paul. First, there is the surprising conclusion: "we are weak in him." Why does Paul not surmise, "we *were* weak in him, but by his resurrection we have now become powerful?" On the surface, this seems the more logical deduction: the resurrection-power transforms the weak Paul to make him powerful. But there are at least two reasons why this "logical" alternative misses the point. The first has to do with the understanding of "weakness." In the context of 11:1—12:13, a "weakness" is not an obstacle to be overcome or a sin to be forgiven, not a limitation one gains the mastery of, as one transcends a physical handicap or an alcohol problem.[66] In addition to the escape from Damascus (for which Paul does not apologize) and the thorn in the flesh (which remains with him), the sufferings and trials of ministry are also categorized as "weakness." The list of hardships concludes with the claim, "Who is weak, and I am not weak?" (11:29). In fact, the "weaknesses, insults, hardships, persecutions, and calamities" (12:10) are for Paul by no means over and gone. Moreover, the Christology of 13:4 is not applied in a then-and-now, sequential fashion (which for Paul would have included mention of the future resurrection), but rather in a dialectical fashion. It is not that Paul was once weak but now made strong; *in the midst of* Paul's "weakness" God's power is revealed.

---

65. The ἀλλά ("but") gives particular force to the second half of the sentence.
66. The same Greek word for "weakness" (ἀσθενεία) of course may signify in other contexts something quite different—a physical illness, a weakness of the flesh, a weakness in faith.

This leads to the second conclusion, in which Paul claims a connection with the other side of the dialectic: "we shall live with him by the power of God toward you" (literally).[67] Readers are not to misunderstand Paul's acknowledgment of weaknesses. They may need in fact to rethink the charges that in person Paul is "weak" (10:10), for viewed christologically the reverse side of human weakness is divine power. When he comes to them in person, the power that is "made perfect in weakness" (12:9) will be *very* evident, and they will have their proof that Christ is speaking through him. What readers need in face of this christological paradox is to turn their attention away from Paul and from the false apostles, to examine themselves and mend their ways (13:5, 11). So confident is Paul of this divine power that he hopes readers will begin to correct their situation in order that when he comes he can be restrained in the use of this apostolic authority (13:10).

As one reflects on this paradox of power-in-weakness, so prominent in the Corinthian letters, a serious question is inevitably raised. Käsemann, for example, speaks of the paradox as a "divine law" and goes on to say, "God gives grace to the world in just this way: in, with, and through weakness."[68] But, in terms of the theology of Paul's letters, is this a universal pattern? Is the power *only* available "in, with, and through weakness"?[69] Our investigation of these autobiographical texts confirms Käsemann's contention—as long as the cross and resurrection are theologically held together. For example, the case made against the false

---

67. The last phrase in the Greek sentence, εἰς ὑμᾶς ("toward you, in dealing with you"), is omitted in Vaticanus, evidently because to the copier it seemed awkward at the end of the sentence. The presence of the prepositional phrase in the text assures that the future tense ζήσομεν ("shall live") is to be taken not apocalyptically but as a simple future, referring to the impending visit to Corinth.

68. Ernst Käsemann, "Die Legitimität des Apostels: Eine Untersuchung zu II Korinther 10–13," in *Das Paulusbild in der Neueren Deutschen Forschung,* ed. K. H. Rengstorf (Darmstadt: Wissenschaftliche Buchgesellschaft, 1964), 500–501.

69. These sorts of questions have been raised by G. G. Collins, "Power Made Perfect in Weakness: 2 Cor. 12:9-10," *CBQ* 33 (1971): 528-37; and Hege Kjaer Nielsen, "Paulus Verwendung des Begriffes Δύναμις. Eine Replik zur Kreuzestheologie," in *Die Paulinische Literatur und Theologie,* ed. Sigfred Pedersen (Aarhus: Forlaget Aros, 1980), 137–58.

apostles in Corinth moves *from the nature of the gospel* to say that in weakness God's power comes to light. It is important that the logic does not begin with Paul's own personal experience and then move to universal patterns ("Since through weakness I discovered divine power, it must be true for everyone else"); it begins with the death and resurrection of Christ. The archetype is Christ, not Paul. Paul becomes simply an example of what union with Christ entails and only in this sense does his experience function as a paradigm for others. The autobiographical passages we have considered serve to interpret something at the heart of Good Friday and Easter.

Admittedly this paradox of power-in-weakness finds more pointed expression in the Corinthian letters. One could possibly argue that it has only contingent significance and does not play a prominent role in the Christian identity of the apostle. But this overlooks the fact that the paradox has its parallel in the Philippian letter, where the power of the resurrection is known in the fellowship of sufferings (3:10), and in the Letter to the churches of Galatia, where the new creation is experienced in openness to persecution for the cross (6:12-17).[70] The paradox may have more immediate relevance for one set of readers than for another, but its frequency in the letters and its expressed basis in the gospel hardly allow it to be dismissed as only occasional.

The acid test of any self-perception comes not in the good times when life is prosperous and easy to affirm, but in the dark hours when obstacles appear the most difficult and when one is tempted to lose heart. Paul's identity as a Christian in the four passages considered in this chapter demonstrates a convincing authenticity precisely because it is shaped in the dark hours, in terms of the often distressing and painful circumstances of his ministry. In the language of hardships, insults, rejections, weaknesses, afflictions, he tells the story of faith, confessing the crucified, risen, and returning Christ as one with whom he is united. His identity is rooted in pain, but it is not the pain itself that has abiding significance. Its prominence in the text serves to point

70. Two of the other three Pauline letters refer to joy amid afflictions—Rom. 5:3; 1 Thess. 1:6.

beyond itself to the presence of the protagonist of the faith story, the one who entered into the pain once at the crucifixion and who continues there in the company of his followers. This lived out theology of the cross in turn becomes a channel of grace both for the community of believers in its confusion and uncertainties, and for a world marked by pain. We need now to follow this theology of the cross a bit further in terms of the character of the church.

THE SUFFERING OF THE CHURCH

In the previous chapter the passages considered provided a basis for reflecting on two of the marks of the church confessed in the creed—its unity and its holiness. We used the passages to suggest what, in the patterns of the Pauline letters, it might mean to confess "one holy . . . church." The passages reviewed in this chapter raise the possibility of an additional mark of the church, not mentioned in the creed—suffering. Could it be that just as unity and holiness are characteristics of God's people, so is suffering?

Definition becomes important in this consideration. The Pauline texts we have examined speak of suffering in a very particular way. They do not intend the tragic and often meaningless suffering caused by ravaging diseases, by unprovoked disasters, by the premature ending or the dehumanizing prolongation of life. The texts rather speak of a variety of physical trials and tribulations, mental stresses and violent rejections, all incurred in the service (διακονία) of the gospel.[71] The afflictions mentioned in the Pauline lists vary from "daily pressure" and "sleepless nights" to "countless beatings and often near death" (2 Cor. 11:23, 27-28); from "watching" to "imprisonments" (2 Cor. 6:5). Often the terms are general, and, as we have seen in 2 Cor. 4:7-15, some seem not so much to report particular incidents as to depict a style of life. In any case, the sufferings mentioned by Paul are the

---

71. Beker draws a distinction between redemptive suffering at the hands of injustice and the tragic, meaningless suffering "at the hands of the power of death." The latter, with its numbing isolation, becomes so devastating because it mocks strategies of justice and change. See J. Christiaan Beker, *Suffering and Hope: The Biblical Vision and the Human Predicament* (Philadelphia: Fortress Press, 1987), 68–69.

result of deliberate, voluntary discipleship and are not just "bad things" that happen.

What we observe of the texts is a strikingly positive interpretation of afflictions. No bitterness or hostility emerges, no sense of bafflement as to why this has to happen, no apparent stifling of an uncontrollable rage at injustice. In none of the contexts is an effort made to identify the persecutors or to lay the blame for the trials on a particular group. While the pain and tribulations are not sought, neither are they unexpected. We need to remind ourselves as to how Paul is able to take his troubles in stride. First, the sufferings are seen as a concomitant experience of participation with Christ. Their "reason" is found in Christ's own death, in which the apostle is incorporated at baptism. In 2 Cor. 13:4, for example, the prepositional phrases ("in him," "with him") unambiguously link Paul to Christ. His weakness and strength are not independent of Christ but expressions of his participation with Christ. Second, the afflictions are viewed in a positive light as they become opportunities to experience the risen life and power of Christ ("that the life of Jesus may be manifested in our bodies," 2 Cor. 4:10), an eschatological gift given ahead of time. If the "reason" for the sufferings is Christ, then the consequence is also Christ.

But in what sense is suffering a mark of the church? Karl Barth is extremely helpful at this point. He asks a simple question: What makes a Christian a Christian? In contrast to much of classic theology, he anwers not in terms of the benefits of salvation (i.e., that a Christian is a recipient of divine grace, of forgiveness, of joy and a new life) but in terms of the Christian's calling as witness, the Christian's life in the execution of a task. This vocation constitutes "the primary determination of Christian existence."[72] But as this calling as witness is exercised, there follows of necessity "a secondary determination of Christian existence"—affliction. It is not as if affliction makes the Christian a Christian; only the call of Christ does that. But affliction

---

72. Barth's notion of the Christian as "witness" is helpfully developed by Shirley C. Guthrie, Jr., in *Diversity in Faith—Unity in Christ: Orthodoxy, Liberalism, Pietism, and Beyond* (Philadelphia: Westminster Press, 1986), 81–136.

cannot be avoided. It may not be a spectacular persecution; it "may consist only in isolated conflagrations of greater or lesser severity which break out and then die down." It may be a relatively tolerable pressure one learns to live with, perhaps "the soft and muffled but for that reason all the more intensive force of a kind of Christianity." But it cannot be escaped:

> Since the vocation to be a Christian is essentially and decisively the vocation to be a witness, a man cannot possibly become and be a Christian without having to experience and endure affliction as the work of the surrounding world. Real Christians are always men [and women] who are oppressed by the surrounding world.[73]

Barth even goes so far as to say if Christians are not oppressed by the surrounding world, then they have to ask whether they might in fact be self-deceived and not Christians at all.

As with unity and holiness, suffering becomes a challenge for the church. To say this of course is to walk on eggshells. There are no exhortations in the Pauline letters to suffer, no seeking of afflictions, no lust for martyrdom (as one finds in Ignatius of Antioch). The topic can be twisted easily into a masochism that searches out rejection and trouble or into a martyr complex that turns personal problems into great persecutions—and into great virtues. Camus observed about Christians, "Too many people now climb on crosses merely to be seen from a greater distance, even if they have to trample somewhat on the one who has been there so long."[74]

Paul himself provides clues about this challenge of suffering in Romans 8. The first half of the chapter is devoted to an affirmation of life in the Spirit—its freedom and its obligations—concluding with a wonderful picture of the church as the family of God, children convinced by the Spirit that they are "heirs of God and fellow heirs with Christ" (8:17). Only a stunning proviso is set alongside the promise: "provided we suffer with him in order that we may also be glorified with him." The adoption cannot be enjoyed nor the divine glory anticipated apart from

---

73. Karl Barth, *Church Dogmatics,* trans. G. W. Bromiley (Edinburgh: T. & T. Clark, 1962), 4/3/2, 618–19.
74. Albert Camus, *The Fall,* trans. Justin O'Brien (New York: Modern Library, 1956), 114.

participation with Christ in the here and now, before the final redemption, when participation means suffering. So shocking is the condition that it necessitates elaboration in the section that follows (8:18-27).

In the elaboration, however, the text speaks not of sufferings as in persecutions and rejections, but to the predicament of creation and humans in it, who find themselves bound in a "groaning" because of the way things are in the world—twisted, subjected to futility, unfulfilled. Christians are not exempt from this plight; in fact they are led by the Spirit to join in the "groaning," to take their place in this earthly choir that gives forth unintelligible sounds of anguish and incompleteness. Christians are hopeful because they trust God's promise, but they can do no more than wait, wait with patience and longing, as they share with the whole created order in travail and anguish anticipating "the glorious liberty of the children of God." Even in their prayers, which might seem to offer moments of escape, the Spirit provokes an intercessory litany of groaning, joining the Christians' voices with the moans of the terminally ill who long for death, with the angry raging of the oppressed who seek freedom, with the whimpers of the hopeless who have no strength left to cry.[75] In fact, so deeply enmeshed are the Christians' prayers with the world's pained pleas for freedom that Paul has to assure the readers that God is able amid the confusing clamor still to discern the mind of the Spirit.

In the final section of the chapter the mood becomes one of confidence and affirmation (8:28-39). God, who did not spare the divine Son, is surely "for us." God refuses to let the adopted family, whose members are conformed to the image of the Son, be cut off for any reason whatsoever. This family, however, now finds itself in an embattled state needing such reassurance. It is threatened not simply by the strains of mortality and a shared humanity; it is faced with tribulation, distress, persecution, fam-

---

75. The RSV misses the force of the text in Rom. 8:26 with the translation "with sighs too deep for words." The Greek phrase στεναγμοῖς ἀλαλήτοις picks up the theme of "groaning" from 8:22, 23. So the NEB: "through our inarticulate groans." Whether or not the phrase signifies the ecstatic cries of glossolalia is unimportant for our consideration.

ine, nakedness, peril, and the sword. A citation from Ps. 44:22 (LXX: Ps. 43:23) depicts the family's plight: "For thy sake we are being killed all the day long; we are regarded as sheep to be slaughtered" (8:36).

The chapter lays out the pattern of suffering for the people of God: from the proviso that the adopted children must suffer with Christ (8:17); to the identification with the groans and cries of a suffering humanity (8:18-27); to a place of vulnerability and perpetual martyrdom (8:35-36). How does the church suffer? By joining with the entreaties of the dispossesed, many of whom have little or no voice of their own, by taking up their clamor for freedom and interceding in their behalf. Douglas John Hall cautions the church not to assume that this identification is "the answer" to human suffering wrapped up in a doctrinal package; that would be arrogance:

> The answer, the only answer that we ourselves know and that we are obliged and glad to share with others, is the ongoing presence of the crucified one. . . . We are part of the response of God to the massive suffering of God's world. In and through the church, visible and invisible, God provides in this world a representative—a priestly—people, a people learning to suffer the becoming of the creature, learning sufficient freedom from self-concern, that they may assume in concrete ways the concerns of their neighbors, their society, their world.[76]

What becomes operative, then, is the mutuality of affliction and comfort, expressed in the prayer of thanksgiving for the church at Corinth, the gift of "the Father of mercies and God of all comfort" (2 Cor. 1:3-7).

As it takes on this priestly role, according to Romans 8 the church discovers itself in a beleaguered spot, open to all sorts of hardship and affliction, itself a victim of hostile forces. It learns that intercession has its hazards, that the world is rarely tolerant of such identification and concern. It is not that the church goes out to hunt for opportunities to suffer; it only takes seriously its proper place in the human community, and suffering comes.

---

76. Douglas John Hall, *God and Human Suffering: An Exercise in the Theology of the Cross* (Minneapolis: Augsburg, 1986), 141.

It may be that the makers of creeds omitted suffering as a mark of the church because it lacks permanence. Unlike unity and holiness, its terminus comes in the eschatological day with "the redemption of our bodies" (Rom. 8:23). But for these in-between days, suffering with the afflictions of unfulfilled people means suffering with a crucified Christ. Though "a secondary determination of Christian existence," it prevents the specter of the people of God standing aloof and unmoved by an anguished world.

A postscript: The Pauline passages about suffering "on account of Christ" have been interpreted from the vantage point of one who finds them unsettling and disturbing. That vantage point is generally shared by most Christians in the church of North America, who have experienced little of the suffering of which the texts speak. But the texts are richly polysemous, and their meaning cannot be contained in any one interpretation. Multitudes of Christians throughout the world who intimately know the afflictions about which Paul writes read the texts not as challenges but as words of comfort. They are glad to be assured that the divine power is made perfect in weakness, that nothing can separate them from God's love. Political tyrannies, unjust social orders, the hostile rejection of family and acquaintances have already introduced them in a profound way to the fellowship of Christ's sufferings. Their experiences sensitize them to hear the texts in this nuanced fashion.

Furthermore, we Christians who do not know much ourselves about suffering "on account of Christ" can ill afford to face those who do suffer or those who experience the consequences of exploitation and oppression, and instruct them to accept their plight passively and patiently. It is one thing to take on ourselves the suffering of Christ and quite another to advise others to be "patient" and "comforted" in their pain. What suffering people need from us is an authentic and obedient witness to the hope of the victory of the crucified and risen Christ over sin, suffering, injustice, and death.

Conclusion

The church finds itself today in a confusing and highly ambiguous situation. For a multitude of reasons the lines separating the church from the broader society have grown so dim as to be hardly visible. Visitors from outer space would find it well nigh impossible to discern the difference between the social and political culture of North America, with its remnants of a civil religion designed to bless the status quo, and the Christian community. One could of course hope that the reason for the indistinctness derives from the church's success in transforming culture, that the social and political structures have become humane and generous as the leaven pervades the loaf. But unfortunately the reverse is often the case. It is more evident that the church has accommodated itself to the prevailing environment rather than shaped it, becoming no more than an echo of a generally accepted system of values. The church has made peace with society's economics, embraced its psychology, and granted legitimation to its standards of morality. The delicate balance of being "in but not of" the world is dreadfully tilted toward "in."

The issue that confronts the church, then, is one of identity, of understanding and articulating who it is, of claiming its distinctiveness. In a sense this is the task of every generation of Christians, whenever and wherever they live. Yet it poses today a peculiar set of problems. Ours is a pluralistic society, priding itself on openness and religious tolerance, eschewing absolute claims. The influences of the Enlightenment are everywhere evident in the skepticism about theological dogma and the dislike of anything that smacks of religious bigotry. Doubt, we are told, has an efficacious role to play in rooting out vestiges of unproven beliefs instilled in us from childhood and in protecting us from indoctrination. To struggle in such a context with the issue of Christian identity, to seek to understand one's own heritage and distinctiveness, and to confront the exclusive demands of the gospel are by no means easy.

Both liberal and conservative elements of the church have their own sets of problems. Liberal Christianity, itself a product of the Enlightenment, has prided itself on its openness to and dialogue with modern scientific, cultural, and social development. It, too, has valued a certain skepticism about dogma and thus has defined what it means to be Christian in terms of what one does more than what one believes, a way of life rather than a set of doctrines. But this becomes problematic when persons of another religion or of no religion at all demonstrate a self-sacrificing love beyond that of Christians. The result is a confusion and uncertainty about what is distinctively Christian.

Conservative Christianity has perhaps worked more diligently to define itself, drawing a bold line of distinction between church and world especially in the realm of personal morality and in beliefs about the authority of Scripture. The line, however, has not been so bold in the public arena. It has, for instance, often been difficult to distinguish between the faith and life of conservative Christianity and the values and goals of the American middle class.

Thus the church confronts a serious crisis—namely, the pervasive confusion about its own identity, a crisis that can be solved only by serious theological reflection.[1] And such serious theo-

1. George Stroup, who discusses in detail this crisis in Christian identity, comments: "The most urgent theological issue is not whether there is some common ground between Christian faith and other religious traditions, theistic or secular, nor the question of whether Christianity is superior to other religious traditions. The crucial theological issue of our day is not whether the Christian community can find acceptance and understanding in other religious communities. On the contrary the question is whether the church can rediscover the sense in which it stands and lives out of a tradition, reinterpret that tradition so that it is intelligible in the contemporary world, and offer a clear description of Christian faith which makes it relevant to the urgent questions and issues of modern society." George W. Stroup, *The Promise of Narrative*

logical reflection must be marked, above all else, by a fresh engagement with the church's sacred text. There in the story of Israel, in the story of Jesus, and in the story of the gospel's impact on the Christian community, is enshrined the tradition of the people of God, a memory out of which the people of this day refashion their identity. In the face of domestication by its surrounding culture, the church will never discover who it is until it recovers and reappropriates that memory in its urgency and energy. The story emerging from the biblical text possesses a remarkable power to challenge conscription, to break through the many layers of acculturation, and to bring vitality to a weary, co-opted church.

The highlighting of this theological task, however, is not to be construed as advocating a retreat from the church's mission in the public arena, nor as a time-out when the church forsakes its social responsibilities long enough to find itself. It is rather that Christian communities need to resist the temptation to follow the latest intellectual fads, usually initiated by the surrounding culture, and "strive without traditionalist rigidity to cultivate their native tongue and learn to act accordingly."[2]

The letters of the apostle Paul provide a remarkable starting place in the quest for Christian identity. What Paul is about in writing to the communities under his care is to help them sing more intelligibly the songs of Zion, comprehend more clearly the grammar of the faith, and discover in the story of the crucified, risen, and returning Christ the parameters of life in God's new creation. As a pastor-theologian, Paul commends, entreats, scolds, warns, instructs, corrects, and consoles his readers to enable them to understand and obey their calling to be the body of Christ. Overhearing Paul's dialogue with these ancient communities puts the modern church in touch with its own founda-

Theology: Recovering the Gospel in the Church (Atlanta: John Knox Press, 1981), 24. Stroup lists four symptoms of the crisis: the curious status of the Bible in the church's life, the church's loss of its theological tradition, the absence of theological reflection at all levels of the church's life, and the inability of many Christians to make sense out of their personal identity by means of the Christian faith.

2. George A. Lindbeck, *The Nature of Doctrine: Religion and Theology in a Postliberal Age* (Philadelphia: Westminster Press, 1984), 133–34.

tional story. In the gospel both the contemporary church and individuals within it discover a consciousness that provides an alternative to the surrounding environment and from it are invited to let their own identity be shaped and reshaped.[3]

THEOLOGY AND THE CROSS

In the Pauline letters the message of the crucified Christ emerges as the focal point of concern. No reason exists for boasting other than the cross, "by which the world has been crucified to me, and I to the world" (Gal. 6:14). Several dimensions of this motif in the letters have surfaced in our study; they have significance for the modern church's struggle for identity. First, *theological reflection begins with the word of the cross.* This is what Luther found so compelling in Paul and what led him to oppose the rationalism of the scholastics. To employ an inferential or speculative methodology that starts with the created order or with a presumed understanding of justice and then moves to talk of God is inevitably to fall into idolatry. The one who is drawing the inferences, no matter how astute or well intentioned, is bound to interpret God in his or her own image. God is finally bound by what the inferences and speculations allow. In contrast, a Pauline epistemology begins with the message of the crucifixion, admittedly offensive to some people and sheer folly to others, but the means by which human wisdom is refuted and God's wisdom and power are made known.

To embrace an epistemology like Paul's today is to move sharply against the grain. Our modern language is saturated with terms drawn from the social sciences, which have assumed an almost imperialistic role in contemporary discussion, reflecting the ethos of modern life. Robert Bellah speaks of the way in which the social sciences have usurped the traditional position of theology, to tell us what kind of creatures we are, to provide images of personal behavior, and to legitimate the social structures that govern us. But it is not so much the language that proves problematic for the Christian faith, Bellah says, as the

3. See Stroup's analysis of the narrative structure of both personal and communal identity and how each is changed by "collision" with the narrative of Jesus Christ. Stroup, *The Promise of Narrative Theology,* 100–98.

accompanying assumptions, often unexamined, about the nature of reality. There is, for example, the relativistic assumption of the social sciences that religious and moral claims cannot be judged true or false, valid or invalid, but simply vary with persons, cultures, societies, and historical moments. And there is the tendency toward a determinism that all human actions are explainable in terms of variables for which scientific work can account.[4] Underlying the enterprise is a fantasy of an objective knowledge of a world of so-called facts that are simply not to be doubted by rational minds, a world in which values and commitments have no place.[5]

Given the pervasive axioms of the social sciences, Christians of the Pauline persuasion claim a way of knowing that cannot be proved true. The theology of the cross is simply not arrived at via empirical observation of the human experience. Instead, it entails a revelation, and with the revelation the *knower* is changed, experiencing a drastic (though not necessarily instantaneous) transformation of identity. This makes the task of communicating the faith to a non-Christian world extremely difficult, because the premises and promises of the church and the premises and promises of the modern American mind substantially differ.[6] For instance, a theology of the cross will be highly suspicious of evangelistic techniques and methods of church growth that offer faith as a quick fix to the personal and social complexities of contemporary life.[7] It is not that a theology of the cross abhors

4. Robert Bellah, "The Recovery of Biblical Language in American Life," address given at New College, Berkeley, Calif., April 11, 1987.

5. See the classic critique of the fantasy of objective knowledge by Michael Polanyi, *Personal Knowledge: Towards a Post-Critical Philosophy* (Chicago: University of Chicago Press, 1958), esp. 269–324.

6. Lesslie Newbigin, *Foolishness to the Greeks: The Gospel and Western Culture* (Grand Rapids, Mich.: Wm. B. Eerdmans, 1986), 63, comments: "From within the plausibility structure that is shaped by the Bible, it is perfectly possible to acknowledge and cherish the insights of our culture. There is an asymmetry in this relationship, as between the paradigms of science, but not a total discontinuity. From one side the other looks quite irrational, but from the other side there is a rationality that embraces both."

7. Lindbeck in proposing his "postliberal theology" abandons the liberal practice of identifying modern questions that need to be addressed and then of translating the gospel into currently acceptable categories. His method advocates a form of catechesis or socialization, helping people learn the language of faith, yet he wonders whether this is possible until "dechristianization reduces

success in any form and harbors a jealousy of larger memberships and bigger budgets. It rather opposes the inherent epistemology that constantly wants to look *past* the cross, not *through* it.[8]

THE GOD REVEALED IN THE CROSS

Second, when one begins with the word of the cross, *the God revealed turns out paradoxically to be radically free and radically engaged.* If God stands as the hidden figure behind the drama of the cross and if the preaching of the cross occasions God's self-revelation, then what we encounter is a free, sovereign God, in no way bound by human categories or expectations. Such a self-revelation exposes human wisdom as idolatrous in its failure to observe either the First or Second Commandment of the Decalogue. The scandalous, even offensive, character of the cross, through which God justifies the ungodly, attests to a God who does not look and act as a respectable God ought to look and act. God's ways are simply not our ways.

At the same time, the event that discloses the free and sovereign God reveals also that God is deeply and lovingly involved with humanity and humanity's predicament. If it is true that "God shows his love for us in that while we were yet sinners Christ died for us" (Rom. 5:8), then God's freedom turns out to be something very different from aloofness and autonomy. What in fact makes God so utterly "different" is precisely the depth of suffering love manifest in the crucified Christ, a love for sinful, helpless, ungodly creatures, and a love that immediately implicates Christ at the very point of human alienation (Rom. 8:3; 2 Cor. 5:21). While God is "other," God is by no means other-worldly. As Karl Barth wrote:

> We are confronted with the revelation of what is and always will be to all other ways of looking and thinking a mystery, and indeed a mystery which offends. The mystery reveals to us that for God it is

Christians to a small minority." While important, this method cannot absolve the Christian community of its responsibility to provide an intelligible account of itself to the world, even if on its own terms. See George Lindbeck, *The Nature of Doctrine*, 132–34.

8. Douglas John Hall, "The Cross and Contemporary Culture," in *Reinhold Niebuhr and the Issues of Our Time*, ed. Richard Harries (Grand Rapids, Mich.: Wm. B. Eerdmans, 1986), 127.

just as natural to be lowly as it is to be high, to be near as it is to be far, to be little as it is to be great, to be abroad as to be at home. Thus that when in the presence and action of Jesus Christ in the world created by Him and characterised *in malam partem* by the sin of man He chooses to go into the far country, to conceal His form of lordship in the form of this world and therefore in the form of a servant, He is not untrue to Himself but genuinely true to Himself, to the freedom which is that of His love.[9]

As it sings its hymns, says its prayers, repeats its liturgy, and reads its sacred text, the Christian community declares that God eludes every effort at domestication, every attempt to be captured as the patron or matron deity of a particular ideology, whether liberal or conservative, Marxist or capitalist. At the same time, this transcendent God refuses to be disengaged from human life, will not be banished from life's distortions, hurts, and injustices, in fact chooses the hostility of the far country over the safety of the father's house.

The worship of a God like this empowers the transformation of the identity of the worshiping community. Praising a free but engaged God warrants a free but engaged people who forsake their insularity for the sensitive pressure points of human life. Such praise projects the Christian community right into those places and among those people who "groan in travail" and who, raging or silent, long to be set free from "the bondage to decay." In responding to human hurt, the church is careful to maintain its freedom, not confusing itself either with the Democratic Party at work or the Republican Party at prayer.

One cannot overemphasize the fact that the theology of the cross speaks of a free and sovereign God who in Christ chooses to be engaged in the very depths of the human situation. The notion of an abstract deity—and therefore of a people of God—unrelated to and untouched by the vicissitudes of history can no longer be accepted. Rather the revelation of God in the cross leads us to speak of God's—and the people of God's—*engagement* in the vicissitudes of history. It leads to talk about social ethics, an area that has often been the Achilles' heel of many

---

9. Karl Barth, *Church Dogmatics*, trans. G. W. Bromiley (New York: Charles Scribner's Sons, 1956), 4/1: 192–93.

theologies of the cross.[10] The Christian community finds in the crucifixion the clue as to where God is present in the world, where divine grace, albeit in a hidden and mysterious way, is active. "In human suffering and degradation, in poverty and hunger, among the two-thirds who starve, in races that are brought low, in the experience of failure, in exposure to the icy winds of the nihil, in the midst of hell—there it looks for the God whose acting is the precondition of Christian obedience."[11] God in no way has given up on the created order, no matter how perverted and self-destructive it has become—and neither can God's people.

THE CROSS AS THE CHURCH'S NORM

Third, *the message of the cross functions as the norm and point of critique of the church's quest for identity.* While we have been emphasizing the role of the theology of the cross in shaping Christian identity, Käsemann's insight as to its polemical function should not be lost. The preaching of the crucified Christ persistently addresses the church's pretensions, its self-satisfaction, its easy accommodation with culture. It not only judges the *world* but stands over against the *Christian community*, probing, testing, humbling any affectation that "calls evil good and good evil."[12] It is when the preaching of the cross has fallen silent that the church allows itself to be assimilated into a bourgeois society, ignoring the distinctives of its calling.

This critical function of the theology of the cross becomes particularly apparent when considering the issue of power. It becomes easy for the church to assume that power, whether exercised within the community or in the broader society, has to do with domination, control, coercion, and regulation, and operates

---

10. The problem has been that with such a polemical stance toward works-righteousness there has been little room for human efforts to make life more humane. A stress on the theocentric character of the theology of the cross, however, makes social ethics possible.

11. Douglas John Hall, *Lighten Our Darkness: Toward an Indigenous Theology of the Cross* (Philadelphia: Westminster Press, 1976), 151.

12. See Thesis 21 of Luther's Heidelberg disputation. *Luther's Works,* ed. Jaroslav Pelikan and Helmut T. Lehmann (Philadelphia: Fortress Press, 1957), 31: 53.

in a context of rivalry and competition. The worlds of politics, finance, and education, with their clearly defined pecking orders, their "ole boy" networks, their carefully managed bases of power, become tempting models. But the Letters to the Corinthians present an alternate world, where God's power is manifested in weakness, where the powerless are chosen to shame the strong, where cloaking the gospel in eloquent wisdom leaves it ineffectual, where competing factions are confronted with the sharing of power. From time to time someone like Mother Teresa emerges to remind the church of this alternate world, this strange dialectic that critiques its own exercise of power.

As it is probed, tested, and corrected by the preaching of the cross, the church then finds itself increasingly at odds with conventional wisdom. It grows uncomfortable with its official role as the spokesperson for the American (or any other nation's) system of values. It nurtures a new understanding of "success" that does not coincide with affluence, social prominence, achievement, and consumption. It shares its power in unheard of ways with those heretofore excluded from power. The church knows that it cannot turn imperialistic and force its renewed identity on the surrounding culture; it does not expect the federal government to act as if it were a Christian institution. Yet it is commissioned by the message of the cross to mourn in public ways the dying of the old and celebrate the inbreaking of the new, to make visible an alternate world.[13]

But how is the church to recognize the preaching of the cross when it hears it? Merely the repetition of certain code words is no confirmation. How is it to validate the probing message that is to renew its identity? Ulrich Luz has provided help by noting both the radicality and difficulty of this critical function of the message of the cross. Its radicality lies in its role as subject rather than object. In the final analysis the church does not interpret the cross, but the message of the cross interprets the church, and

13. The notion of nurturing an alternate consciousness in contrast to the dominant consciousness of society is explored most thoroughly by Walter Brueggemann, particularly in terms of the prophets. See *The Prophetic Imagination* (Philadelphia: Fortress Press, 1978).

from that vantage point the church interprets humanity and the world. The Christian community itself is called into being by the preaching of the crucified Christ and becomes object to the critiquing activity of the subject. But therein lies also its difficulty. The message of the cross is not an abstract, disembodied entity; it is expressed in human words, voiced by prophets and preachers, shared by saints and sinners, reflected on by theologians. It is an interpreted word. What, then, is the criterion for a theology of the cross? How can *its* truthfulness be judged?

In a sense there can be no litmus test to prove its validity. The people of God (including its theologians and preachers) are constituted in and by the word of the cross, and therefore it appears a bit problematic that the same people can validate the truth of the constituting message. Luz, however, proposes from the Pauline letters two "secondary truth-criteria."

First, the message must be consistent with the *story* of the cross of Jesus of Nazareth. Luz acknowledges that Paul expresses little about the particularities of Jesus' life and death, yet he cites traditional formulas like Phil. 2:6-11, which, with respect to Jesus' death, are clearly understood as historical assertions. The scandal of the cross for Paul grows out of a specific historical event, a death inflicted in a particular way, and a theology of the cross must cohere with the shape of the event itself.[14]

Second, the message must be actually allied with an existence under the cross. Paul's own life, evidencing a constant bearing in his body of the death of Jesus, becomes a witness for the truthfulness of his message. Thus the question to be raised about any contemporary proclamation is whether those who proclaim it also embody it. Luz concludes: "Then the truth of the theology that poses as a theology of the cross would lie not simply in its contents or in its resolves, but would be determined by its charac-

---

14. This point is also forcefully made by Paul Meyer, who rightly argues that the historical event of the crucifixion and not a theology of the cross lies at the center of the New Testament. See Paul W. Meyer, "The This-Worldliness of the New Testament," *Princeton Seminary Bulletin* 2 (1979): 228–30. See also Hans Weder, *Das Kreuz Jesu bei Paulus: Ein Versuch über den Geschichtsbezug des christlichen Glaubens nachzudenken* (Göttingen: Vandenhoeck & Ruprecht, 1981), esp. 225–51.

ter in the broadest sense, namely by the character which it assumes in the people who advocate it."[15] The church whose theology is shaped by the message of the cross must itself take on a cruciform life if its theology is to carry credibility.

THE CROSS AND GOD'S GRACE

The theology of the cross, with its demand for honesty and realism, is very likely to conjure up images of pessimism and despair, what Barth referred to as "Nordic morbidity."[16] At its best, the community formed by such a message refuses to shrink from pain, seeks out the dispossessed and distraught, and makes no effort to hide its own weaknesses. On the surface it may seem that only a thin line separates it from a masochism that thrives on trouble and pain. For this reason, it is important that the church seeking its identity in the word of the crucified Christ not neglect the fourth dimension—namely, *that the cross reveals God's saving grace.* At the heart of a cross-centered theology is good news that has to do with liberation from the law's curse, the expiation of human sin, the justification of the ungodly.

The complexity with which salvation appears in the Pauline letters contributes to its depth and richness. In our consideration of texts we have encountered a variety of images mutually supportive of one another and confronting readers with a mindboggling picture of God's saving grace in the death and resurrection of Christ. From these images three aspects of salvation itself are particularly instructive to the Christian community as it seeks a renewed identity.

1. Salvation is a cosmic, world-encompassing act of God. "In Christ God was reconciling the world to himself" (2 Cor. 5:19). Repeatedly the word "all" appears in texts that depict the scope of God's redemptive work (e.g., 2 Cor. 5:14-15; Rom. 3:23-24; 5:18). The world may not know or act as if it is the object of such incredible compassion, but it becomes important that the *church* knows that God's salvation is inclusive and *acts* like it. Why is it important for the church? Is it not enough to say that God loves

15. Ulrich Luz, "*Theologia crucis* als Mitte der Theologie im Neuen Testament," *EvTh* 34 (1974): 129–30.
16. Karl Barth, *Church Dogmatics*, 4/1: 559.

and Christ died for me? The problem comes precisely as Christians begin to take seriously the alternate world articulated in the Pauline letters and discover themselves in conflict with the prevailing mores and values of contemporary society.

One avenue open to the church at this point is to become an enclave or a sect, providing an option that rejects culture and avoids all unnecessary involvements beyond the enclave. The surrounding society turns out to be the evil empire, which is treated with hostility or indifference. Church members become cynical about political issues, because they are convinced that all politicians are crooks. This avenue, however, ignores the inclusive scope of Christ's saving activity and the fact that the world (including that of politicians) is the object of divine love. When it does this, it italicizes the boundary between the church and society, and in some of its forms degenerates into an unwarranted self-righteousness as it fails to take note of the many ways the church itself has been invaded by the world. In fact, Christians belong squarely in the public arena, oftimes in a subversive role, questioning its securities and certitudes, but always to the end that the *world* discovers God's salvation.

2. To speak of salvation in such universal terms as Paul does could lead to the mechanistic view that God saves people whether they like it or not, whether or not they believe in and serve God. One, therefore, cannot dispense with the Pauline emphasis on faith. Luke Johnson defines faith as "that acknowledgement of God's claim on the world (and on one's life) which is the opposite of idolatry. It refers to that responsive hearing of God's word which allows his way of making humans righteous to be the measure of reality, rather than human perceptions. It bespeaks that acceptance of God's grace as the source of authentic life which is the opposite of self-aggrandizement."[17] Behind the human response lies the pioneering faith of Christ, characterizing the life of every person who lives in him.

Faith, both Christ's and ours, becomes, then, the distinguishing mark of the church. It sets apart this particular people from

---

17. Luke Timothy Johnson, "Rom. 3:21-26 and the Faith of Jesus," *CBQ* 44 (1982): 83–84.

other people who claim a different set of loyalties and a different mark of identification. But if Johnson's definition is heeded, faith never gives the church a reason for self-righteousness, for taking a superior attitude toward the world, for claiming a monopoly on compassion. It recognizes salvation as a gift, the motivation for which lies exclusively in divine generosity. It is "the opposite of self-aggrandizement."

3. While salvation is effected by the world-encompassing act of God, it also remains a *task* for the church. The community at Philippi, having read of Christ's obedience unto death, is immediately enjoined to work out its own salvation "with fear and trembling" (Phil. 2:12). The divine grace evident in the death and resurrection of Jesus does not cease with the first century, but continues in the historical process amid the human struggles carried on in persons and communities. Wherever that divine grace is present, it is present not via edict or compulsion but through a suffering love. Thus throughout the Pauline letters the language of the crucifixion becomes the language of the Christian life. The death of Jesus continues to be borne in the bodies of God's people. But this "dying daily" emerges from and is a dimension of God's gracious salvation. It is the occasion for Jesus' risen life to be manifested, both in the lover and the loved.

THE CROSS AND GOD'S VICTORY

This leads us to the final aspect of our study, which figures appropriately in the church's quest for identity. *The theology of the cross, intertwined as it is in the Pauline letters with the promise of God's ultimate triumph, is also a theology of hope.*[18] But it results in a hopefulness far different from the naive optimism peddled today by the advocates of positive thinking, both inside and outside the church. They lack the sober realism given birth at the cross and therefore anticipate a too easy triumph of good over evil. Their confidence is ultimately anchored in what they perceive as an unlimited human capacity to overcome obstacles. Their case is argued in terms of individuals who "conquer" per-

---

18. This of course Jürgen Moltmann developed with his two volumes, *Theology of Hope* and *The Crucified God.*

sonal tragedies, to athletic teams that win against all odds, to salespersons who produce phenomenal results. The difficulty with the gospel of positive thinking is its inability to contemplate or cope with failure. If success results from a positive attitude and extraordinary human exertion, then failure has to be attributed to negative thinking and insufficient effort, a simplistic explanation of tragedy, to say the least.

In contrast, the hope consistent with a theology of the cross trusts not in the undaunted human spirit but in the final triumph of God. The Pauline letters repeatedly warn against an already "realized" eschatology and point to the *future* resurrection of the dead. The dialectic of power-in-weakness finds its resolution in God's final defeat of the powers of evil and death. Admittedly, expressing this hope in such mythological categories has its problems. Many fear that the church, as it has on occasion, will misconstrue this eschatological hope and embrace an otherworldly hope that denies any meaning to the present world. They either dismiss eschatology as a biblical embarrassment or "demythologize" it. The alternatives offered unfortunately create even more hazardous difficulties, usually by abandoning God's purposes in creation or by reducing hope to hope for the existence of the individual.[19] The cross itself, however, prevents such an otherworldliness and keeps those who hope firmly anchored in history, realistic about the present *and* hopeful about the future.[20] It will not allow the community formed by it to forsake the created order, but empowers the community to develop ways and means to express God's purposes, without either cynicism or misplaced optimism.

---

19. See the conclusion to *Suffering and Hope*, where Beker acknowledges the major objections to his apocalyptic interpretation of Paul and counters with his affirmations. J. Christiaan Beker, *Suffering and Hope: The Biblical Vision and the Human Predicament* (Philadelphia: Fortress Press, 1987), 85–91.

20. See Meyer's comment: "The eschatological tradition has not continued unbroken; it has passed through a crucible fired by a public act not only available but also inevasible to every onlooker and every inquirer, the crucifixion of Jesus of Nazareth. It has irreversibly become 'this-worldly.'" Paul W. Meyer, "The This-Worldliness of the New Testament," 222.

Indexes

AUTHORS

SCRIPTURE

(extended treatment of passages are listed in italic)